Planning
the
Built
Environment

Planning
the
Built
Environment

Larz T. Anderson

PLANNERS PRESS
AMERICAN PLANNING ASSOCIATION
Chicago, Illinois
Washington, D.C.

ISBN (paperback): 978-1-884829-42-0
ISBN (hardbound): 978-1-884829-43-7
Library of Congress Catalog Card Number 99-76705
Printed in the United States of America

Copyediting and interior composition by Joanne Shwed,
Backspace Ink

Interior figure illustrations by Thomas A. Ekkens

Contents

PART III—TRANSPORTATION

List of Figures

List of Tables

Acknowledgements

Many of the ideas discussed in this book were conceptualized and developed by Professor Laurence C. Gerckens of Ohio State University.

In the 1970s, Professor Gerckens taught a series of "Elements" courses in Ohio State's graduate program in City and Regional Planning. These were intended to develop the basic skills necessary for the practice of urban planning. For these courses Professor Gerckens developed several course manuals, a number of data sheets, and a series of student exercises. His students found his teaching to be stimulating and his course materials valuable.

When Professor Gerckens was promoted up the academic administrative ladder, I was privileged to continue teaching several of his "Elements" courses, using the course outlines and materials he had developed.

As time passed, I edited and updated his work, dropped some of it, and added to it here and there. Later on I taught similar "Elements" courses in the graduate planning program at Virginia Tech[1] based on the course materials Gerckens and I had developed at Ohio State.

The text that follows owes its genesis to Professor Gerckens. He should not, however, be held responsible for any errors of omission, commission, or distortions of fact.

OTHERS WHO HAVE HELPED

Tom Vlasic, of the consulting firm Spangle Associates, provided very valuable and welcome comments on the subdivision process.

John Blayney, of Sonoma, made many constructive suggestions concerning the content and organization of this book, and I thank him for them.

Joanne Shwed, of Backspace Ink, did a nice job of editing this text; she clarified it where needed, and weeded out my unhyphenated compound adjectives.

Thomas A. Ekkens ably converted my sketches into nice, clean graphics.

Richard Carlile, of Carlile and Macy (Engineers and Planners) generously provided some subdivision maps.

Gordon Baechtel, of Baechtel-Hudis (Consulting Civil Engineers), kindly provided some more subdivision maps.

Nancy Adams, Transportation Planner for the City of Santa Rosa, gave welcome assistance with the collection of traffic and transportation data.

Staff members of the Sonoma County Permit and Resource Management Department were most helpful and constructive when responding to my requests for reproductions of maps and more maps.

Note
1. Formally known as Virginia Polytechnic Institute and State University.

Introduction

This book, as suggested by its title, is about planning the physical components that constitute much of our built environment.

The term "planning" refers primarily to the design of the functional, rather than the aesthetic, aspects of those physical components.

The term "built environment" refers to the structures and facilities that we build in urban and suburban areas, as a part of the physical pattern we use in our current civilization. These include roads, utility systems, schools, subdivisions, housing, and some accompanying physical features.

This built environment can be considered to be composed of a number of subcategories, which include:

- the natural environment
- the built environment
- the social environment
- the economic environment

Those who are involved with designing various aspects of urban areas realize that all of these environments are interrelated; that actions taken in one category of environment usually impact other parts of the total environment. This book will, however, consider primarily the built (or physical) environment, because to do justice to a comprehensive review of the totality of our urban environment might well call for a team of experts to work for decades, and produce a large and complex tome.

The professionals who are most often involved with designing the physical components in our urban areas are (in alphabetical order): architects, civil engineers, landscape architects, traffic engineers, and urban planners.

It is the author's observation that, for the design of components of the built environment, there are many assignments which one person (or a team) qualified in one profession can often undertake and complete satisfactorily (perhaps brilliantly) without the participation of people from other professions. These assignments are often small in scale and have few, but well-defined, objectives (for example, a single structure that is to be built for a specific use, and in accordance with established, clearly defined development regulations).

There are also many assignments where, although they could be satisfactorily done by members of one profession, the quality of the resulting design would probably be substantially improved if it were undertaken by a team which has representation from several of the design professions (for example, a small subdivision).

There are still more assignments where it is absolutely essential that professionals from a variety of fields work together if a truly satisfactory design is to be produced. These jobs are often large in scale, involve a number of topics, and have multiple objectives which are often conflicting (for example, the development of a section of an urban area, in order to create a large, "planned-unit development" which has a variety of land uses).

The purpose of this book is to acquaint students (and to reacquaint experienced professionals) in one of the design fields with some of the basic procedures used by professionals in other design fields. For example: If you are now (or want to be) an urban planner, it would be helpful for you to know something about water and sewer systems, traffic generation, and site planning. This is not to imply that you should become a civil engineer, a traffic engineer, and a landscape architect. On the other hand, you should know enough about these other fields so that the work you do will be compatible with the work they will do, and that you know enough about their vocabulary and design constraints in order to communicate and work effectively with them.

Many chapters in this book conclude with lists of "Recommended Reading" and "Sources of Further Information." The "Recommended Reading" lists are important sources that augment this text; readers are strongly urged to review them if they are available. (They should be considered "required reading" if this book is used as a classroom text.) The "Sources of Further Information" are provided for those readers who wish to delve further into the topic under discussion; they should not be considered as "required reading."

A number of exercises are provided in Appendix A that are directly related to many of the topics discussed in this book. These exercises have proven to be valuable learning experiences for students, and to be a far more effective teaching technique than lecturing or assigning readings; they are what some educators refer to as "experiential learning."

In writing this book, consideration of how to use computer programs in the design process has been consciously omitted. There are many excellent and affordable computer programs that are very useful to design professionals. However, to the inexperienced, computers may be considered to be beige boxes that, when some numbers are typed in, will print out other numbers that they assume are valid and need not be questioned. It is hoped that those who read this book will understand which factors should be considered when designing segments of the built environment, and will learn how to make appropriate calculations concerning them. Only when we understand the analysis and design processes should we rely on computer programs; only then should they be used to take over what is often complex, time-consuming, and tedious work.

Land

1

Landforms

DEFINITION

Landform—The form, structure, and character of the surface of the land.

Landforms are usually the result of the interactions of various natural physical processes with the surface of the earth.

These processes include stream erosion, wind erosion, glacial action, earthquakes, volcanic action, the freeze-thaw cycle acting on surface materials, the leaching chemicals from rocks and soils, and the deposit of wind- or water-borne materials. These processes are usually (but not always) very, very slow.

Mankind also makes significant impacts on landforms through actions such as draining lakes and marsh areas, flooding lowland areas, massive grading operations, and diverting rivers. Man-made impacts on landform are usually very small in size, but very rapid when compared to the scale and pace of geologic change.

THE IMPORTANCE OF THE STUDY OF LANDFORMS TO DESIGNERS OF URBAN AREAS

Landforms are important to designers because they often place substantial limitations on the location, intensity, and character of urban development. For example, in some areas it is difficult or expensive to build because of steep slopes, extensive rock formations, or the presence of water; in other locations, it is dangerous to build because of natural hazards such as flooding, landslides, earthquake hazards or shoreline erosion.

On the other hand, landforms often identify opportunities because they may show locations that are most suitable for urban development, areas suitable for the exploitation of natural resources (through farming, mining, and forestry), or areas where the natural features are of such ecological importance or social value that they should be preserved.

HOW LANDFORMS AFFECT URBAN DEVELOPMENT

Mountains and steep hillsides—Roads and buildings are difficult and expensive to build in mountainous or steeply sloping hillside areas. Their construction is relatively expensive because of the cost of excavating the uphill section of a road right-of-way (ROW) or a level building site, and the cost of filling and compacting the downhill section. Aside from the economics of development, grading in hillside areas may have very serious adverse environmental impacts: it can cause severe soil erosion and can disrupt much vegetation.

Rocky hillside areas may experience rock-falls, especially in the freeze-thaw cycle of winter-spring. Avalanches may occur in areas with heavy snowfalls. Some soils tend to lose their cohesion when they are saturated with water. If they are on a steep hillside, the force of gravity pulls them downhill which may result in a landslide.

Vee-shaped valleys—The bottoms of these valleys usually have rivers or streams which pose flooding problems, and the steep sides of the valleys may be expensive building sites. Flash flooding is often a serious threat in these valleys.

Flood plains—Many plains are subject to periodic flooding, especially those located where there is no place into which the flood waters can drain. These areas are often suitable for agriculture but may be hazardous for urban development.

Bare rock—These include areas where the depth to bedrock is slight. Installation of underground utilities is difficult and expensive. Grading for level building sites or parking lots is expensive. In some cases, it may be more economical to leave the landform alone and build structures above it.

Sand—Wind blows sand around. You may find that sand intrudes on urban development and may cover it over as the years go by, or the sand around and under the development may be blown away.

Lakes—It is possible but often expensive to build urban development on barges or house-boats. Or, piles can be driven down to a firm bearing soil (or to the point of resistance) and used for foundations, but that's expensive, too. Installing underground (or underwater) utility lines is also a severe problem. Of course, there are environmental costs to be

considered; they are usually significantly adverse.

Marshes, bogs, and mud flats—These have problems that are similar to those present in lakes, although the water is thicker in them. Some of these areas can be drained and developed, or filled and developed. Note, however, that areas which have water on their surface (seasonally or more frequently) are classified as "wetlands," and most of them are considered to be valuable ecological resources. Current legislation places severe restrictions on how they may be used or modified.

Shoreline areas—Shorelines adjacent to the Pacific Ocean are sometimes inundated by tsunamis ("tidal waves"). On the Atlantic and Gulf coasts, hurricanes occasionally do great damage to shoreline development.

Earthquake areas

- *Sites which are crossed by a fault zone*—Often, when an earthquake occurs, the land on one side of the fault moves, while the land on the other side of the fault does not. This plays havoc with any building foundations and underground utilities that straddle the fault line.

- *Sites which are not directly on, but are in the vicinity of, a fault zone*—These areas may experience severe shaking, which may cause substantial damage to aboveground structures in the area. Underground utilities may be compressed and then stretched by the shaking motion, which may cause severe damage or failure.

- *Sites which undergo liquefaction*—When some soils contain substantial water, they may undergo "liquefaction" when shaken by an earthquake, causing them to act like a liquid for a brief period of time. This can result in slides or slumps of the soil, and destroy the foundations of any structures built on them.

THE INFLUENCE OF LANDFORMS ON THE LOCATION OF CITIES

The earliest cities appear to have been built in areas where it was easy to grow crops. This often meant that their locations were on or adjacent to the flood plains of rivers such as the Nile, Tigris, Euphrates, and Indus.

Many of the earliest North American cities were built in coastal areas where there were good harbors. The cities of Boston, New York, and Charleston are examples. Cities (such as Montreal and St. Louis) were also built in inland areas which were accessible by ships and barges using navigable rivers.

Later, as the interior of the country was being settled, canals were built to provide water-borne transportation. The alignment of these canals, of course, had to observe the local landforms. Most often they followed existing river beds and, when the river was no longer navigable, they had to avoid mountains and rock outcroppings. The growth of a number of cities in the United States was greatly accelerated by the construction of these canals.

The canal-building era in the United States was soon eclipsed by the railroad-building era, which started about 1830 and lasted into the 20th century. Rail lines strongly influenced urban growth in America: many cities that had good transportation (by water or rail) flourished; those without tended to stagnate or decline.

The location of rail lines, like the location of canals, has to observe the restrictions imposed by local landforms. Rail lines are generally built with a maximum grade of 1 percent, so they are most often found on level to gently sloping terrain, or following the alignment of river valleys which zigzag across the face of hillside areas, or cutting or tunneling through hills and mountains. Since rail-line locations are so strongly influenced by landforms, in many cases the locations of many cities were also influenced by landforms.

With the development of automobiles and trucks in the 20th century, it became feasible to locate large cities in areas not served by rail lines or waterways. It should be noted, however, that most cities which have major commercial or industrial uses relying on the shipment of heavy or bulk cargo must have access to rail or water-borne carriers. Cities that do not require bulk cargo shipments can now rely on highway transportation. (An example of this is the "Silicon Valley" metropolitan area in California.) We observe that today's city location is far less restricted by landforms than it was 50 years ago. Nevertheless, we still select sites for city development where the landforms are friendly to urban development (such as on gently sloping plains that are not subject to flooding).

THE INFLUENCE OF LANDFORMS ON THE FORM OF CITIES

Many city planners acknowledge that the forms of most cities are strongly influenced by economic considerations. At the same time, they also acknowledge that economic considerations are often strongly influenced by the character of local landforms.

For example, activity centers in American cities are usually located in areas with good access; areas with good access are located where roads or rail lines can be built at a moderate cost. This rules out mountainous areas, lakes, and marshes for the location of high-intensity urban uses.

Gently sloping terrain, which is well drained and has easy-to-build-on soils, is usually the most suitable for agricultural uses. Economic forces, if left to work in an unfettered manner in urban areas, tend to displace the very low-intensity uses (such as agriculture) with medium-intensity uses (such as subdivisions) which, in turn, may be outbid by high-intensity uses (such as business parks or shopping centers).

While it is true that (almost) any terrain can be made buildable for urban development, the economic cost of doing so in some areas may make it prohibitively expensive, to say nothing of the environmental costs. For example, mountains can be leveled (for a price), lakes and marshes can be filled (for a price), and sites can be constructed above rock formations (for a price). It seems that areas with difficult landforms are avoided for urban development largely because of economic considerations. As a result, when there are no regulations to the contrary, land uses which generate high economic returns tend to get first choice of location; low-intensity land uses, which generate a low economic return per unit of land area, get what's left over.

In North American cities, we can observe the interaction of economic forces with landforms. For example:

- Port development often takes place on level lands adjacent to navigable waterways.
- Central business districts are often found in areas that have good accessibility and fairly level building sites.
- Rail lines, freeways, and major streets are located where the terrain does not require excessive grades.
- Areas that are subject to occasional flooding are occupied by land uses which do not expose residents to danger and which, if inundated, do not incur an unreasonable economic cost. Land uses such as agriculture or parklands are sometimes found here.
- The slope of the terrain usually identifies which land uses are economically and

environmentally suitable. Level terrain can accommodate many types of land uses; steeply sloping terrain is suitable for relatively few. The effect of the slope of terrain on land uses will be discussed at greater length in Chapter 3.

- The elevation above sea level of various sections of an urbanizing area may strongly influence the location and timing of land development because of constraints imposed by utility systems. Water supply, sewage disposal, and storm drainage systems rely primarily on "gravity flow" for their operation. If a city has built a water supply system that serves all land uses below the 1,000-foot elevation, those areas above 1,000 feet cannot be served without the construction of new pumping stations and storage facilities, which may require a considerable economic investment. If a city has a sewage treatment plant that receives an inflow of sewage at an elevation of 500 feet above sea level, those areas below that level cannot be served by gravity-flow sewers; this means that pumping stations and force mains would have to be built, perhaps at a considerable economic cost, if areas below the treatment plant are to be developed. This subject will be discussed in greater detail in Chapters 4 and 5.

The constraints of landform, combined with economic forces, have had a noticeable effect on the forms of North American cities. Cities that are located on gently sloping, well-drained plains can (and do) expand outwards from their centers, almost without limit; the result is what is sometimes known as "spread city." (The Los Angeles area is often pointed out as an example of this.) Cities that are built in valleys, and which are bounded on several sides by mountains or steep hillsides, usually develop in a linear pattern along the valley floor and often extend for miles. Cities that contain pockets of difficult-to-develop landforms within their boundaries (such as lakes, bogs, steep hills, flood plains, and rock outcroppings) tend to develop urban patterns with holes in them, leaving vacant areas or areas of low-intensity land uses.

DEFINITIONS OF SOME FREQUENTLY USED GEOLOGICAL TERMS

Alluvial fan—A cone-shaped deposit of alluvium made by a stream where it runs out onto a level plain or meets a slower stream.

Alluvium—An unconsolidated terrestrial sediment composed of sorted or unsorted sand, gravel, and clay that had been deposited by water.

Arroyo—A steep-sided and flat-bottomed gully in an arid region that is occupied by a stream only intermittently, after rains.

Bedrock—The solid rock that underlies gravel, soil, or other superficial material.*

Butte—A conspicuous, isolated, flat-topped hill or small mountain, especially one with very steep or precipitous sides.*

Canyon—A steep-walled chasm, gorge, or ravine; a channel cut by running water in the surface of the earth, the sides of which are composed of cliffs, or series of cliffs, rising from its bed.**

Cliff—A high, steep face of rock; a precipice.*

Delta—An alluvial deposit, usually triangular, at the mouth of a river.**

Divide—A ridge of high ground separating two drainage basins emptied by different streams.

Drainage basin—A region of land surrounded by divides and crossed by streams that eventually converge to one river or lake.

Drumlin—A low, smoothly rounded, elongated hill composed of glacial till.*

Dune—A mound, ridge, or hill of wind-blown sand.*

Erosion—A group of processes whereby earthy or rock material is loosened or dissolved and removed from any part of the earth's surface. It includes the processes of weathering, solution, corrosion, and transportation.**

Esker—A glacial deposit in the form of a continuous winding ridge, formed from deposits of a stream flowing beneath the ice of a stagnant or retreating glacier.

Fault—A fracture or fracture zone along which has been displacement of the sides relative to one another and parallel to the fracture.*

Flood plain—A level plain of stratified alluvium on either side of a stream, submerged during floods and built up by silt and sand carried out of the main channel.*

Gully—A small ravine; any erosion channel so deep that it cannot be crossed by a wheeled vehicle or eliminated by plowing.**

Hill—A prominence smaller than a mountain. In general, the term "hill" is properly restricted to more or less abrupt elevations of less than 300 meters; all altitudes exceeding this are considered mountains.**

Hillock—A small, low hill; a mound.**

Karst—A type of topography that is formed over limestone, dolomite, or gypsum by dissolving or solution, and is characterized by closed depressions or sinkholes, caves, and underground drainage.*

Landslide—The rapid downslope movement of soil and rock material, often lubricated by ground water; the tongue of stationary material deposited by such an event.

Meander—Broad semicircular curves in a stream that develop as the stream erodes the outer bank of a curve and deposits the sediment against the inner bank.

Mesa—A tableland; a flat-topped mountain or plateau bounded on at least one side by a steep cliff.*

Moraine—A glacial deposit of till left at the margin of an ice sheet.

Mountain—A tract of land considerably elevated above the adjacent country. Mountains are usually found connected in long chains or ranges; sometimes they are single, isolated eminences. Generally, a mountain is considered to project at least 300 meters above the surrounding land.**

Plain—A region of generally uniform slope, comparatively level, of considerable extent, and not broken by marked elevations and depressions; it may be an extensive valley floor or a plateau summit.**

Plateau—A relatively elevated area of comparatively flat land which is commonly limited on at least one side by an abrupt descent to lower land.*

Ravine—A depression worn out by running water; larger than a gully and smaller than a valley.**

Sinkhole—A small, steep depression caused in Karst topography by the dissolution and collapse of subterranean caverns in carbonate formations.

Spurs—The subordinate ridges which extend themselves from the crest of a mountain, like the ribs from a vertebral column.**

Subsidence—A sinking of a large part of the earth's surface.**

Terrace—A relatively flat, horizontal, or generally inclined surface, sometimes long and narrow, which is bounded by a steeper ascending slope on one side and by a steeper descending slope on the opposite side; also known as a *bench*.**

Till—A body of unconsolidated sediment that may contain a variety of fragment sizes (from clay to boulders) which has been deposited by glacial action.

Tsunami—A great sea wave produced by submarine earthquake or volcanic eruption; commonly misnamed "tidal wave." *

Valley—Any hollow or low-lying land bounded by high ground, usually traversed by a stream or river which receives the drainage from the surrounding heights.*

Note

Definitions marked with * are adapted from the American Geological Institute, *Dictionary of Geological Terms.* 3rd ed., 1984. Reprinted with permission.

Those marked with ** are adapted from the American Geological Institute, *Dictionary of Geological Terms,* 1976 ed. Reprinted with permission.

Sources of Further Information

American Geological Institute. *Dictionary of Geological Terms.* 3rd ed. Robert L. Bates and Julia A. Jackson, editors. Garden City, NY: Anchor Press/Doubleday, 1984.

Griggs, Gary B., and John A. Gilchrist. *Geologic Hazards, Resources, and Environmental Planning.* 2nd ed. Belmont, CA: Wadsworth, 1983.

Hendler, Bruce. "Caring for the Land" (Planning Advisory Service Report No. 328). Chicago: American Society of Planning Officials, 1977.

Press, Frank and Raymond Siever. *Earth.* 2nd ed. San Francisco: W. H. Freeman and Co., 1978.

2

Maps

The three-dimensional qualities of the earth's surface can be communicated in a limited degree through words such as, "There's a mountain over there." However, this only communicates "what" and not precisely "where" or "how big." To communicate specific qualities, quantities, and locations, graphic description is often required. For this, we use maps which have been prepared by surveying an area and drawing a representation of that area to a specific scale.

SOME BASIC DEFINITIONS

Map (noun)—A graphic representation (usually on a flat surface) of the earth's surface or a part of it.

Map (verb)—To prepare a map.

Survey (verb)—To measure and map out such calculations as the size, shape, position, and elevation of an area of land.

Scale (noun)—The ratio of the actual measurements of something to those of a drawing or map or model of it.

MAP SCALE

There are three ways in which the scale of a map may be indicated:

1. A ratio (also known as a "representative fraction") such as 1:24,000. In this example, 1 unit of length on the map is equal to 24,000 units of horizontal distance on the terrain. A specific example: if a road is shown on a map as being 1 inch long, then the actual distance it represents on the terrain is 24,000 inches; therefore, the road is interpreted to be 2,000 feet long.

or

2. A linear scale, such as 1 inch = 2,000 feet. In this example, 1 inch on the map represents 2,000 feet on the terrain.

or

3. A graphic scale, such as:

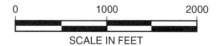

It is common practice to include all these descriptions of scale on a map. It should be noted that if a map is photographically enlarged or reduced, only the graphic scale will remain valid.

Maps are produced at a wide variety of scales. There are a series of standard scales for maps; the standard scales depend upon the country in which the map is produced and the purpose of the map. Table 2.1 indicates

Table 2.1. Scales of Maps Typically Used in Planning Studies

Type of Planning Area	Map Scale	
	Representative Fraction	Linear Scale
Project planning	1:600	1 inch = 50 feet
Planning regulations	1:1,200	1 inch = 100 feet
Subarea plans	1:2,400	1 inch = 200 feet
Small cities	1:6,000	1 inch = 500 feet
	1:12,000	1 inch = 1,000 feet
Large cities	1:24,000	1 inch = 2,000 feet
	1:25,000	1 inch = about 2,000 feet
Counties	1:62,500	1 inch = about 1.0 miles
	1:100,000	1 inch = about 1.6 miles
	1:125,000	1 inch = about 2.0 miles

typical map scales in current use in urban planning studies.

PLANIMETRIC MAPS AND TOPOGRAPHIC MAPS

Two types of maps that are often used by urban and regional planners are *planimetric* maps and *topographic* maps. Planimetric maps show the positions of features without showing the hills and valleys of the land (i.e., they show no contour lines). They usually include rivers, lakes, roads, transportation routes, and political boundaries. The common road map is an example of a planimetric map. (See Figure 2.1.)

Topographic maps show the detailed surface features of an area including its elevation, physical features (such as forests, rivers, and lakes), and constructed features (such as roads, railways, buildings, and canals).

Topographic maps indicate the elevation of the terrain by means of contour lines. Each contour line shows the elevation (usually in feet above sea level) of the terrain. Figure 2.2 is an example of a topographic map.

Topographic maps are a basic resource for physical planning and design. They provide essential information needed for the design of projects concerned with land areas, landforms, elevations, or gradients. They supply a great deal of information that is used in studies made by planners, engineers, urban designers, hydrologists, foresters, miners, geologists, economists, and others interested in the broader aspects of the conservation or development of natural resources.

INTERPRETING TOPOGRAPHIC MAPS

The form of the earth's surface is most commonly indicated through the inclusion of *contours* on a map. When these contours are shown, the map becomes a *topographic map.*

Contour lines on topographic maps connect points on the land surface that have the same vertical elevation.

Contour intervals are the vertical distances between contours. For example, if one contour shows the elevation of 560 feet and the adjacent contour is 565 feet, then the contour interval is said to be 5 feet.

Figure 2.1. An Example of a Planimetric Map

SCALE IN FEET

Figure 2.2. An Example of a Topographic Map

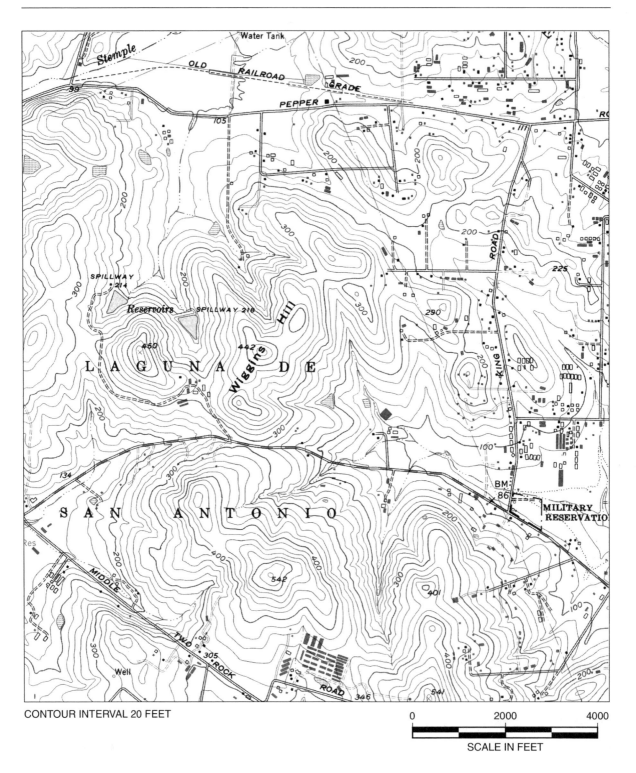

CONTOUR INTERVAL 20 FEET

SCALE IN FEET

Figure 2.3. Contours Indicating a Steep Slope

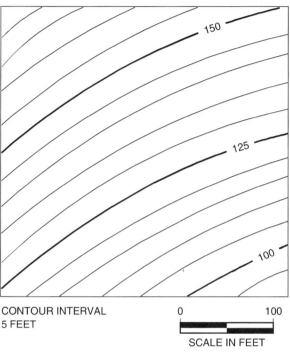

CONTOUR INTERVAL
5 FEET

0   100

SCALE IN FEET

Figure 2.4. Contours Indicating a Moderate Slope (mapped with a 5-foot contour interval)

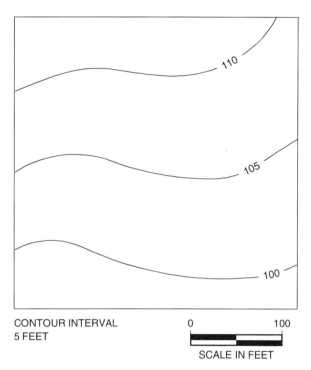

CONTOUR INTERVAL
5 FEET

0   100

SCALE IN FEET

Contour lines usually show the elevation in feet or meters above a *datum plane*, which is usually (but not always) mean sea level.

The ground elevation is usually noted on every fifth contour line. It is good practice to show this fifth contour in a bolder line than the intervening four contour lines in order to increase the legibility of the map.

There is no standard contour interval for all topographic maps. The interval may range from 3 inches for land surveys in Arizona deserts to 100 feet for maps of the rugged sections of the Rocky Mountains. It is essential to identify the contour interval of a topographic map as one of the first steps in its interpretation.

CHARACTERISTICS OF CONTOURS

- All points on a contour line have the same elevation.

- Contour lines never cross other contour lines except where there is an overhanging cliff, a natural bridge, or a pierced or arched rock.

- Contour lines never split.

- When contour lines are relatively close together, they indicate a change of vertical elevation of the earth's surface in a relatively short horizontal distance, often indicating a steep slope.

Figure 2.3 is a map of a hypothetical terrain that has a fairly steep slope, made evident from the spacing of the contours. One can tell from the scale of the map that there is about a 25-foot change of elevation in a distance of 100 feet; this is generally considered to be a fairly steep slope. (The subject of slope will be discussed further in Chapter 3.)

Figure 2.5. Contours Indicating a Moderate Slope (mapped with a 1-foot contour interval)

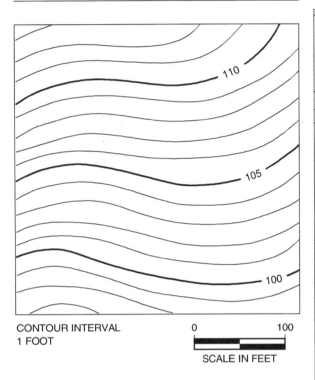

CONTOUR INTERVAL 1 FOOT

0   100

SCALE IN FEET

Figure 2.6. Contours Indicating Ridges and Valleys

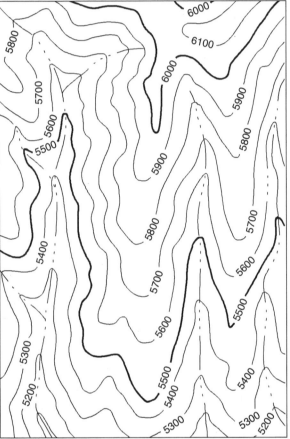

CONTOUR INTERVAL 100 FEET

When the contour lines are far apart, they indicate that there is little change in surface elevation in a given horizontal distance and that the surface is relatively flat.

Figure 2.4 illustrates some terrain which has a gentle slope indicated by the widely spaced contours. Here you will observe a 5-foot change of elevation in a distance of 100 feet, usually considered to be not steep.

Figure 2.5 illustrates the same gently sloping terrain that was shown in Figure 2.4, but it has closely spaced contours. This is because the contour interval on the map is only 1 foot rather than 5 feet. The lesson to be learned here is that it is important to check the contour interval of the topographic map, as well as its visual character of the contours, when you are evaluating how steep the terrain is.

Figure 2.6 illustrates terrain that has ridges and valleys.

Valleys are always indicated by contours that point uphill (see Figure 2.6). Within a valley, the contour lines run up the valley on one side, often turn at a watercourse, and run back down on the other side.

Ridges have contour patterns that are somewhat similar in their general appearance to those of valleys, with this major exception: contours in valleys usually have a distinctive "V" shape, with the apex of the V occurring at

Figure 2.7. Contours Indicating a Hilltop

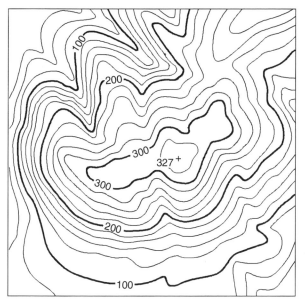

CONTOUR INTERVAL 20 FEET

Figure 2.8. Contours Indicating a Depression

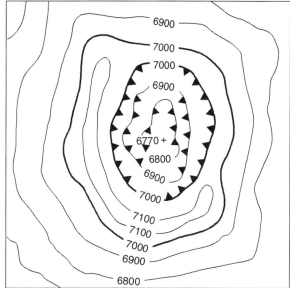

CONTOUR INTERVAL 100 FEET

a watercourse (such as a stream). Ridges, on the other hand, usually have contours that are more in the shape of a rounded "U"; they rarely have the V form. This distinction is the result of geologic processes, primarily from the eroding effect of precipitation falling on the surface of the earth.

Contour lines that enclose an area occur only around elevated areas such as the tops of hills, or around depressed areas such as sinkholes and craters.

Figure 2.7 illustrates a hilltop with its typical closed contours. When mapping a hilltop, it is good practice to provide the spot elevation of its highest point.

Depressions in the surface of the earth are also indicated by concentric closed contours. It is good practice to indicate the spot elevation of the lowest point of the depression and use "hachure" marks on the downhill side of the contour. (See Figure 2.8.)

THE DIRECTION OF THE FLOW OF WATER OVER TERRAIN

In which direction does water flow? There are two answers to this question. The first, and most obvious, is that water flows downhill. The second is that water flows downhill *at right angles to the contour lines* of the hill. That is, water runs straight downhill; it never flows diagonally across the face of a uniform slope. This bit of information is important to remember when making studies that involve the flow of water, as is often required when preparing plans for water supply, flood control, storm drainage, soil erosion, or many environmental protection programs.

A USEFUL TOOL FOR READING MAPS

An *engineer's scale* is often used as an aid in reading maps. This is a "ruler" which is usually triangular in cross section and slightly over 12 inches in length. The standard markings on an engineer's scale are 10, 20, 30, 40, 50, and 60 divisions per inch. The scale can therefore be easily used to measure maps that have a linear scale which is one of these figures (such as 50 feet to the inch) or a multiple of one of them (such as 500 or 5,000 feet to the inch).[1] Engineer's scales are also available for use with metric-scaled maps and drawings. These are similar in size and shape to those described above, but their scales are marked in representative fractions such as 1:500, 1:1,000, and 1:2,000.

USGS MAPS

The basic source for topographic maps in the United States is the United States Geological Survey (USGS), which is a division of the U.S. Department of the Interior. The USGS produces topographic maps that cover the entire United States. Each map is bounded by parallels of latitude and meridians of longitude. The maps are most frequently those in the 7-1/2-minute series. These are often referred to as "quadrangles," "quads," or "topos." In this series of maps, most of the maps cover 7-1/2 minutes of latitude and 7-1/2 minutes of longitude, at a scale of 1:24,000. The sheet size of each quad for areas on the mainland of the United States is typically about 22 × 28 inches.[2]

These maps are available at USGS offices, and from many local distributors such as bookstores and mountaineering supply stores. Other series of maps produced by the USGS include those at scales of 1:100,000, 1:250,000, 1:500,000, and 1:1,000,000. These maps are readily available directly from the USGS and infrequently from local private distributors.

The USGS maps contain three basic types of data: cultural features (such as roads, railroads, cities, and towns), water features (such as lakes, rivers, streams, and major intermit-

tent channels), and topographic relief (shown with contour lines and spot elevations). The contour intervals vary from map to map depending on the scale and terrain of the country. Many of these maps include additional information such as woodland areas, limits of urbanized areas, highway classifications, and the boundaries of major public land areas.

It is important to check the date of each USGS topographic map, which is shown in its lower right-hand corner. In growing urban areas, it is probable that substantial changes will take place on the surface of the land within a few years after the date of publication. The USGS attempts to keep their maps of growing metropolitan areas up to date, and often publishes revised maps which show new development in a purple overprint.

Free index maps for individual states are available from the USGS. The standard topographic map is sold for $4 by the USGS, and usually from $4 to $5 by private retail outlets (1999 prices).

The USGS will supply, on a special-order basis, copies of individual film positives or negatives used in making the color plates for topographic maps. For example, a separate negative (or positive) can be obtained for topographic contours only, for place names only, or for water features only.

For some areas, the USGS has prepared "orthophoto" quads. These are black-and-white aerial photographs which have been processed so that they are distortion-free, and are printed at a scale of 1:24,000 with the same boundaries as the 1:24,000 topographic maps. The current practice of the USGS is to produce orthophotos in digital form rather than as a conventional photographic image. The digital format, which is supplied on a compact disk (CD-ROM) for a computer, allows the user to instruct a computer to print out the image at a scale which suits local needs.

In addition to using USGS topographic maps, at a scale of 1 inch = 2,000 feet, many cities have their own topographic maps prepared. These maps are typically at a scale of 1 inch = 100 or 200 feet.

MEASURING MAPPED LAND AREAS

It is often necessary for the designer to measure mapped land areas. Examples: How much space would this planned freeway interchange occupy? How large is this proposed park? Can a 60-acre shopping center fit on this site? Sometimes these measurements must be precise and accurate; sometimes they can be reasonable approximations.

There are four major methods used to measure land areas on maps. These are:

1. using a planimeter
2. using a computer-aided design and drafting (CADD) program
3. using geometric figures to approximate mapped areas
4. using gridded overlays

The first two methods usually yield precise measurements of areas, but they require special equipment and may be time-consuming to use. The second two methods produce approximate measurements, but they are quick and easy to use and do not require expensive equipment.

A planimeter is a small device which consists of two hinged arms (each about 12 inches in length); the end of one arm is kept anchored on the map. The second arm is hinged to a specific point of the first arm; its free, outer end has a pointer which is used to trace the boundaries of the map area to be measured. On older planimeters, this tracing motion actuates a graduated dial which indicates the size of the area measured. On newer planimeters, the size of the area measured is indicated on a digital readout. When using a planimeter, each area should be measured twice. If the two measurements are not the same, an error has been made somewhere and a third measurement should be taken to identify which of the first two measurements was correct. For further instructions on how to use a planimeter, see Colley, pp. 124-126.

Many (but not all) CADD programs have the ability to precisely measure mapped areas. They usually work best in computers with fast processor chips and substantial memory. A digitizing tablet with a mouse is also required. Most civil engineering offices that are engaged in design work, and many landscape architecture offices, use CADD programs. There is considerable variation in how CADD programs work, so discussion of them will not be included here.

It is possible to approximate the size of irregular mapped areas by comparing them to the area of geometric forms constructed on top of them. For example, to measure the area of a parcel of land that is somewhat rectangular in shape, draw a true rectangle on top of it and then calculate the area of the rectangle. You must leave as much blank area inside the geometric figure as you have excess areas lying outside its boundaries. Besides rectangles, triangles and circles are often convenient to use. (Area of a triangle equals 1/2 base times altitude; area of a circle equals pi times radius squared.) See Figure 2.9 for some examples of these calculations.

A simple way of measuring mapped land areas is to:

1. Prepare a grid pattern on a sheet of transparent film (such as clear acetate or mylar).
2. Lay the gridded sheet on top of the mapped area to be measured.
3. Count the number of grid cells that cover the mapped area.

Figure 2.9. Estimating the Areas of Irregular Mapped Shapes Using Geometric Figures

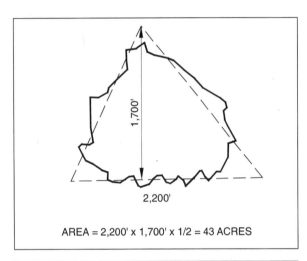

AREA = 2,200' x 1,700' x 1/2 = 43 ACRES

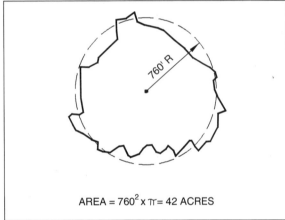

AREA = 760^2 x π = 42 ACRES

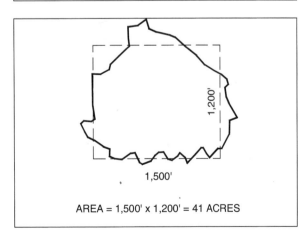

AREA = 1,500' x 1,200' = 41 ACRES

4. Multiply the number of grid cells counted by the area that each cell represents; this will give an approximation of the size of the mapped area.

When preparing a grid pattern, you must decide how large to make each grid cell. The appropriate size depends upon the scale of the map that you wish to measure and the degree of accuracy desired. For example, if a grid cell with an area of 100 acres is used, you can't expect your measurements to be more precise than to the closest 100 acres. On the other hand, if grid cells with an area of 1 acre each are used, the precision may approach plus or minus 1 acre. However, if 1-acre cells are used, it will require counting 100 times as many cells than if 100-acre cells were used.

Figure 2.10 provides some grids, drawn at a scale of 1 inch = 2,000 feet. On the left-hand side of the page are some plain grid cells. In the center of the page, the cells have had dots placed in their centers. On the right-hand side of the page, the grid-cell boundaries have been eliminated and each dot now *represents* the area of one entire grid cell.

If you choose to draw some grids for measuring land areas, you would do well to use a full page (at 8-1/2 × 11 inches) drawn at a single scale for use as a measuring grid. The areas shown in Figure 2.10 are far too small to be useful in measuring maps; they are included only to illustrate how grids can be made.

The grid pattern should be prepared at the same scale as the map you intend to measure. For example, if you want to use a 10-acre grid, you know that each grid cell should contain 10 acres × 43,560 square feet per acre, which equals 435,600 square feet. This can be represented by square cells the sides of which have a length equal to the square root of the area of the cell, which is 660 feet in this case. (The square root of 435,600 is 660.)

Figure 2.10. Grids for Measuring Areas on a Map at Scale 1" = 2,000'

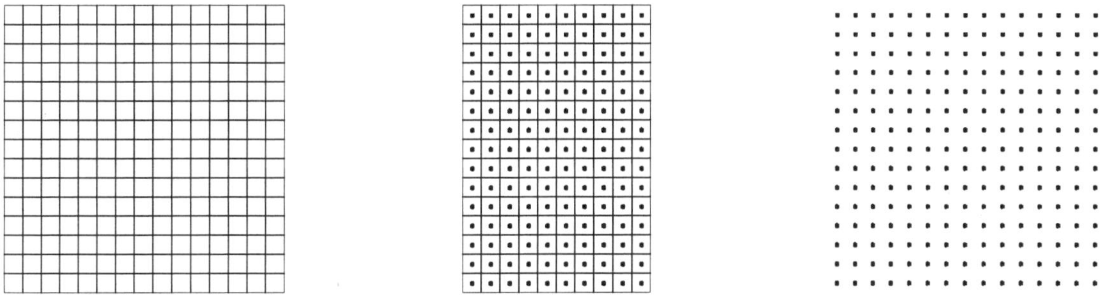

GRID SIZE 200' x 200'
(EACH GRID CONTAINS 40,000 SQ. FT., OR 0.918 ACRES)

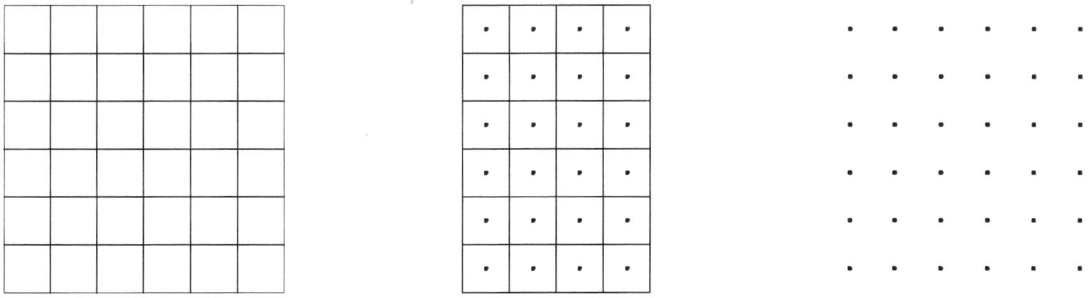

GRID SIZE 500' x 500'
(EACH GRID CONTAINS 250,000 SQ. FT., OR 5.74 ACRES)

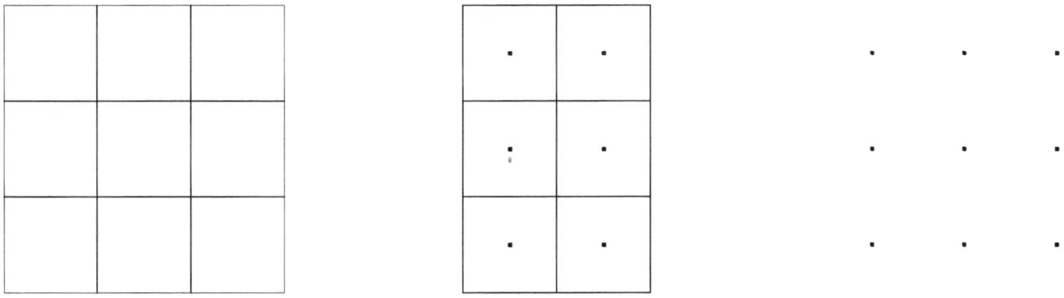

GRID SIZE 1,000' x 1,000'
(EACH GRID CONTAINS 1,000,000 SQ. FT., OR 22.96 ACRES)

When you have developed this information, take your engineer's scale and lay out a grid with cells that measure 660 feet on each side, at the scale of the map you are measuring. Or, if you choose to use dots to represent grid cells, space the dots 660 feet apart. You can choose to draw your grid showing the boundaries of all grid cells *or* prepare a grid in which each dot represents one grid cell. You will find that the dot representation makes life a lot easier when it comes to counting grid cells.

You can draft your grid pattern directly on drafting film; an easier way is to draft it on plain paper, and then use a photocopy machine to transfer your grid onto transparent film (often used for making overhead projection sheets).

To use your grid, place it on top of the map you wish to measure and tape it in place temporarily. (You must not move it around on top of the map once you have started counting grid cells.)

The next step is to count the number of grid cells that represent the land area you are measuring. This is no problem where each cell on your grid is fully filled by land area. On the edges of the area being measured, however, you are going to have to make judgment calls on whether a cell is more or less than *half filled* by the land area; if it is more than half filled, you count the cell; if it is less than half filled, you don't. (If you are using a grid made up of dots that represent cells, the number of these agonizing decisions is greatly reduced.)

To calculate the area of the land you have measured, simply multiply the number of cells you have identified as covering the land by the area that each cell represents.

Notes

1. Although you may think of the engineer's scale as a form of ruler, it is considered bad form to use it for drawing straight lines because your pen or pencil may damage the delicate edges of the scale.

2. (A) A minute of latitude is equal to 1 nautical mile, which is 6,076 feet in length. There are 60 minutes to a degree. (B) The length of a minute of longitude is equal to 1 minute of latitude multiplied by the cosine of its latitude. For example, at the equator, 1 minute of longitude has a length of 6,076 feet; at 45 degrees latitude, it has a length of 4,296 feet; at the North and South Poles, it has a length of 0 feet.

USGS Additional Information

The USGS's "Topographic Mapping" is a 20-page brochure describing the mapping process and topographic maps (free upon request).

Additionally, the USGS's "Topographic Map Symbols" is a folded brochure (sheet size 11 × 15 inches) that graphically shows the symbols used on USGS topographic maps (free upon request).

The USGS publications listed above, as well as maps and information on geology and hydrology, are available from any of the offices of the Earth Sciences Information Centers (ESICs), which are located in the following locations:

Reston–ESIC
507 National Center
Reston, VA 20192

Anchorage–ESIC
4230 University Dr., Room 101
Anchorage, AK 99508-4664

Denver–ESIC
P.O. Box 25286
Denver, CO 80225

Menlo Park–ESIC
345 Middlefield Rd.
Menlo Park, CA 94025-3591

Rolla–ESIC
1400 Independence Rd.
Rolla, MO 65401

Salt Lake–ESIC
222 W. 2300 South, 2nd Floor
Salt Lake City, UT 84119

Sioux Falls–ESIC
Eros Data Center
Sioux Falls, SD 57198-0001

Spokane–ESIC
U.S. Post Office Building, Room 135
904 W. Riverside Ave.
Spokane, WA 99201-1088

Washington, DC–ESIC
U.S. Department of Interior Building
1849 C St., NW, Room 2650
Washington, DC 20240

The home page of the USGS on the internet is:
http://www.usgs.gov/

This address can lead to many sources of mapping and earth science information.

Sources of Further Information

Colley, Barbara C. *Practical Manual of Land Development.* 3rd ed. New York: McGraw-Hill, 1998, pp. 19-48, 61-62.

Russell, James E. *Site Planning.* Reston, VA: Reston Publishing Co., 1984. See Chapter 2, "Topographic Maps," pp. 39-52.

3

The Constraints of Slope on Land Development

VISUALIZING SLOPE

Slope is defined as the slant or steepness of the terrain. In most planning and engineering work, slope is usually expressed in terms of percent. Percent of slope is the change in vertical elevation between two points divided by the horizontal distance between the two points. (Note that horizontal distance is different from the distance measured along the sloping surface of the land.)

Slope is almost never described in terms of angular degrees. In construction work, slope is often described in terms of the ratio of the horizontal run to the vertical rise, such as a "2-to-1 slope." Figure 3.1 illustrates the interrelationship of various methods of describing slope.

It is important for the urban planner to be able to visualize various categories of land slope. In many areas, the following slope categories are considered meaningful and appropriate:

0–3 percent	flat
3–10 percent	moderately sloping
10–15 percent	hillside
15–30 percent	steep hillside
over 30 percent	very steep

Another way of visualizing slope is to think of the grades of various types of streets. A modern freeway in rolling terrain may have a maximum grade of 4 percent. City streets in midwestern cities rarely exceed 5 percent in grade; sometimes they get as steep as 10 percent. Cincinnati has streets in the hilly sections of the city that are from 10 to 12 percent slope, but they are quite a problem in the wintertime when snow and ice are present. In San Francisco, the cable cars are used on streets with a 15 percent grade and the very steepest street is 24 percent. (This street horrifies tourists and the adjacent sidewalk has steps in it.)

THE CONCEPT OF SLOPE ANALYSIS

Within the framework of our contemporary economic system, and our construction practices and technology, there are certain slopes (and ranges of slopes) upon which certain types of construction can be most economically undertaken (that is, on some slopes, the cost of construction to meet the requirements

Figure 3.1. Alternative Methods of Describing Slope

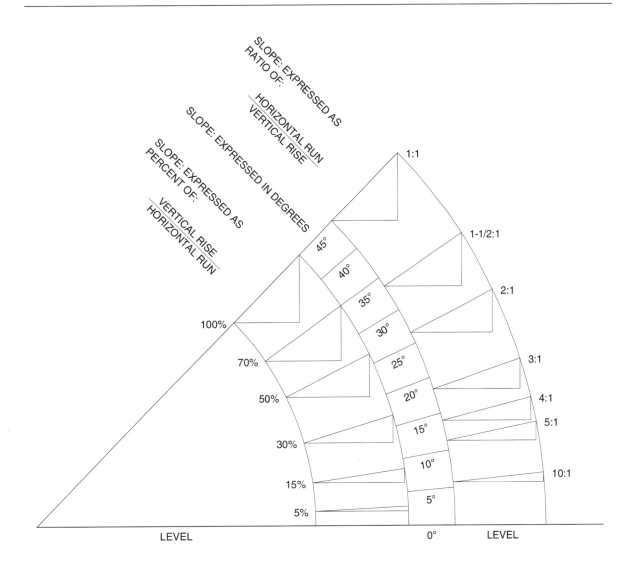

of a specific urban land use will be minimized). This cost of construction, as reflected in the consumer cost, includes not only the cost of structures but also the costs of site preparation, site development, utility services, and the provision of necessary drainage facilities, access roads, and parking spaces.

By classifying the ground slopes in an area, a *slope analysis* of that area can be determined.

This slope analysis can provide guides to the land uses and patterns that could exist in the area if economy in physical construction, based on ground slope qualities, were the only influence on urban form and structure. Obviously, this is not the only influence; slope analysis by itself does not determine urban form and structure.

A graphic slope analysis is essential when planning an urban area. Such an analysis can indicate subareas within which certain land uses should be avoided, if possible, because of high development costs. It can also identify those subareas within which land development can be most economically undertaken, if other factors appear to indicate that development for these uses is desirable or mandatory.

A slope analysis is often the first physical planning study undertaken when urban development on a vacant site, or the expansion of an urban area, is contemplated. This slope analysis is often accepted as the basic study which, to a great degree, determines the future uses of land. The determination of economically feasible land uses, by the nature of the landform, is then modified by the application of social, economic, and other goals and constraints; however, the form of the land is usually the *first* consideration made in an urban planning site analysis.

A graphic slope analysis commonly consists of a topographic map on which the terrain is divided into a number of distinct "slope categories." For example, all terrain which has a slope between 1 and 3 percent is outlined on the map and identified as being in that particular slope category. On the same map, terrain in other slope categories (such as from 3 to 5 percent and from 5 to 10 percent) is also identified and marked.

THE EFFECT OF SLOPE ON LAND USES

Experience in the construction of cities has shown that, for each slope category, there are some uses of land that are particularly suitable. There are some that are impractical because of the economic cost of construction. Table 3.1 indicates the uses that are generally considered appropriate for each slope category. Note, however, that the information given here is not to be considered as the ultimate and universal truth. In many cases,

where there is a strong social motivation, and an economic ability and a willingness to pay for added costs of construction, the limitations of land slope can usually be overcome.

In doing so, however, consideration should be given to ecological impacts. Sloping terrain is difficult to develop without disrupting the natural setting, and has the potential for causing serious erosion problems; the steeper the slope, the greater the threat.

MAKING A SLOPE ANALYSIS

A *slope analysis* is an analysis in map form of the natural slope of an area, noted in percentages. A topographic map and an engineer's scale are needed to prepare a slope analysis.[1]

Percent of slope is the ratio of the vertical rise of land to the horizontal length of that rise (a rise of 1 foot in 100 feet is a 1 percent slope; 5 feet in 50 feet is a 10 percent slope; etc.).

In order to analyze slopes and record the analysis in map form, two operations are necessary. First, a *classification system* of useful slope divisions must be selected. The system which is usually employed depends upon the character of the terrain being analyzed. When the terrain is generally quite flat, the following slope categories are often used:

0–1 percent
1–3 percent
3–5 percent
5–10 percent
10–15 percent
over 15 percent

When the terrain is generally quite hilly, these categories are often used:

0–5 percent
5–10 percent
10–15 percent
15–30 percent
30–50 percent
over 50 percent

Table 3.1. The Effect of Slope on the Feasibility of Various Land Uses

NOTE: The following rules are somewhat dependent upon the cost of modifying the slope of individual sites. That is, how expensive is it to make a steeply sloping area into a reasonably level site? In sandy soils, this can often be done quite inexpensively; in mountainous terrain, the cost can be prohibitive.	
Slope Category: Under 1/2%	Almost *no* land uses are feasible in this slope category because of the problems of surface drainage of rain. There are some exceptions, of course, such as rice paddies, orchards where irrigation is done by flooding basins around the trees and, of course, flood control basins.
Slope Category: 1/2 to 1%	
Industry	Large-scale, linear production uses. (Slopes greater than this either interfere with production line methods or increase construction costs.)
Commerce	Expensive due to drainage problems.
Residence	Expensive due to drainage problems.
Roads	Expensive due to drainage problems. Dangerous due to standing water, fog, and ice.
Airports	Expensive due to drainage problems. Dangerous due to standing water, fog, and ice.
Recreation	Picnic areas and informal, small-group field sports. (Difficult ground drainage and expensive artificial drainage systems make provision for organized or intensive sport-recreation use expensive.)
Agriculture	Truck crops in flood plain areas, general farming, elsewhere. Excellent for crops grown using flood irrigation methods.
Slope Category: 1 to 3%	
Industry	Moderate and small plants without extensive linear production; trucking terminals; warehouses (3% grade the upper limit for uninhibited trucking operations).
Commerce	Commercial developments of all types, specially well suited to large-scale shopping center development and parking lots (good natural drainage, easy slopes, easy truck and auto access).
Residence	All types (single-family, multifamily, townhouse, high-rise), but 2% minimum grade needed in areas where ground frost is probable.
Roads	In any pattern. Slopes of this category impose no limitations on the geometry of the road system.
Airports	All types (best slope, drainage good, easy grades, no inhibition of operations by standing water or ice).
Railroads	Moderately inexpensive railroad construction.[1]
Recreation	Playgrounds and playfields, intensive picnic, intensive informal field sports, camping (sufficiently flat for organized field sports, yet sufficiently sloped for good natural drainage). Must have slope over 2% where ground frost is probable.
Agriculture	General farming.
Slope Category: 3 to 5%	
Industry	Intensive, small-scale industry with minimum trucking needs (truck access difficult and perhaps impossible with icing).
Commerce	Small-scale, individual commercial structures. (Parking areas must be terraced.)
Residence	Single- and multifamily residences; townhouses; high-rise apartments (with terraced parking lots or parking garages).

Table 3.1. The Effect of Slope on the Feasibility of Various Land Uses (Continued)

Roads	Truck roads must run parallel with, or diagonal to, the contours; high-speed roads similarly limited.
Airports	Often feasible, but runways and taxiways should not have a slope in excess of 2%; this means running them parallel with or diagonal to the contours.
Railroads	Must run parallel with or diagonal to the contours. Switching and marshalling operations are difficult.
Recreation	Playgrounds and playfields[2]; picnic areas; informal field sports; camping; golf courses; nature trails; natural hiking areas.
Agriculture	General farming.

Slope Category: 5 to 10%

Industry	Intensive, small-scale industry on slopes up to 7%. (Truck access becomes difficult and expensive when the slope exceeds 7%.)
Commerce	Small-scale, individual, commercial structures on slopes from 5 to 8% (with virtually no parking demand or, if provided, in parking garages). Economic construction practically precluded on sites with slopes over 8%.
Residence	Detached, single-family residences, townhouses, and multifamily residences are all feasible, but parking lots must be terraced, or parking garages must be provided.
Roads	Truck roads and high-speed roads must run parallel with or diagonal to the contours. In areas of slope over 8%, road routing is virtually dictated by the terrain. The topography creates serious problems of access from the road to the abutting properties, due to the cut and fill of the roadway.
Airports	Usually economically impractical, unless you can find a long ridgetop that parallels the prevailing wind direction, and which can be levelled without excessive expense.
Railroads	Must run virtually parallel with the contours, but even then creates serious embankment problems and high costs.
Recreation	Golf course, picnicking, camping, hiking. (Large, level fields, such as tennis courts or football fields, are expensive to construct and may be environmentally damaging.)
Agriculture	General farming. (Care must be taken for erosion control.)

Slope Category: 10 to 15%

Industry	Economically impractical.
Commerce	Economically impractical, except for unusual, specialized shopping areas to serve "planned-unit developments." (Parking areas must be terraced or in structures.)
Residence	Hillside subdivision for single-family homes (which take special design if terrain is not graded to form building pads). Townhouse construction is economically impractical. Apartment construction is often feasible, especially when a "cluster design" is utilized. Special care must be taken in the design of access roads and parking areas for apartments.
Roads	Any road design takes special care in this terrain. All types of roads can be constructed, but at greater economic and ecological cost than is experienced for roads built in more level areas.
Railroads	Same as in slope category 5 to 10%, but problems are more severe.
Airports	Economically impractical.
Recreation	Hiking, camping, picnicking. Sports which require level play areas (such as playfields) are economically impractical. Golf courses are unplayable.

Table 3.1. The Effect of Slope on the Feasibility of Various Land Uses (Continued)

Agriculture	Pastures and forests are most appropriate. Cultivation should be avoided due to erosion problems. Some specialized crops (such as vineyards) are suitable.
Slope Category 15 to 30%	
Industry	Economically impractical.
Commerce	Economically impractical.
Residence	Single-family home subdivisions are possible, if special care is taken in the design of access roads and the location of septic tanks (if used), and if only clearly suitable building sites are used. (Note that, in some areas, septic tanks are prohibited in areas with a slope in excess of 20%.) Townhouse construction is usually economically impractical. Apartment construction is possible only on special sites, and only if suitable provision can be made for access roads, parking areas, water supply, and sewage disposal; this is usually expensive.
Roads	Same as for 10 to 15% slope category, except problems are extreme. Cuts and fills on the uphill and downhill sides of the roads are often so extensive that they are very damaging to the local ecology.
Railroads	Same as in slope category 5 to 10%, but problems are more severe.
Recreation	Trails and camping. No uses are possible which require level areas or the concentration of people. Provision of utilities (water supply and sewage disposal) is often difficult and expensive.
Agriculture	Pasture and forest uses are suitable; vineyards are also suitable, if they do not involve substantial grading.
Over 30%	
Urban uses	All urban uses which require the construction of roads and the provision of utilities are both prohibitively expensive and extremely damaging to the terrain. As a general rule, land with a slope of over 30% should not be disturbed. If, however, it is determined that, for social or economic reasons, development in this terrain is necessary, it must be planned with extreme care; cuts and fills must be kept to an absolute minimum; soil surveys must be made prior to any planning or development.
Recreation	Trails. (This terrain is too steep for camping.)
Agriculture	Uncultivated pastures and forests.
A note on fire protection	Access roads for fire protection are very important in mountainous terrain. If they are to be built, it is best to locate them along ridge tops, and sometimes along valley floors, rather than cutting across the faces of steep slopes.

1. Rail lines are usually built with a maximum grade of 1%, so in sloping terrain rail lines are generally designed to cross contours diagonally, rather than run directly up (or down) the slope. Rail lines with grades as high as 2.5% have been built, but heavily loaded trains are slowed to a crawl on them; they are generally found only in mining areas of mountains.
2. Not suitable in areas that have a slope in excess of 4%.

The first step in the preparation of a slope analysis is to inspect the topographic map, consider the output requirements of the slope analysis, and then decide what slope categories you should use. If detailed information about buildable areas is required, you should have a fairly refined analysis of the land areas between 1 and 20 percent slope. If the purpose of your slope analysis is to compute water runoff from a drainage basin, you would probably choose to use quite a different set of slope categories for your analysis.

You should be aware of the following:

- Only on rare occasions will there be justification for more than six slope categories.
- The more slope categories you include, the greater the number of measurements you must make, and the longer it will take you to complete the slope map.
- The degree of accuracy of many topographic maps, and the number of judgment decisions required in making slope analyses, lead one to prefer generalized slope maps with few categories, rather than detailed slope maps with many categories.

The second step is to prepare a graphic aid called a *slope scale*. This is a sort of ruler which shows the distances between contours for each slope classification. It is constructed to the scale of the map and according to the contour interval of the map.

A slope scale is constructed in the following manner: For every slope category in the selected classification system, a corresponding *horizontal distance between contours* must be found and marked off along a straight line. Each distance must be marked off at the scale of the map being used.

It is an easy task to calculate the horizontal distance between contours when the percent slope of the terrain and the contour interval are both known. We know, by definition, that:

$$\text{percent slope} = \frac{\text{vertical rise} \times 100}{\text{horizontal distance}}$$

Transposing elements of this equation, we can show that:

$$\text{horizontal distance} = \frac{\text{vertical rise} \times 100}{\text{percent slope}}$$

If we substitute in this equation the contour interval (the vertical distance on the terrain represented between two adjacent contour lines on the topographic map), we get:

$$\frac{\text{horizontal distance}}{\text{between contours}} = \frac{\text{contour interval} \times 100}{\text{percent slope}}$$

Example #1

Given: Contour interval = 2 feet
Slope of terrain = 7 percent
Find: Horizontal distance between contours

From the preceding equation:

$$\frac{\text{horizontal}}{\text{distance}} = \frac{\text{contour interval} \times 100}{\text{percent slope}}$$

$$= \frac{2 \text{ feet} \times 100}{7} = 28.57$$

To make a slope scale which identifies terrain with a slope of 7 percent, one need only to make a scale on which two tick marks are spaced 28.57 feet apart, using the scale of the map to be analyzed. (We would actually use the figure of 29 feet, because of significant figures.)

Example #2

Given: Map scale of 1 inch = 200 feet
Contour interval = 5 feet
Find: Distances ("X") on the slope scale for 1 percent, 3 percent, 5 percent, 10 percent, and 15 percent slopes

Table 3.2. Sample Table Illustrating the Construction of a Slope Scale

Slope (percent)	Equation for Distance "X"	Distance "X"	Length on Slope Scale, When Map Scale is 1 inch = 200 feet* (inches)
1	(5x100)/1	500	2.50
3	(5x100)/3	167	.83
5	(5x100)/5	100	.50
10	(5x100)/10	50	.25
15	(5x100)/15	33	.17

* Preparing this last column is not really necessary. It is easier just to use an engineer's scale to mark off the distance "X"s directly on the slope scale, using the appropriate map scale.

$$\text{distance ''X''} = \frac{\text{contour interval} \times 100}{\text{percent slope}}$$

We can make a simple table, as illustrated in Table 3.2.

Figure 3.2 illustrates two different methods of making a graphic slope scale for the figures developed in Example #2. The upper diagram shows a 3 × 5 inch card with different slopes marked on each edge. The lower diagram shows how the slope marks can be combined on one edge of the card.

Specific Steps in Making a Slope Analysis

Using your slope scale, mark on a topographic map the areas that are in each slope category. For example, mark all locations where the contours indicate a slope of exactly 5 percent. Next, mark all the locations where the slope is exactly 10 percent. Using this procedure you will have identified all those areas that are between 5 and 10 percent in slope, and they should be labeled as such. You can then proceed to mark the locations where the contours indicate a slope of exactly 15 percent, and then label those areas that lie between the 15 percent mark and the 10 percent mark as having a slope of between 10 and 15 percent. This process is continued until all the lands in the various slope categories have been identified.

When marking the contours, hold the slope scale as close to right angles to the contours as you can; do *not* measure diagonally. (An exception to this rule is made when you are using your slope scale to lay out the route of a road, and you are given an exact grade that the road must follow.)

When you find an area on the map where you cannot measure the slope of the terrain because either the upper or the lower contour is missing, you may choose to leave the area blank. This often occurs on hilltops and valley floors.

After you have identified the slope of all areas on the map (other than those for which you have insufficient information), the next step is to "rationalize" the boundaries of the slope areas (round out the boundaries of the slope areas so that they enclose logical areas, rather than strange-shaped areas which have angular boundaries).

Preparing a Slope Map for Display

A second copy of the topographic map should be obtained and the rationalized boundaries of the slope areas should be traced onto it. This can best be done on a light table, although you can do almost as well by

**Figure 3.2. Slope Scales for a Topographic Map
(which has a scale of 1 inch = 200 feet)**

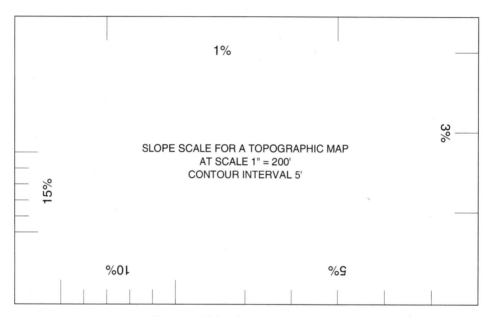

Form "A" (with separate scales)

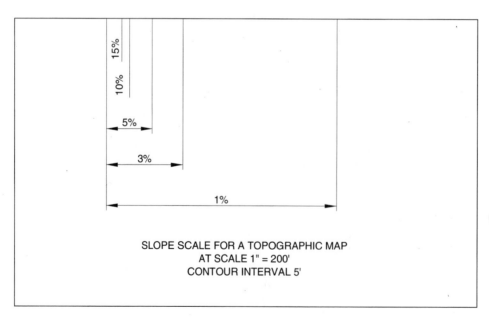

Form "B" (with combined scales)

holding the two maps together in front of a well-lit window.

The "rationalized" map should then be colored, using a carefully selected range of colors. The lightest colors are generally used to indicate the flattest areas; the strongest colors are used to indicate the steepest areas. It is preferable to use colors in the same general color family (such as pinks-to-red, light-greens-to-dark-greens, and tans-to-browns) when illustrating features on a map that have some obvious relationship.

Figures 3.3, 3.4, and 3.5 give examples of the steps involved when preparing a slope map using the techniques outlined above, other than the map coloring.

Note

1. Some computer programs for Geographic Information Systems (GIS) can produce slope maps after appropriate data are keyed in.

Figure 3.3. A Basic Topographic Map

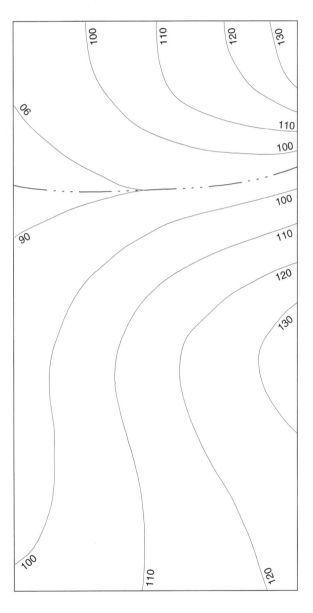

Figure 3.4. A Topographic Map Marked to Show Boundaries Between Slope Categories

Figure 3.5. A Slope Map with Rationalized Slope Boundaries

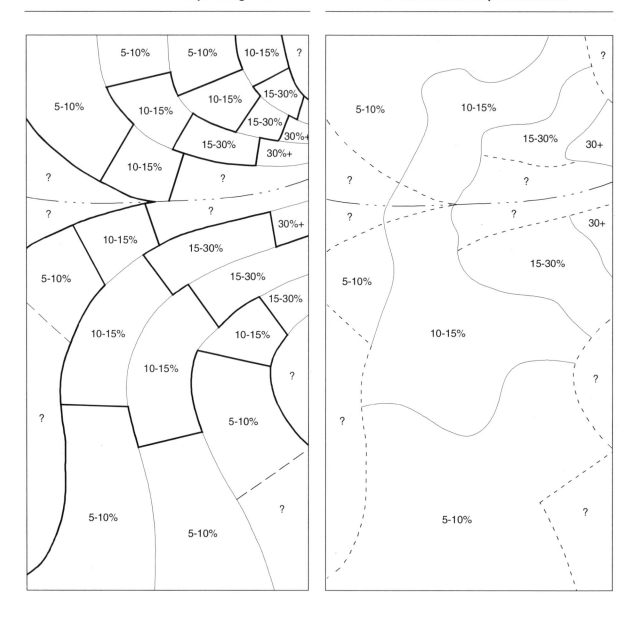

Utilities

4

Water Supply and Distribution

A BRIEF HISTORY OF WATER SUPPLY AND DISTRIBUTION IN THE UNITED STATES

Philadelphia (Pennsylvania) was the first large city in the U.S. to establish a public water supply system; the city sank its first two public wells in 1682, and by 1744 had an excellent water system. The City of Winston-Salem (North Carolina), however, was the first city to install a city-wide system of pipes to distribute water, and had an effective network of bored-log pipes in operation in 1776. Wooden pipes were used for water distribution until the advent of pumps, when it was found that these pipes did not satisfactorily withstand the increased water pressure; therefore, the more expensive cast-iron pipes were substituted after 1800. Cast iron soon became the predominant material for water supply mains with reinforced concrete being used for large-diameter pipes. In recent years, plastic pipes have also come into widespread use.

Starting in 1832, the City of Richmond (Virginia) pioneered the use of sand filter beds to remove sediments and other impurities from water supplies in the U.S. In 1857 Louis Pasteur announced the germ theory; this stirred many public-spirited people to become concerned with the quality of municipal water, and considerable attention was then given to water filtration and treatment. The chlorination of water was first undertaken in the U.S. in 1908 in Jersey City (New Jersey) as a means of making a water supply that had been tainted with sewage safe to drink. The addition of chlorine to water supplies has now become the most widely practiced method of disinfecting water in the U.S.

THE BASIC WATER SUPPLY AND DISTRIBUTION SYSTEM

The basic water supply and distribution system is shown schematically in Figure 4.1.

Sources of Water

Water comes from:
- underground sources such as wells or springs
- surface sources such as continuously flowing rivers
- natural or man-made reservoirs
- lakes

Figure 4.1. Schematic Diagram of a Typical Urban Water Distribution System

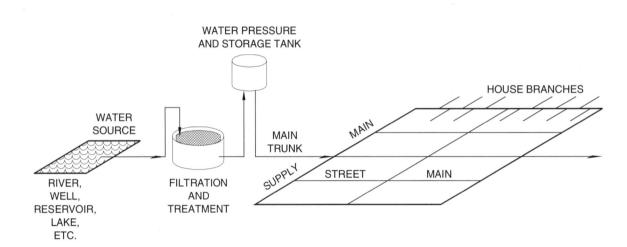

Water Filtering and Treatment

A water filtering and treatment plant is usually required between the source of water supply and the water distribution system. A filtering system is used to filter out sediments and other solid materials. Water treatment is used to provide the water with a desirable chemical balance and to eliminate any undesirable biological contaminants.

Pressure Tower and Storage

Water is pumped from the treatment plant to a pressure and storage tank. This tank may be in the form of an elevated tower, or a reservoir on (or under) the surface of the ground at an elevation well above the elevation of the water users. The purpose of this water pressure and storage tank is to establish adequate water pressure throughout the water system, and provide an adequate supply of water for normal use and fire fighting. The water supply must be available and usable not only under routine conditions but also at times when no power is available to run water pumps.

Local Distribution

Water leaves the pressure tower in a *main trunk* (the largest pipe in the system), which branches out into *supply mains*, then to *street mains* which, in turn, have *house branches* providing water to each building. Because the water is under pressure, water lines may go up and down hills, if consideration is given to the change of water pressure due to change of elevation.

MACRO INFLUENCES OF WATER SUPPLY ON URBAN FORM

1. Where a source of water supply does not exist, urban development will not occur. Where supply is limited, urban development will be limited to the population which the water supply can serve.
2. Water quality can restrict urban development. Where supply sources are so polluted as to make them unpalatable,

they may be useless, or require such a great expenditure to make them potable as to be unsupportable. Pollution may be man-made or natural (such as sulfur springs).

3. Urban development usually occurs below the elevation of the water supply. Development can be located at an elevation near or above the elevation of the water source only if water towers (with pumped storage) are installed to provide adequate water pressure at the desired elevations.

4. Water trunks, mains, and branches must be protected from winter freezing and therefore must be located well below the surface of the ground in areas where winters are severe. If bedrock exists near the surface of the ground, the cost of excavation may be so great as to preclude water service, or delay it until the demand for the use of the land is sufficient to justify the increased costs.

5. The available water pressure at house branches will limit the development of sites. If pressure is adequate to serve only 2 floors of housing, the cost of serving 3- or 4-story housing will usually be too great to be justified. Multistory buildings (6-22 stories), however, often provide auxiliary pumps and storage facilities at a justified cost.

6. Areas that are not served by a central water system may be served by individual springs or wells. Ground-water sources may be so meager as to make individual well service impossible, resulting in nondevelopment.

7. Where individual wells and sewerage systems (septic tanks and leaching fields) are used on one property, only low-density (large-lot) development

can be permitted to occur. This is because it is necessary to physically separate septic fields from water supply wells in order to prevent contamination of the wells.

8. Arid desert areas are difficult to urbanize because, among other reasons, there are usually inadequate water supplies. Frigid polar areas are also difficult to urbanize because, among other reasons, it is very difficult to establish a source of flowing water there and workable water distribution systems. Desalinization plants and water recirculation systems are technologically feasible and can provide water to desert, polar, and other waterless areas, but their current economic cost is so high that it prohibits their use except for very unusual situations, such as military outposts.

THE DEMAND FOR WATER

The primary uses of water in the United States are for agriculture, industry, and municipal water systems. Agriculture uses about 900 gallons per capita per day (gpcd), industry about 900 gpcd, and municipal water systems about 150 gpcd. The demand for agricultural water varies widely with location. In areas with heavy and reliable rainfall, little irrigation water is needed to raise crops. In the arid western section of the United States, however, agricultural areas use 90 percent of all the water produced. Of all the water used by agriculture, about 40 percent is returned to streams or aquifers; the remaining 60 percent enters the atmosphere through evaporation or transpiration.

The demand for industrial water also shows great variation from place to place and from industry to industry. Paper mills and steel mills use prodigious quantities of water, while fabricating industries use relatively little. Most of the water used by industry comes directly from streams, lakes, or wells, rather than from municipal water systems. Approximately 98 percent of industrially used water flows back to streams or aquifers, with only 2 percent being evaporated to the atmosphere or consumed in the industrial process.

Per-capita water consumption by municipal water systems also varies. Water used in private homes typically ranges from 20 to 80 gpcd, with an average of about 40 gpcd. Municipal water systems usually supply local commercial uses, as well as small industries that do not have their own direct source of water; these customers typically use about 70 gpcd, with notable variation from place to place. Municipal use of water for fire fighting, street cleaning, and park watering averages about 10 gpcd. Losses from municipal water systems, even with careful management, generally run 20 percent or more. Therefore, the total water consumption for municipal water systems runs about 150 gpcd (40 gpcd to private homes; 70 gpcd to commerce and industry; 10 gpcd to public use; and 30 gpcd to unaccounted-for losses). About 90 percent of the water from municipal systems is returned to streams and aquifers, usually after some type of sewage treatment.

Water for fire fighting in urban areas almost always requires a substantially larger water storage capacity (and larger water mains) than does the normal day-to-day demand for water. The requirements for water for fire fighting are determined by reviewing the combustibility of specific areas of the city, and then calculating the flow of water that would be required to suppress a fire in that area.

Example

A water supply system for a city (or part of a city) of 10,000 population would typically provide:

Fire flow: 3,000 gallons per minute for 10 hours = 1,800,000 gallons

Municipal flow: 150 gpcd × 10,000 persons × peak demand factor of 1.5 × 10 hours / 24 hours = 937,500 gallons (round to 900,000 gallons)

Total storage required: 2,700,000 gallons

WATER PRESSURE

A water pressure of about 50 pounds per square inch (psi) is usually required in the water system adjacent to each urban use. In some water systems the pressure may, however, be as low as 20 psi, or as high as 80 psi. If the water pressure in the system exceeds 80 or 90 psi, a "pressure-reducing valve" must be installed between the water system and the user. If the water pressure is less than 20 psi, each water user will need to install an on-site pump and storage system. Water pressure inside each building (in contrast to water pressure in the water main outside the building) should be at least 15 psi at each fixture (preferably 20 psi). This means that the designers of multistoried buildings must often plan for a fairly complex network of pumps, storage tanks, and pressure-reducing valves within individual buildings.

DESIGN GUIDELINES FOR CENTRAL WATER SUPPLY SYSTEMS

Water mains peripheral to the area for residential development deliver water under pressure to the area. Water pipes carry this water onto the site and then to each dwelling unit. Unlike the storm sewer and sanitary sewer piping systems (which are gravity systems), the water supply piping system is a pressurized system.

In a gravity system of pipes, fluids flow downhill, propelled solely by the force of gravity. In a pressurized system, fluids are pushed through the pipes to produce a desired pressure at the point of release (for example, at the end of a fire hose), or it may be used to raise the fluid to a higher elevation. The water supply network of pipes serving residential areas should be in a grid or a loop pattern; they should include no long dead-end lines. See Figure 4.2.

The grid and loop patterns allow for segments of the water system to be closed off for repairs; the dead-end line does not. Dead-end lines sometimes experience serious pressure drops in periods of high water demand; they may also suffer from water stagnation in periods of low water demand. Water pipes may be curved or bent at virtually any angle. They must be laid deep enough in the ground so that they will not freeze in the wintertime (typically at least 4 feet below the surface of the ground in midwestern United States). Residential street branches of water supply pipes should be no less than 2 inches in diameter. No street main should be less than 6 inches in diameter, and no branch main should be less than 8 inches in diameter. Any water main that serves a fire hydrant should be at least 6 inches in diameter, because smaller pipes cause too great a pressure loss when fire-flow volumes pass through the pipes.

In earlier years, water supply lines were kept well separated from sanitary sewer lines; these days, a number of major building codes now approve of installing sanitary sewers and water supply lines in the same trench.[1] It is recommended, however, that the water line be placed at least 12 inches above the sewer line, with a lateral separation of 18 inches.

Fire hydrants should be located along all water lines at the location of each street intersection and between intersections as necessary to assure that hydrants are no more than 1,000 feet apart (500 feet between hydrants is more desirable because this reduces the pressure loss in small-diameter fire hoses). Fire hydrants should be located at least 50 feet from any structure, in order to assure their accessibility in the event that a nearby structure catches fire.

CALCULATING THE POTENTIAL SERVICE AREA OF A WATER SUPPLY SYSTEM

If you build a water storage tank on top of a hill—or erect a tank on top of a tall tower—what areas can be served by it?

We know that water weighs 62.4 pounds per cubic foot. What amount of pressure does this water exert? If we visualize 1 cubic foot of water (a cube $12 \times 12 \times 12$ inches), we note that the weight of the water (62.4 pounds) presses down on the bottom of the cube. Since the bottom of the cube measures 12×12 inches, its area is 144 square inches. We can therefore calculate that the water pressure at a depth of 1 foot is 62.4 pounds divided by 144 square inches, or .433 psi.

We also know that we must have some water pressure when we turn on the faucet in our house, or else the water won't flow out of the pipes. A frequently used figure for the minimum desirable water pressure is 20 psi.

Suppose you build a two-story house right at the foot of the water tower. How high must the tower be in order to serve the second story of the house with water at 20 psi? We can set up a ratio:

$$\frac{1.00 \text{ feet height}}{.433 \text{ psi}} = \frac{X \text{ feet height}}{20 \text{ psi}}$$

Figure 4.2. Schematic Diagram of Grid, Looped, and Dead-End Water Distribution Systems

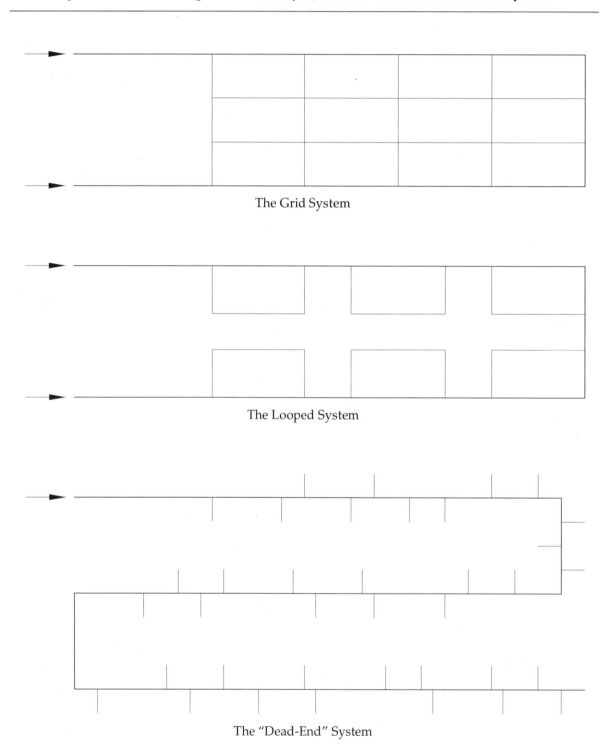

The Grid System

The Looped System

The "Dead-End" System

Figure 4.3. Recommended Separation of Water and Sewer Lines

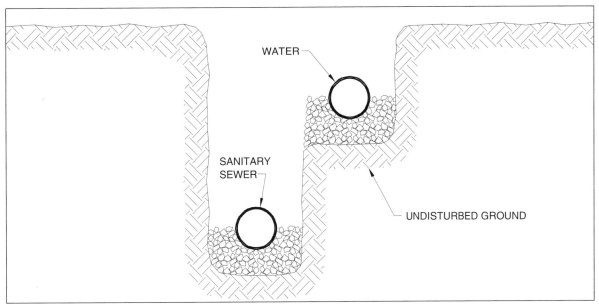

Source: Dewberry and Davis. *Affordable Housing Development Guidelines for State and Local Government*. Washington, DC: U.S. Department of Housing and Urban Development, Office of Policy Development and Research, 1991, p. 109.

Solving for X,

$$X = \frac{20}{.433}$$

= 46.2 feet (46 feet, with significant figures)

We now know that the bottom of the water tower must be at least 46 feet above the second story of the house. And how high is the second story of a house? As a rule of thumb, we can say that each story is about 10 feet high; therefore, the top of the second story of a house is about 20 feet. We can therefore deduce that the bottom of the water tank would have to be 46 feet + 20 feet, or 66 feet above the ground.

Suppose we move the house away from the bottom of the water tower. How far could we go before we run out of adequate water pressure? Theoretically, we could go an infinite distance, so long as we didn't raise the elevation of the house. In reality, however, we would observe a loss in water pressure as the house is moved away from the water source. This loss of pressure is caused by conditions such as the friction of the water moving in pipes, going through valves, and making sharp turns. As a rule of thumb, engineers use the figure of a loss of 5 feet of "head" for every 1,000 feet of pipe, or 2.2 psi per 1,000 feet.

Sample Problem #1

A water tower is located on a totally flat plain; the bottom of the tank is 100 feet above the ground. What is the maximum service radius of the tower, if a residual pressure of 20 psi is required at the first floor of residences to be served?

Solution

We need 20 psi at 10 feet above grade. Pressure at the 10-foot elevation, disregarding line loss, would be equal to 90 feet of head (100 feet − 10 feet). 90 feet of head = 38.97 psi (90 feet × .433 psi/feet). Since we have 38.97 psi at the first story, and we need to retain only 20 psi, this means we can afford to lose 18.97 psi (38.97 − 20) in line loss. We can therefore set up the following ratio:

$$\frac{2.2 \text{ psi pressure loss}}{1{,}000 \text{ feet of water line}} =$$

$$\frac{18.97 \text{ psi pressure loss}}{X \text{ feet of water line}}$$

Solving for X,

$$X = 8{,}622 \text{ feet}$$

We therefore say the service radius from the water tower is about 8,600 feet, under the conditions cited.

Sample Problem #2

A water tank is located on a continuous slope of 5 percent. The bottom of the tank is 160 feet above grade. Find the maximum extent of service to:

A. downhill areas

B. uphill areas

C. areas at the same elevation as the base of the tank

Assume that 20 psi is required on the first floor of each residence; this is 10 feet above the surrounding terrain. Also assume a line loss of 5 feet of head (2.2 psi) per 1,000 feet of distance from the base of the water tower.

Figure 4.4 diagrams the three design situations.

Solutions (refer to Figure 4.4)

Situation (A): Service to areas downhill from the tank—The difference in elevation

Figure 4.4. Sketches of the Situations Described in Sample Problem #2

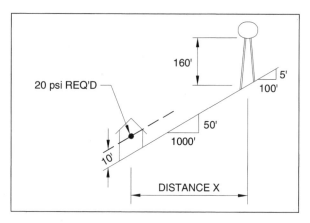

Situation A. Water service to areas downhill from the water pressure tank

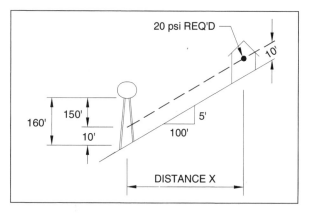

Situation B. Water service to areas uphill from the water pressure tank

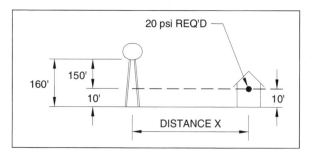

Situation C. Water service to areas at the same elevation as the base of the water pressure tank

along the downhill slope is 5 percent, or 5 feet of vertical distance for every 100 feet of horizontal distance, or 50 feet of vertical distance for every 1,000 feet of horizontal distance.

This means that a water line running downhill for a distance of 1,000 feet will develop an added 50-foot "head" of water pressure, if pressure loss due to friction is disregarded. But, we know that there is a line loss of 5 feet of head for every 1,000 feet of pipe length. Therefore, if the pipe runs downhill a distance of 1,000 feet, the water pressure will increase by a head of 45 feet (50-foot increase less a 5-foot decrease). We can therefore conclude that there is no limit to the distance downhill from the tank that can be served since the water pressure increases the further downhill the pipe goes.

Situation (B): Service to areas uphill from the tank—We require 20 psi in the house 10 feet above the ground, from a water tank 160 feet high. This is equivalent to 20 psi at ground level from a tank 150 feet high. We can calculate the water pressure from a tank 150 feet high; it is 150 feet × .433 psi/feet of height = 65 psi. We can afford a reduction from the original 65 psi down to 20 psi; the difference is a loss of pressure of 45 psi (65 − 20 = 45). This pressure loss may be from pipe friction, or change of elevation, or both.

Let us take a sample distance of 1,000 feet and see what our pressure losses are. Loss due to pipe friction will be 2.2 psi (a given approximation). Loss due to increase in elevation will be equal to a loss of head of 50 feet (1,000 feet × 5 percent grade = 50 feet). This is equal to 50 feet × .433 psi/foot = 21.6 psi. So, in 1,000 feet we lose 2.2 + 21.6 psi = 23.8 psi. If we lose 23.8 psi in 1,000 feet, how far can we go before we lose 45 psi?

$$\frac{23.8 \text{ psi}}{1,000 \text{ feet}} = \frac{45 \text{ psi}}{X}$$

$$X = \frac{45 \times 1,000}{23.8}$$

= 1,890 feet (1,900 feet when rounded)

Situation (C): Service to areas at the same elevation as the base of the tank—Water pressure in the house, disregarding pipe friction, is equal to a head of 150 feet (160 feet tank height less 10-foot elevation to water outlet in house). This head of 150 feet is equal to a water pressure of 150 feet × .433 psi/foot = 65 psi. But, if a water pressure of 20 psi is required in the house, this means that we can afford to lose 45 psi in friction losses (our original 65 psi − 20 psi residual pressure in house = 45 psi). We know that we lose 2.2 psi in friction losses for every 1,000 feet of pipe length. How many feet of pipe length can we have before we lose 45 psi? We arrive at the answer by solving the equation:

$$\frac{2.2 \text{ psi loss}}{\text{in } 1,000 \text{ feet}} = \frac{45 \text{ psi loss}}{\text{in } X \text{ feet}}$$

$$\text{so } X = \frac{45 \text{ psi} \times 1,000 \text{ feet}}{2.2 \text{ psi}}$$

= 20,000 feet

The precise calculated answer is 20,454.545 feet, but we must round off our answer to two significant figures.

The foregoing examples of water system design were provided to illustrate basic concepts of how water distribution systems work. In actual practice, engineers use computer programs to assist in determining desirable pipe sizes, analyze the flow of water in a network of pipes and valves, and determine the optimum network.

DEFINITIONS

Acre-foot—Unit quantity of water; an amount which would cover 1 acre to a depth of 1 foot; consists of 326,000 gallons.

Aquifer—A subsurface zone that yields economically important amounts of water to wells. (The word "aquifer" is synonymous with the term "water-bearing formation.") An aquifer may be porous rock, unconsolidated gravel, fractured rock, or cavernous limestone.

Domestic use—Water use in homes and on lawns, including use for washing, cooking, flushing toilets, laundry, washing cars, air coolers, and swimming pools.

Evaporation—The process by which water is changed from a liquid to a gas or vapor.

Flood—Any relatively high stream flow overtopping the natural or artificial banks in any reach of a stream.*

Flood plain—The lowland that borders a river, usually dry but subject to flooding when the stream overflows its banks.

Ground water—The water zone below the surface of the earth in which the rocks and soil are saturated, the top of which is the "water table."

Hydrology—The science of the behavior of water in the atmosphere, on the surface of the earth, and underground.

Impermeable strata—A layer of soil or rock which is not permeable to the passage of water (e.g., clay).

Infiltration—The flow of a fluid into a substance through pores or small openings. The common use of the word is to denote the flow of water into soil material. (In sanitary engineering, the term refers to the flow of water from adjacent soils into a sewer line.)

Leaching—The removal into solution of soluble minerals from solids into percolating waters.

Percolation—The passage of water through the open pores of soils, or the fissures in rock.

Permeability—The property of soil or rock to pass water through it. This depends not only on the volume of the openings and pores, but also on how these openings are connected to one another.

Saturated zone—The zone of soil in which water occupies the pores between the solid soil particles.

Sediment—Fragmental mineral material transported or deposited by water or air.

Transpiration—The process by which water vapor escapes from the living plant and enters the atmosphere.*

Water table—The upper surface of the saturated zone.

Note

1. Dewberry and Davis.

Definitions marked with * are adapted from the American Geological Institute, *Dictionary of Geological Terms*, 1976 ed. Reprinted with permission.

Recommended Reading

Lynch, Kevin and Gary Hack. *Site Planning*. 3rd ed. Cambridge, MA: MIT Press, 1984, pp. 243-245, 463.

Sources of Further Information

Colley, Barbara C. *Practical Manual of Land Development*. 3rd ed. New York: McGraw-Hill, 1998. See Chapter 10, "Water Supply Lines."

De Chiara and Koppleman. *Urban Planning and Design Criteria*. 2nd ed. New York: Van Nostrand Reinhold, 1975, pp. 519-528.

Dewberry and Davis. *Affordable Housing Development Guidelines for State and Local Government*. Washington, DC: U.S. Department of Housing and Urban Development, Office of Policy Development and Research, 1991.

5

Wastewater Management

DEFINITIONS

Wastewater management is the process of removing, reconditioning, and reusing water that has been used by man once or more, and is no longer wanted in its present location and condition. The term "wastewater management" has come into common usage only in fairly recent times; previously, the term "sewage disposal" was generally used. The term "sewage disposal" is no longer widely used because we now realize that we really can't "dispose" of sewage. We can move it from one location to another, but we can't eliminate it from the world's ecosystem. Furthermore, we now realize that sewage, which is primarily water, has a potential for reuse after being treated to remove the undesired elements from it. After all, water is a valuable resource, both in an economic and an ecological sense, regardless of its source.

Sewage is liquid waste containing dissolved and/or suspended solid wastes, which is conducted away from residences; institutions; and commercial, agricultural, or industrial establishments. Solids in sewage typically constitute about 1/10 of 1 percent by weight.

There are two major methods of treating sewage:

1. Collecting the wastewater through a network of pipes and letting it flow by gravity to a wastewater treatment plant; releasing the treated liquid residue (effluent) to a river, stream, lake, or ocean; and disposing of the solid residue (sludge) by whatever means is available, economical, and not environmentally damaging. This system is used in most U.S. urban areas. Many urban areas, however, now make use of the treated effluent for irrigating crops, for recharging underground aquifers, or for watering parks and golf courses, rather than just discharging the water into a nearby river or ocean.

2. Allowing the wastewater from an individual source (such as a house or store) to flow by gravity to a septic tank where it is biologically digested by a natural process, and then allowing the effluent to flow through a leaching field into the nearby soil. The sludge is removed from the septic tank every two

or three years. This system is primarily used in rural areas.

Basic Definitions

Sewage—Wastewater flow from residential, commercial, and industrial establishments.

Sewer—A pipe or other conduit used to carry off wastewater or storm waters.

Sewerage—The system of pipes, pumps, and treatment facilities used to transport, treat, and discharge sewage or storm waters.

Sewerage Definitions

The terminology concerning sewerage has not been standardized, and one will find a variety of different definitions for such terms as "main" and "trunk." The following definitions are in fairly widespread usage and will serve to show the general relationships between the various parts of the sewerage system. Please refer to Figure 5.1.

House lateral—A pipe carrying wastewater from a house to the sewerage system.

Street main—A sewer that receives the discharges from house laterals.

Branch trunk sewer—A sewer that connects one or more street mains to a trunk sewer.

Trunk sewer—A sewer that forms one of the major branches in the sewerage system; receives wastewater from one or more branch trunk sewers.

Interceptor—The major sewer line that collects the flow of sewage from other sewers and carries it to a wastewater treatment plant.

Lift station—A pump which raises the vertical elevation of wastewater, usually without substantial horizontal displacement.

Force main—A pipe in which wastewater flows under pressure, usually from a pump to some uphill destination.

Invert elevation—The elevation of the lowest part of the interior of a pipe.

Infiltration—(1) General definition: the movement of water through the soil surface and into the soil. (2) Definition in relation to pipes: the movement of water through cracks or defective joints into a sewer line.

Outfall—The sewer line that carries treated effluent from a wastewater treatment plant to the point of effluent discharge.

Other Definitions

Effluent—The liquid residue from a wastewater treatment plant.

Sludge—Precipitated solids produced by sewage treatment plants. Sludge occurs as a watery mixture of effluent and solids, but is usually dewatered to become a slush or a solid before disposal.

Package plant—A small, self-contained, wastewater treatment plant, partially or completely preassembled by a manufacturer; usually designed to be operated with a minimum of supervision; usually provides secondary treatment of wastewater.

Manhole—A lined circular pit which provides access to underground utility lines. Manholes are usually 4 feet in diameter, and are as deep as required to reach the utility line. In drainage systems, manholes have two purposes: they provide access to the drain for cleaning, and serve as junction boxes for tributary drains.

Biochemical Oxygen Demand (BOD)—A measure of the amount of oxygen required for the biological degradation of a specific quantity of organic solids in a specific amount of water over a given period of time. BOD is usually expressed in terms of milligrams of oxygen per liter of water required in a five-day period.

Figure 5.1. Schematic Diagram of a Sewerage System and a Wastewater Treatment Plant

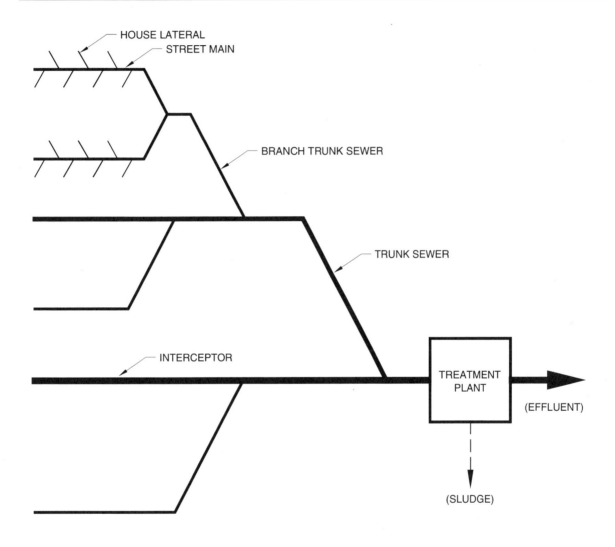

THE BASIC SANITARY SEWER SYSTEM IN URBAN RESIDENTIAL AREAS

In a typical case, wastewater that is originated in a house in an urban area would leave the site by means of a house lateral and flow into the street main; from here, it would flow into a branch trunk sewer, then into a trunk sewer, then through the interceptor to the wastewater treatment plant. In the waste-

water treatment plant, the wastewater is treated, as the name implies.

Wastewater treatment plants usually give "primary" and "secondary" treatment to sewage; in some circumstances, "tertiary" treatment is also given. "Primary treatment" consists of screening and settling out the solids from the sewage. "Secondary treatment" may take place following the primary treatment; it is a biological process in which the organic materials in the sewage are oxidized and digested. (The oxygen demand of raw sewage is usually the major environmental problem of sewage.) In this step, the acidity/ alkalinity of the sewage is also controlled. "Tertiary treatment" may follow secondary treatment, and is a process in which detrimental inorganic chemicals such as salts and heavy metal compounds are removed. Nitrates and phosphates are usually the major targets of tertiary sewage treatment.

The fluid that is discharged from the wastewater treatment process is called "effluent." Effluent is usually discharged into flowing streams, rivers, or the ocean. If the effluent has been sufficiently treated, it will not produce damage to the quality of the receiving waters. All too often, in the past, inadequately treated effluent has produced serious environmental damage.

While the majority of wastewater treatment plants discharge their effluent into flowing streams, large lakes, or the ocean, some effluent is used as irrigation water for agriculture or ponds for recreation use. When effluent is used for agriculture, it is used either to flood fields or is distributed with a sprinkler system. The effluent usually has had secondary treatment, so it is neither unsanitary nor malodorous. Health regulations, however, generally forbid its use on food crops that are eaten without cooking (such as fruits), put some restrictions on its use for food crops that are always cooked before eaten (such as selected vegetables), but very few restrictions when it is used for nonfood crops (such as cotton).

TYPES OF WASTEWATER FLOWS

Communities produce several different types of wastewater that must be disposed of. These include:

- *domestic* (also called *sanitary*) wastewater from residences, institutions, stores, and similar uses
- *industrial wastewater* from industrial plants; some of this may contain industrial products (such as chemicals), or may be predominantly cooling water used in industrial processes
- *infiltration*, which is unwanted water that leaks into the sewer systems
- *combined systems*, where domestic and industrial wastewaters are combined with storm water flows in the same sewerage system. (For a discussion of storm water flows, see Chapter 6.) Combined systems are not favored because, in times of runoff from local precipitation, the wastewater treatment plant must either run a great deal of rainwater through the treatment plant (an unnecessary expense), or allow the treated domestic and industrial wastewater to bypass the treatment plant along with the rainwater; neither situation is desirable.

The volume and character of sewage flow in combined systems vary widely from installation to installation and season to season. It is not practical to make general statements concerning them; each system requires an individual analysis.

AMOUNTS OF WASTEWATER FLOWS

The amount of domestic wastewater that is produced in an area depends upon how much water is supplied to the area, and what proportion of that water finds its way into the sewerage system. It is not uncommon for an urban area to receive about 150 gallons per capita per day (see Chapter 4). However, perhaps 20 percent of this goes to unaccounted-for losses, and a substantial amount may be used for such tasks as watering lawns and washing cars, and not find its way into the wastewater system. As a general rule of thumb, from 60 to 75 percent of the water introduced into an area will find its way out of the area in the form of wastewater. This is, however, an unreliable rule of thumb; it is not valid if there are many private wells introducing water into the system, or if there are many septic tanks receiving the wastewater.

The amount of industrial wastewater produced depends very largely on the type of industry in the area and the water demand for each. Warehousing, for instance, produces very little wastewater. Canneries, on the other hand, produce great amounts of wastewater. A site-by-site analysis of wastewater production is needed in order to predict future wastewater flows from industrial areas. Where one is planning for future industry, an allowance of 5,000 gallons per acre of undeveloped land per day is often used.

The amount of water that infiltrates the sewerage system and passes into the wastewater treatment plant is dependent upon the condition of the sewerage, and upon the amount of water adjacent to the sewer lines. Old sewers, with cracks or poor joints, are more prone to infiltration than are well-constructed modern sewers. Sewers laid below the water table in the soil (especially in marshy areas) are more prone to infiltration than are pipes in dry areas. Sewers that have manholes located in areas subject to flooding are quite likely to receive some storm water infiltration. In some areas, homeowners have connected the downspouts from their roofs to sanitary sewers (rather than to storm sewers, or let the runoff flow into the adjacent yard or street); this is also a form of infiltration that should be minimized.

LIFT STATIONS AND FORCE MAINS

The usual practice in sewer design is to utilize gravity flow from the point of origin of the wastewater to the treatment plant (see Figures 5.2 and 5.3). In flatland areas, however, if sewers were to be installed at a uniform depth below the surface of the ground, the pipes would not have enough of a slope to induce the wastewater to flow through them; if the pipes were to be installed with an adequate slope, excessively deep (and expensive) trenching would be required at the downhill end.

In many flatland areas, lift stations are installed (see Figure 5.4), sometimes in conjunction with force mains (see Figure 5.5). In the design of a sewerage system with a lift station, one plans for the installation of a sewer line starting at an appropriate depth (usually about 6 feet below the surface of the ground) and slopes it downward as it flows toward the wastewater treatment plant. When the depth of the trench required for the sewer becomes too deep (14 or 16 feet), a pump is installed to lift the sewage back up to an elevation 6 feet from the surface once again, and the sewer line then continues its downhill flow.

To the uninitiated, this sounds like a simple and logical solution. There are problems with this approach, however, that cause the majority of municipal engineers to eschew it whenever possible. The problems are present because pumps are involved. The specific problems are:

- Pumps must be operable at all times, even when there is a failure of electric power. This usually requires the installation and maintenance of a reliable, standby internal combustion engine.
- More than one pump must be installed, so that one pump can be in use while another one is being repaired.
- Raw sewage contains a great deal of grit that quickly wears out pumps, and it may include many miscellaneous objects

Figure 5.2. Profile of a Gravity-Flow Sewerage System in Gently Sloping Terrain

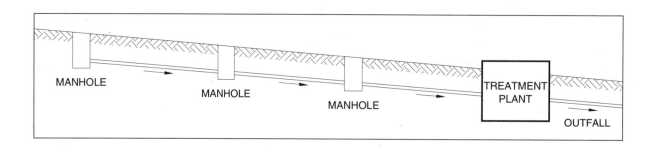

Figure 5.3. Profile of a Gravity-Flow Sewerage System in Steeply Sloping Terrain

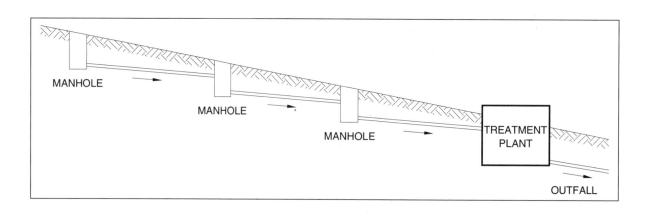

Figure 5.4. Profile of a Gravity-Flow Sewerage System with a Lift Station in Level Terrain

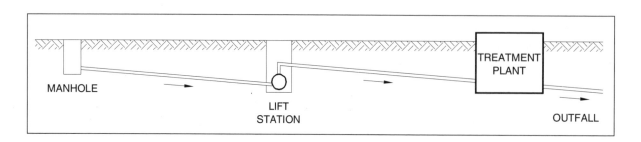

Figure 5.5. Profile of a Sewerage System With a Force Main

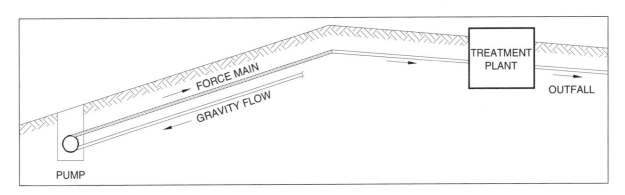

(such as hubcaps, dead animals, or disposable diapers) that readily clog pumps; each pump station must have an effective screening apparatus, which requires cleaning and maintenance on a regular basis.

Sometimes someone wants to develop land that is at a lower elevation than an established wastewater treatment plant. This means that sewage from the area must be pumped uphill, through a force main, to the treatment plant. This force main cannot be used as a conventional sewer line that can be tapped into from adjacent properties because the sewage in the pipe is under pressure. If one wishes to make a connection to the force main, a special pump must be installed that can push the sewage from the adjacent property into the force main. A common procedure is to avoid a multiplicity of these special pumps by installing a gravity-flow line parallel to the force main, and letting the sewage it collects flow by gravity to the pump at the lower end of the force main (see Figure 5.5).

Many municipal engineers are convinced of the validity of Murphy's Law ("if something can go wrong, it will"). They therefore prefer to rely on good old gravity flow in wastewater systems rather than on pumps that require constant maintenance.

THE WASTEWATER PLANNING PROCESS

A generalized description of the process used to plan for wastewater collection and treatment is:

1. Determine the size and location of the service area.
2. Identify the probable future land uses in the service area.
3. Estimate the quantity and characteristics of the flow of sewage that land uses in the service area will produce.
4. Design the wastewater collection and treatment facilities:
   A. pipe sizes, slope, and location
   B. treatment plant capacity and location
   C. effluent discharge location and sludge removal process

There are many policy issues involved in Steps 1 and 2; the urban planner should participate in these phases of the wastewater planning process. Sanitary engineers (specialists in the field of civil engineering) usually have the primary responsibility for the full scope of the wastewater planning process.

When engineers design sewer systems, they generally draft a preliminary layout on paper in order to visualize "the big picture," and then turn to the computer to work out the details. As B.C. Colley says:

> Sophisticated CADD software systems are available that will make calculations, offer alternatives, and draft the designs [of sewer systems]. Software that does not require CADD is also available for making hydraulic calculations and offering alternatives. These calculations can also be entered into a spreadsheet program that will allow the designer to try different pipe sizes and slopes instantly.[1]

DESIGN GUIDELINES FOR SEWERS

Pipe Capacity

The ability of a pipe or an open channel to carry fluids (such as sewage) is dependent upon:

- the size of the pipe or channel
- the slope of the pipe or channel
- the roughness of the interior surface of the pipe or channel

These factors have been combined in what is known as the "Manning equation"; most civil engineers are familiar with this. While urban planners and landscape architects will rarely have a working knowledge of it, many of them should be aware of the implications it has on the design of wastewater systems in urban areas.

The volume of fluid that a pipe carries is measured by multiplying the velocity of flow times the cross-sectional area of the flow. There are limits to the desirable velocity of flow. Experience indicates that if the flow of sewage in a full pipe is less than 2 feet per second (fps), any sediments or solids in the waste tend to settle out when the pipe is partially full and may clog the pipe. On the other hand, if the flow is faster than about 10 fps,

the solids carried in the water tend to erode away the interior surface of many types of pipes causing their destruction. Therefore, sewer systems are generally designed for a minimum flow velocity of 2 fps and a maximum velocity of 10 fps.

Pipe Size

Pipe size should be determined by the flow requirements of the wastewater system and by the slope of the terrain in which the pipe is located (see discussion above), with the following exceptions:

- Many state and local codes require that house laterals be at least 4 inches in diameter.
- All lines other than house laterals should be at least 8 inches in diameter to facilitate cleaning.
- Large-diameter pipes should not feed into smaller diameter pipes; this is to assure that a bulky object carried by a large pipe does not clog the entrance to a small-diameter pipe.

Pipe Depth

- In areas where buildings are expected to have basements, the invert elevation of street mains should be about 6 feet below the surface of the ground.
- In areas where buildings are *not* expected to have basements, street mains may be about 4 feet below ground.
- When a building site is a considerable distance from a street main, or is notably uphill or downhill from it, a design analysis should be made to make sure that a satisfactory connection to the main is possible.
- Digging a pipe trench through bedrock is very expensive; therefore, sewer lines should avoid areas where bedrock is close to the surface.

• Installation of sewer lines in soils below the water table usually requires pumping of the trench during construction. Furthermore, pipes in these situations may suffer from high infiltration rates, especially if the earth is not firm, and the pipes shift and crack open a few joints.

• Deep trenches (12 to 16 feet) are expensive to excavate and should be avoided, if possible, especially in areas with a high water table, and in soils that tend to crumble or slump. Pipes laid in the bottom of deep trenches are difficult to tap into, for future connections.

Manhole Spacing

• A manhole should be located at each of the following locations:
  — at the end of each sewer line (other than house laterals)
  — at every change of direction in the sewer line which exceeds 10 degrees
  — whenever the sewer line has a change in slope, elevation, or size
  — at the junction of two or more sewer mains

• Manholes should be spaced no further apart than 500 feet if the sewer line is too small for a person to enter.

• Most jurisdictions require that sewer lines run in straight lines between manholes. Some jurisdictions allow curves in the horizontal alignment of sewer lines; when this is done, manholes are required at the beginning and end of each curve.

Location of Wastewater Treatment Plants

These days, the majority of new wastewater treatment plants are built to connect with existing sewerage systems; this is very often a strong determinant in their location.

The location of wastewater treatment plants is limited to those areas which are lower than the area to be sewered and slightly higher than the point of effluent discharge, if the use of pumps and force mains is to be avoided.

Wastewater treatment plants produce objectionable odors from time to time, and are considered by many members of the general public as being visually unattractive. These factors lead designers to locate treatment plants downwind from populated areas and out of sight of the general public, whenever possible.

SIMPLE EXAMPLES OF DETERMINING THE EXTENT OF AREAS THAT CAN BE SEWERED

Example #1

Given: A wastewater treatment plant is located on a flat plain; the invert elevation of the inlet to the plant is 15 feet below the ground. The invert elevation of the sources of sewage is 6 feet below the ground. The minimum slope for sewer lines is 0.25 percent.

Required: What is the maximum length of sewer pipe from the treatment plant that can be used to serve the surrounding area?

Solution: The sewer line can have a drop in elevation of 15 feet – 6 feet = 9 feet. If a 0.25-foot drop is allowed in 100 feet of pipe, how many feet of pipe will there be for a 9-foot drop? We can solve this by setting up a ratio, and solving for "X":

$$\frac{0.25}{100} = \frac{9}{"X"} ; X = \frac{9 \times 100}{0.25} = 3,600 \text{ feet}$$

We see that the length of pipe from the treatment plant to the source of the sewage may be 3,600 feet. Note that this does not mean that the farthest source of sewage would be 3,600 feet, as the crow flies.

Example #2

Given: A wastewater treatment plant is located on the surface of the earth in an area which has a uniform slope of 2 percent. The invert elevation at the inlet to the treatment plant is 22 feet below the surface; the invert elevation of the sources of sewage is 6 feet below the surface. The minimum allowable slope of the sewer line is 0.12 percent.

Required: What is the maximum length possible of an 18-inch-diameter pipe between the treatment plant and the source of sewage:
  A. directly uphill?
  B. at the same elevation as the plant?
  C. downhill from the plant?

Solution:
  A. *Uphill:* As one moves uphill away from the treatment plant, the slope is 2 percent; this is substantially greater than the minimum grade required of 0.12 percent. Therefore, the sewer lines can run uphill for an infinite distance under these conditions.
  B. *At the same elevation as the treatment plant:* The 22-foot invert elevation is 16 feet below the 6-foot invert elevation of the source of sewage. Using the same procedure as in Example #1:

$$\frac{0.12}{100 \text{ feet}} = \frac{16}{\text{"X" feet}} \;;$$

$$\text{"X"} = \frac{16 \times 100}{0.12} = 13{,}333 \text{ feet}$$

  The answer is 13,000 feet, when rounded off to significant figures.
  C. *Downhill:* For every 100 feet we move downhill away from the treatment plant, we lose 2 feet of elevation. This loss of elevation must be made up as sewage flows back toward the treatment plant. In addition to the 2-foot change in elevation per 100 feet of distance, we must allow for 0.12 feet to promote the flow of sewage back to the

treatment plant. We therefore have a difference in elevation of 2.12 feet for every 100 feet of downhill distance from the treatment plant.

We know that we can afford to lose a total elevation of 16 feet in the run from the source of sewage to the treatment plant (22 feet invert elevation of the plant minus the 6-foot invert elevation of the source of sewage). Setting up a ratio, as we did in Example #1:

$$\frac{2.12 \text{ feet}}{100 \text{ feet}} = \frac{16 \text{ feet}}{\text{"X" feet}} \;;$$

$$\text{"X"} = \frac{16 \times 100}{2.12} = 754 \text{ feet}$$

The answer is 750 feet, when rounded to significant figures.

SEPTIC TANK SYSTEMS

General Description

A septic tank is an underground chamber into which sewage flows, where it will be digested by biological action. The solids in the sewage sink to the bottom of the tank where they are gradually digested; the fluids leave the tank in a partially digested state and flow into an adjacent leaching field. The deposit of solids in the septic tank should be pumped out every two or three years.

A diagram of septic tank systems is provided in Figure 5.6.

A leaching field is a network of perforated pipes laid in a bed of sand and gravel. Effluent from the septic tank flows through the pipes, and the sand and gravel into the adjacent soil. During this movement, further bacteriological action digests the organic compounds in the effluent, leaving water of a generally safe and inoffensive quality. Most of this water percolates down through the soil to

Figure 5.6. Schematic Diagram of a Septic Tank System

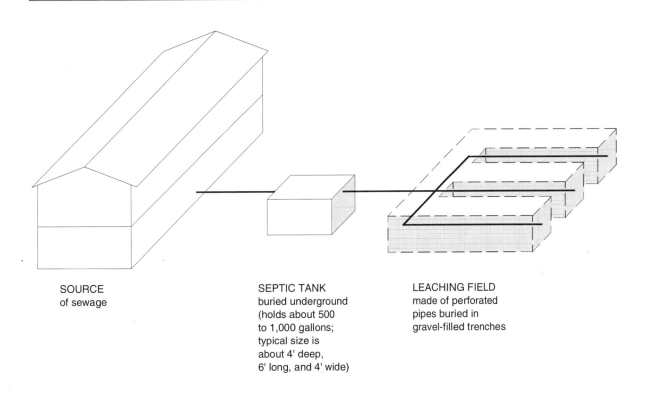

SOURCE
of sewage

SEPTIC TANK
buried underground
(holds about 500
to 1,000 gallons;
typical size is
about 4' deep,
6' long, and 4' wide)

LEACHING FIELD
made of perforated
pipes buried in
gravel-filled trenches

the water table, although some of it may be drawn up to the surface through the root system of plants.

The most important factor in the septic tank system is the soil in which the leaching field is located. Effluent must be able to percolate through the soil and be digested before it reaches the water table. (If it is not digested by this time, it will pollute the ground water.) Some soils (such as clays) are almost impervious to the flow of water and are, therefore, unsuitable for septic tank systems. On the other hand, beds of sand and gravel are also unsuitable because the effluent passes through them too rapidly, possibly ending up at the water table.

"Percolation tests" are made of soils to determine their suitability for septic tank sys-

tems. To make a percolation test, a hole is bored in the ground (usually about 6 inches in diameter and 3 feet in depth), water is poured in the hole, and an observation is made of how rapidly the water passes from the hole into the adjacent soil. The rate at which the water level drops is used as an indication of whether or not the soil is suitable for a leaching field and, if generally suitable, how large the field should be.

Septic tank systems are ecologically very desirable when they work right; they are a threat to public health, and offensive to the nose, when they don't. These systems "fail" if the sewage solids are not pumped from the septic tank on a regular basis, and pass into the leaching field where they clog the pores of the sand and gravel bed, and the adjacent soil. When this happens, the undigested efflu-ent will often be forced to the surface of the earth and make its presence known with its own distinctive odor.

The size of the required field usually deter-mines the minimum required lot size in rural areas. Modern zoning ordinances require enough land in each building site for the building itself, plus front, rear, and side yards to assure privacy, plus at least *two* times the area that is required for a leaching field, as determined by a percolation test on *each lot*. (The requirement for twice the area for a leaching field is to provide replacement space when the original field fails.) Leaching fields are difficult to install in steeply sloping ter-rain. Leaching field layout is usually no prob-lem (if the soil percolates adequately, that is) in lands with a slope of up to 10 percent. In lands with slopes between 10 and 20 percent, leaching fields should be avoided because of the high probability that the sewage will per-colate to the surface.

DESIGN GUIDELINES FOR SEPTIC TANK SYSTEMS

Leaching fields should *not* be installed in the following locations:

- in areas with a water table within 4 feet of the surface of the ground
- in areas with bedrock within 4 feet of the surface of the ground
- in areas subject to seasonal flooding
- within 100 feet of any well (a greater distance is needed if the soil is highly permeable)
- within 50 feet of any dwelling unit
- in terrain where the slope is in excess of 20 percent

There are a number of alternative combina-tions of septic tank systems, water supply sys-tems, and sewers that should be considered.

- *Private septic tank systems and public water supply.* Where septic tank systems serve each residence on its own site and a pub-lic water supply is provided, net residen-tial density usually can be no greater than 4 dwelling units per acre (DU/ac). This condition results from the need for at least 50 feet between any part of the septic tank leaching field system and any dwelling unit on the same property or on a surrounding property.

- *Private septic tank systems and private wells.* Where both sewer and water systems are provided on site for each dwelling unit via septic tanks and wells, net residential density can be no greater than 2 DU/ac, and may have to be much lower. This condition results from the need for at least 50 feet between any part of the sep-tic tank/leaching field system and any dwelling unit, in combination with the need for at least 100 feet between any part of the septic system and the nearest well. Where sandy soils exist, this dis-tance must be increased to 250 feet. In addition, the wells on each site must be uphill from the septic system on the site.

- *Public sewer and private wells.* Where dwelling units are served by a public sewer system but water is provided by individual wells, there are no more limi-tations on residential development than there are when both water and sewer are public facilities. However, it is highly desirable that the water supply should be from a centrally provided source unless this is impossible or grossly uneconomi-cal. Private wells are almost impossible to adequately inspect for water quality control purposes. Private water systems rarely make adequate provision for fire-fighting demands in terms of both the volume of water available without electric power and fire-safe connections for fire-fighting equipment.

PACKAGE PLANTS

Package plants are small, prefabricated, wastewater treatment plants, usually designed to serve from 10 to 500 dwelling units or their equivalent; these plants generally provide secondary treatment to sewage. The per-dwelling-unit cost of a package plant is often very competitive with the cost of large community wastewater treatment systems, and is usually superior to that of septic tank systems.

Package plants have the advantage over large wastewater treatment systems in that they permit development of small areas without a massive investment.

Despite their economic attractiveness, package plants have not met with widespread acceptance. There are two main reasons for this:

1. lack of assurance that the package plant will be well operated and maintained; and

2. their potential for promoting "leap-frog" urban development patterns.

Regarding the maintenance problems, public health regulations usually require that wastewater treatment plants have skilled operators present at all times. If this manpower were to be spent on operating small package plants, the per capita cost of operation would be very high. Furthermore, recent experience has shown that even large wastewater treatment plants with substantial budgets for staffing are often unsatisfactorily operated. Health officials are fearful of the quality of operation that part-time, unskilled operators would produce with package plants. Experience to date with the operation of package plants leaves much to be desired. All too frequently, unskilled operators cannot tell if the plant is operating correctly. In those

instances when the operator knows that the plant is not working right, the raw sewage is allowed to bypass the plant until the operator gets around to calling for skilled assistance to get the plant back in proper working order; the resulting discharge of raw sewage has occasionally gone on for weeks or months at a time.

Some urban and regional planners are concerned about the potential impact of package plants on urban form. In areas where roads and a water supply are available, package plants make intensive urban development possible. This had dire implications for those agricultural areas that planners contend should be maintained as open space.

THE RELATIONSHIP OF WASTEWATER MANAGEMENT AND URBAN DEVELOPMENT

1. Sewers (when combined with roads and water supply) induce urban growth. Areas that are sewered are far more likely to be developed than are virgin areas because:

    A. Property owners desire to get a return from their investment in the utility systems; and

    B. Sewered lands are less susceptible to unforeseen delays in the issuance of development permits.

2. Although an area may be served by sewer lines, its growth may be inhibited by inadequate capacity of the sewer pipes which have been provided, or by the inadequate capacity of the wastewater treatment plant. It is not unusual, in some areas, to have a "moratorium" imposed on the issuance of building permits until the capacity of sewer lines or the wastewater treatment plant is increased.

3. Once land has been subdivided and developed on the septic tank system pattern, it is very difficult (often impossible) to install a sewer system and increase the density of development. Scattered ownership and conflicting landowner goals are examples of conditions which most often make it politically infeasible to reach an agreement among owners on a sewer development program. This is because those property owners who have septic systems that are in good working order see no need to pay for sewers which they do not (at the present time) need.

4. Traditional sewer designs, which rely on gravity flow of sewage, mean that only those lands which are uphill from a wastewater treatment plant can be sewered and developed on an intensive urban pattern.

5. The introduction of lift stations and force mains to a sewer system (with their long-term commitment to relatively high maintenance and operating expense) can open up large areas to urban development.

6. Because of the strong influence that sewers have on the pace and location of urbanization, all people who are concerned with urban development patterns, and with the preservation of open spaces, should pay close attention to proposals for the construction of roads, water supply, and sewers.

ALTERNATIVE FORMS OF WASTEWATER MANAGEMENT

There appear to be four phases of wastewater management that are appropriate to consider:

1. production
2. transportation
3. treatment
4. sludge and effluent disposal

Alternatives in Wastewater Production

When considering wastewater production, two separate concepts should be considered:

1. reduction of the amount of wastewater produced
2. segregation of the types of wastewater

Reduction of the amount of wastewater produced is closely tied to the subject of water conservation. There are a number of new ideas in this field, some of which originated during recent drought years. Some others were developed specifically in order to reduce the flow of sewage into treatment plants, so that the plants would not need to be enlarged or replaced.

Segregation of wastewater flows is the concept in which "black water," which contains a high concentration of organic materials (such as excreta), is kept separate from "grey water," which contains little organic material. Grey water generally comes from washing or cooling operations. Black water requires thorough treatment before its effluent can be released to the environment; grey water, on the other hand, needs little or no treatment. Under this concept, grey water may be used for irrigation purposes, or it might be released into storm sewers; black water would be transported (by gravity flow, a vacuum system, or a pressure system) to a treatment plant.

Alternative Methods of Transporting Wastewater

As previously discussed, most wastewater flows are in gravity-flow systems. Some consideration is currently being given to the use of a vacuum pipe system, in which the wastewater is sucked by pumps into the treatment plant. Also under consideration is the use of a pressure system in which the wastewater would flow by gravity from multiple sources to a pump at a pump station; the pump would then push the wastewater into a force main, through which it would be transported to the treatment plant.

Both the vacuum and the pressure systems have advantages and disadvantages when compared with a gravity-flow system. Some advantages are that:

- The location of the sewer lines would not need to be constrained by the downhill flow concept; this means that large areas of land that are not now sewered could be opened up for urban development.

- Smaller pipes could be used which would often be less expensive to install.

The disadvantages of the vacuum and the pressure systems are that:

- They both use pumps (which cost money to install and maintain) and are subject to breakdowns.

- The vacuum system might be difficult to maintain because of infiltration problems (any cracks in the pipe joints would suck air or water into the system).

- The pressure system might suffer from exfiltration (loss of wastewater through faulty joints in the pipes). This is not desirable because of the noxious character of sewage. The pipes for carrying sewage under pressure would be similar to pipes used to distribute water under pressure, but would have to be better installed and maintained. It should be remembered that water mains typically lose 20 percent or more through unaccounted-for leaks.

Alternative Methods of Sludge and Effluent Disposal

Sludge disposal is a very real problem for most cities because there is so much of it. Conventional methods of sludge disposal are:

- burying it in a sanitary landfill
- burning it
- dumping it at sea

The first two methods may have some adverse environmental impacts, depending upon the characteristics of the sludge and on the care with which the process is undertaken. The third method is always environmentally damaging and is now prohibited in most areas. A method of sludge disposal now used in some agricultural areas is the spreading of sludge over a field and disking it into the upper layer of soil; in this manner, it becomes an effective fertilizer. This method appears to be desirable, if the sludge does not contain undesirable elements (such as heavy metals or toxic chemicals) that would adversely affect the crops grown on the land or the ground water under the surface of the earth.

The use of effluent as irrigation water has been previously mentioned. Other alternative uses of effluent are in ponds for landscaping purposes and in small lakes for recreational uses. Another use of effluent is in "groundwater injection." In this process, the treated effluent is pumped into a deep well so that it reenters the supply of ground water. This process appears to have a number of advantages, providing that the quality of the effluent is such that it will not degrade the quality of the ground water.

Note

1. Colley, Barbara C. *Practical Manual of Land Development.* 3rd ed. New York: McGraw-Hill, 1998, p. 195. Used with permission.

Recommended Reading

Lynch, Kevin and Gary Hack. *Site Planning.* 3rd ed. Cambridge, MA: MIT Press, 1984, pp. 239-243.

Tabors, Shapiro, and Rogers. *Land Use and the Pipe.* Lexington, MA: Lexington Books, 1976. This book is out of print, but it is excellent. It is recommended that you peruse it if you can find a copy in your local library.

Sources of Further Information

Colley, Barbara C. *Practical Manual of Land Development.* 3rd ed. New York: McGraw-Hill, 1998. See Chapter 8, "Sanitary Sewers," pp. 175-201.

Crites and Tchobanoglous. *Small and Decentralized Wastewater Management Systems.* New York: McGraw-Hill, 1998. Cited by Kahn, Allen, and Jones as "The bible of small scale wastewater engineering, this is a 1,000 page textbook for both students and engineers, and contains up-to-date information on decentralized wastewater treatment systems."

Herubin, Charles A. *Construction Site Planning & Development.* Englewood Cliffs, NJ: Prentice-Hall, 1988. See Chapter 7, "Sanitary Sewers," pp. 109-124, and Chapter 10, "Subsurface Sewage Disposal," pp. 163-186.

Kahn, Allen, and Jones. *The Septic System Owner's Manual.* Bolinas, CA: Shelter Publications, 2000. A comprehensive, useful, and nicely written treatise. Highly recommended for those who rely on septic systems, or plan urban development that utilizes them.

Tchobanoglous and Burton, editors. *Wastewater Engineering: Treatment, Disposal, and Reuse.* 3rd ed. New York: McGraw-Hill, 1990.

6

Storm Drainage

INTRODUCTION[1]

Water vapor in the air falls to the earth in some form of precipitation. Some of this precipitation is returned directly to the atmosphere through evaporation and transpiration from trees and plants. Precipitation that is not returned to the atmosphere either directly sinks into the earth or remains on the surface. Both the absorbed water and the water that remains on the surface is acted upon by gravity and seeks the lowest level by the easiest path. This results in the creation of surface streams, lakes, and ponds. The water that remains on the surface of the earth, its safe handling as it flows to its common level at the sea, and its effects on the location of cities as well as on their form and structure, is the subject of this chapter on *storm drainage.*

STORM DRAINAGE
AND CITY LOCATION

Land transportation routes have tended to locate adjacent to waterways because of the availability of terrain next to them which had gentle slopes. Many rural settlements and later, urban communities, have been developed adjacent to waterways because of the use of waterways as carriers of commerce, the availability of water for irrigation and domestic purposes, and the frequent availability of flat or slightly sloped lands which were easy to build on. This was particularly true of sites that were located at the intersection of two water routes and their adjacent land transportation routes.

In earlier periods of our urban history, the primary source of industrial power was water power; this reinforced the direct relationship between industrial location and waterways.

Most of the principal cities of the world are located at seaports or on river routes. The more prosperous of these are located at the intersection of major river routes, river routes with ocean ports, river routes emptying into vast lakes, or river routes connecting with major land transportation routes. Although there has been a decreased reliance on waterborne shipping, and a general abandonment of water power as the basis for industrial production, the need for a water supply and the disposal of sewage effluent still virtually dictates that major urban centers be located adjacent to large lakes, flowing rivers, or an ocean.

INFLUENCES OF STORM
DRAINAGE ON URBAN FORM

Drainage considerations greatly affect the macro-form of cities in the following ways:

River Crossings

Rivers and large streams create natural circulation barriers that inhibit movement from one geographic area to another. Because of the considerable expense of bridging waterways, river crossings are less frequent than the roadways at each side of the river. This results in traffic concentrations at bridge locations which, in turn, creates a condition conducive to commercial concentrations. The need to gather streets at bridge locations results in an influence of the river crossing on the street patterns at the ends of bridges. The location and timing of waterway crossings has therefore had a very strong influence on the spatial form and evolution of many cities.

Underground Utility Lines

Underground utilities are laid out to make as few stream crossings as possible because of water infiltration difficulties, the high cost of underwater construction, and the difficulties inherent in insulating utility lines carried across bridges. Because of this, utility service has often been denied to large geographic areas for long periods of time, greatly influencing their patterns of development.

Bridges and Service Access

The location of bridges often determines the desirability of an area, as it influences the routes used between such urban activities as employment, shopping, residence, and schools. An area might have access because of the existence of a bridge, but residents may still require long and devious paths from their homes to work and shopping locations. Bridge access also strongly influences the service areas of schools, hospitals, and fire stations. A residential area might be 1/4 mile from a school (as the crow flies) but, because a river is located between the area and the school, and because the only river crossing is

2 miles downstream, it may actually be beyond the effective service radius of the school.

Poorly Drained Land

Poorly drained areas will often influence urban development in such a manner as to leave them basically undeveloped, until the economic demand for their intensive use is sufficient to absorb the increased cost of building on them. In the meantime, due to their low desirability (and therefore low price), they tend to attract marginal developments requiring little construction such as junkyards, storage yards, and some agricultural uses. This development may leave a social stigma on the area long after the drainage condition has been rectified.

Flood Plains

Flood plains attract urban development! Because of the tendency for pathways to follow waterways, flood-plain areas are common locations for railroad lines. This results in the availability of railroad service and a water source in relation to flat ground, a condition conducive to industrial development. This industry, in turn, creates a demand for close-in, low-cost housing for its workers. This system of interaction results in concentrations of urban development in floodable areas that are subject to immense flood damages in terms of both dollars and human lives. Because of these huge losses, and the fact that industrial plants are often the largest elements in the tax base of cities, millions of dollars have been spent by the Army Corps of Engineers to keep floods away from people and structures that have been located in flood plains. It would appear to be far more logical to keep people and structures out of floodable areas, recognizing the need for waterways to expand during times of maximum runoff.

It should be noted that as urbanization takes place in flood plains, the flood plains (i.e., the areas subject to occasional flooding) expand. This is because the new development increases the amount of impervious surfaces, which increases the runoff, which increases the area needed to accommodate the runoff.

DEFINITIONS[2]

Aquifer—Water-bearing geologic formations that permit the movement of ground water.

Coefficient of runoff—Percentage of gross rainfall which appears as runoff.

Channel flow—The flow of runoff waters through an open channel (contrast with *sheet flow*).

Design storm—A particular storm that contributes runoff which the drainage facilities were designed to handle. This storm is selected for design on the basis of its probable recurrence (i.e., a 50-year design storm would be a storm for which its maximum runoff would occur on the average of once every 50 years).

Drainage basin (frequently known in the U.S. as *watershed*)—That portion of the earth's surface from which precipitation drains to an identified body of water such as a stream, river, lake, or ocean; its boundaries are defined by *drainage divides*.

Drainage divide—The rim of a drainage basin; the dividing line that consists of a series of ridges from which water flows in either of two directions: into or away from the drainage basin. These ridges may be subtle or pronounced.

Erosion—The wearing away of a surface by some external force. In the case of drainage terminology, this term generally refers to the wearing away of the earth's surface by flowing water.

Flood plain—A strip of land adjacent to a river or channel which has a history of being inundated by flood waters.

Ground water—Water that is present under the earth's surface. Ground water is situated below the surface of the land, irrespective of its source and transient status. Subterranean streams are flows of ground waters, and are usually determined to be integral parts of the visible streams.

Hydrology—The science dealing with the occurrence and movement of water upon and beneath the land areas of the earth. It overlaps and includes portions of other sciences such as meteorology and geology.

Hyetograph—Graphical representation of rainfall intensity against time.

Infiltration—The passage of water through the soil surface into the ground.

Invert—The bottom of a drainage facility along which the lowest flows would pass (usually referred to as *invert elevation*).

Outfall—Discharge or point of discharge of a culvert or other closed conduit.

Overland flow—Flow of surface waters before reaching a natural watercourse.

Permeability—The property of soils which permits the passage of any fluid. Permeability depends on grain size, void ratio, shape, and arrangement of pores.

Precipitation—Rainfall, snow, sleet, fog, hail, dew, and frost.

Runoff—The portion of precipitation that appears as flow in streams; drainage or flood discharge which leaves an area as surface flow or pipeline flow, having reached a channel or pipeline by either surface or subsurface routes.

Scour—Wearing of the bed of the stream by entrainment of alluvium and erosion of native rock; also caused by excessive velocities at the entrance of a concentrated stream of water into unstable material.

Sedimentation—Gravitational deposit of transported solid materials found in flowing or standing water.

Sheet flow—Any flow of water which is spread out and not confined, e.g., flow waters flowing across a flat, open field (contrast with *channel flow*).

Storm sewer—A sewer for carrying off precipitation.

Surface runoff—The movement of water on the earth's surface, whether flow is over surface of ground or in channels.

Swale—A shallow, gentle depression in the earth's surface. Swales tend to collect runoff waters and are considered, in a sense, drainage courses. Waters in a swale, however, are usually not channelized enough to be considered stream waters.

Time of concentration—The time required for storm runoff to flow from the most remote point of a drainage area to the measurement or collection point; it is usually associated with the design storm.

Watershed—A defined area drained by a stream or stream system. (Although this term is widely used in the U.S., professional hydrologists recommend that the term *drainage basin* be used instead.)

Water table—The surface of the ground water below which the void spaces within the soil are completely saturated.

ANNUAL DISTRIBUTION OF PRECIPITATION

We all know that in some years we have very mild weather with little rainfall; in other years we have moderate weather with average rainfall; still in other years we have severe weather with heavy rainfall. Meteorologists have compiled, from weather records, the probability of having various intensities of precipitation. For selected locations, they can tell us the probable annual precipitation that will be brought by storms which occur in time periods such as once in 100 years, once in 50 years, and once in 20 years. The storm that brings the precipitation projected for once in a 100-year period is often referred to as a "100-year storm." This is a statement of the *probability* that a storm will occur which brings at least as much as the predicted precipitation once during that period; it does *not* mean that it is predicted to occur regularly every 100 years. There may be two "100-year storms" within a 5-year period, or no "100-year storms" for 200 years, but the probability is that there will be one such storm on the average of once every 100 years.

SUMMARY OF "THE STORM DRAINAGE SYSTEM"

The storm drainage system carries runoff from the roofs of buildings, street paving, and other ground surfaces, to an outfall into a natural channel. This system usually consist of four elements:

1. *natural channels* (such as rivers, streams, and swales)

2. *excavated drainage ditches* (channels that have been dug in order to drain water away from lands; open ditches are generally accepted in agricultural areas, but are often considered hazards in urban areas)

3. *street gutters* (gutters that carry storm waters to drop inlets, which are entries to the storm sewer system)

4. *storm sewers* (described below)

STORM SEWERS

Storm sewers should only be provided where natural channels and drainage ditches cannot handle the quantity of runoff without a threat to public safety, or where the expense of installing storm sewers is substantially less

Figure 6.1. Schematic Diagram of a Storm Sewer System

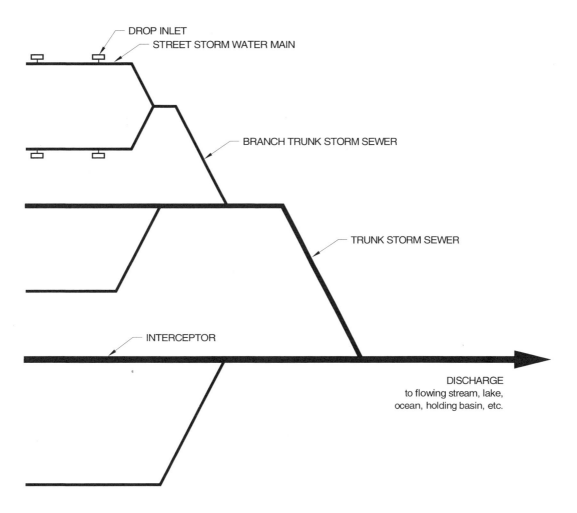

than the potential economic cost of flood damage to private and public properties.

The storm drainage system is almost always a gravity system. (In some cases, pumps are installed to move storm waters. Since these are expensive to build and operate, and cannot always be relied upon to function when needed, they are installed only when there are no reasonable alternatives.) In gravity drainage systems, there must be a continuous downgrade from the highest point on the system to the point of outfall.

The storm drainage system is most commonly a linear branched system generally following the fall of the terrain from the highest point on the system, at the outer edges of the smallest branches, to the lowest point on the system where the trunk of the system empties into a natural channel. Each component of the storm drainage system must be located either in a public street right-of-way (ROW), on public land (such as in a park), or on private property in easements acquired for the purpose. (See Figure 6.1.)

Design guidelines for storm sewer pipe sizes, pipe slopes, and manhole spacing are generally the same as for sanitary sewers (see Chapter 5), with the following exceptions:

Pipe Size

Pipe size should be determined by the calculated flow requirements of the drainage system, except that the underground drains should *not* be expected to carry the greatest anticipated storm flows, such as those that occur every 50 or 100 years. The economic cost of storm sewer construction is so great that, in residential areas, the sewers are generally planned to accommodate storms that recur every 1 or 2 years and, in commercial areas, storms that occur every 5 or 10 years (see Linsley and Franzini). Storm water in excess of the amount that flows in the pipes must be accommodated by surface flows such as that in gutters, swales, ditches, ponds, and retention basins. It is recognized that this surface water may sometimes be a nuisance, but the economic cost of avoiding the nuisance is usually considered to be too high.

The minimum pipe size of storm drains is usually 10 or 12 inches in diameter, although a few cities permit 8-inch drains; these large sizes are required to avoid clogging of the pipes by debris.

Pipe Depth

Storm sewers should be buried below the frost line. Since storm sewers drain surface areas, they often can be at fairly shallow depths, in contrast to sanitary sewers which must drain the basements of adjacent structures.

Frequency of Inlets

Inlets of storm sewers are expensive to install, so the tendency is to minimize their numbers. Nevertheless, it is often necessary to install four drop inlets at each four-way street inter-section, in order to avoid excessive pavement flooding. Inlets are also spaced close enough to avoid excessive flows in the street gutters; this means, under many circumstances, about once every 800 feet. (Excessive flow in a gutter is generally considered to be a flow that is deeper than 6 inches, wider than 6 feet, or faster than 10 feet per second.)

CALCULATING RUNOFF

That portion of precipitation that is not absorbed by the soil, transpired by plants and trees, or returned to the atmosphere by evaporation is called "runoff." Runoff collects via "sheet flow," and flows following the easiest route to the lowest level of the ground. Ridges that separate sheet flow systems are known as "divides." Water falling to one side of a divide will enter one flow system; water falling to the other will enter another system. It is by the determination of the location of divides, based on analysis of sheet flow over landforms, that the area of a drainage basin is delineated.

DETERMINANTS OF RUNOFF QUANTITY

There are a number of determinants of runoff quantity. These include:
- the amount and intensity of precipitation
- soil types
- percent of the area covered by impervious surfaces
- topography
- vegetation
- condition of the soil
- size and shape of the watershed

The Amount and Intensity of Precipitation

There is a great deal of difference, as far as storm drainage is concerned, between a brief, intense rainstorm and a long, gentle rainstorm. For instance, a rainfall of 2 inches that is spread out over a week averages 1/84 of an inch per hour; this could probably be easily handled by most storm drainage systems. On the other hand, a storm that deposits 2 inches of rain in 1 hour would probably be beyond the capacity of most storm drainage systems (that is, if the precipitation enters the system very quickly, because factors such as soil type and condition, size and shape of the watershed, impervious surfaces, or vegetation do not impede it).

With regard to runoff, the total amount of rain that falls is not nearly as important as the intensity of its fall. Engineers design storm drainage facilities to accommodate the amount of runoff generated by the most intense rainfall (expressed in inches per hour) usually for a short period of time such as in the peak 20 or 60 minutes. They base this on the "design storm," which may be a "2-year storm," a "10-year storm," or another yearly description.

Although rainfall is considered by most people to be the primary source of flooding, precipitation in the form of snowfall also contributes to runoff as the snows melt. If snows melt slowly, the runoff from snowbanks is gradual and usually will not cause a surprise flooding problem. However, if the ambient air temperature is high and a warm rain falls on the snows, the runoff can be sudden and significant, and may cause a serious flooding problem.

Soil Types

Impervious soils, such as clay and silt, result in a great amount of runoff because little water is absorbed by the soils. Sandy soils and gravel, on the other hand, absorb great amounts of the water falling on them, resulting in little runoff. The conversion of a site from an agricultural land use, or from a natural vegetation cover to urban development,

often results in great changes in runoff quantity due to decreased ground absorption.

Percent of the Area Covered By Impervious Surfaces

Paved streets, buildings, and parking lots are quite impervious. Most urban developments have a high "runoff coefficient." The runoff coefficient for a parcel of land is an expression of the amount of water falling on the surface that will *not* be absorbed. A development that will not absorb 90 percent of the water that falls on it has a runoff coefficient of 0.90. A runoff coefficient of 0.32 means that 32 percent of the water that falls on the area will be runoff.

Variations in soil type and the amount of development on the surface of the land result in variations in surface permeability which, in turn, result in variation in the quantity of runoff. General runoff coefficients are given in Table 6.1.

The coefficients in these two tabulations are applicable only for storms of 5- to 10-year recurrence intervals, and were originally developed when many streets were uncurbed and drainage was conveyed in roadside swales. For recurrence intervals longer than 10 years, the indicated runoff coefficients should be increased, because more of the rainfall in excess of that expected from the 10-year recurrence interval rainfall will become runoff and should be accommodated by an increased runoff coefficient.

Topography

The greater the ground slope, the greater the runoff. In general, areas with slopes from 10 to 30 percent have approximately 20 percent greater runoff than areas with slopes from 0 to 9 percent grade, all other determinants of runoff quantity being equal.

Areas of steep slope have increased runoff because the water is moving across the surface of the land too rapidly to be absorbed by the soil. Areas with little slope (0 to 1 percent) have ground drainage problems for the opposite reason: since there is no chance for the water to move, the soil is rapidly saturated, resulting in standing pools. The optimum

Table 6.1. Typical Runoff Coefficients for 5- and 10-Year Storm Frequencies

Description of Area	Runoff Coefficients
Business	
Downtown	0.70 to 0.95
Neighborhood	0.50 to 0.70
Residential	
Single family	0.30 to 0.50
Residential (suburban)	0.25 to 0.40
Apartment areas	0.50 to 0.70
Industry	
Light	0.50 to 0.80
Heavy	0.60 to 0.90
Parks, cemeteries	0.10 to 0.25
Railroad yard	0.20 to 0.40
Unimproved urban areas	0.10 to 0.30

Character of Surface	Runoff Coefficients
Pavement	
Asphalt or concrete	0.70 to 0.95
Brick	0.70 to 0.85
Roofs	0.75 to 0.95
Lawns, heavy soil	
Flat, 2%	0.13 to 0.17
Average, 2 to 7%	0.18 to 0.25
Steep, 7%	0.25 to 0.35
Forested areas (depending on soil)	0.05 to 0.20

Source: Department of Transportation, State of California. *Highway Design Manual.* 5th ed. Sacramento, CA: the author, 1998.

topographic condition for ground drainage is gently rolling hills that permit water to move slowly but continuously over the surface of the ground, maximizing absorption potential while minimizing the possibility of surface erosion.

Vegetation

Vegetation retards the flow of water over the surface of the ground (increasing the potential for absorption) and makes the ground more absorbent by opening up the soil through root growth. The heavier the vegetation, the lower the runoff coefficient, all other determinants of runoff quantity being equal.

Condition of the Soil

This determinant of runoff quantity is primarily a function of the probable timing of the maximum intensity storm in relation to other storm activity, spring thaws, and ground temperature. The amount of runoff is strongly affected by the condition of the soil, which is affected by recent precipitation and current soil temperature. For example, soil that has already been saturated by previous rainfall is not able to absorb additional water; therefore, runoff from it will be high. Also, soil that is frozen and contains moisture in the form of a subterranean layer of ice cannot absorb more water, so it too yields a high runoff.

Size and Shape of the Watershed

The preceding six determinants of runoff dealt with the *amount* of water that will flow from a watershed; the size and shape of the watershed strongly influence the *length of time* that it takes for precipitation to flow through the watershed.

Some watersheds are so large (for example, the Ohio Valley) that it takes days (even months, if the precipitation is in the form of snow) for precipitation which falls on its upper reaches to flow down to its outfall. On the other hand, in a small watershed (of an acre or so in area), precipitation will often run off it in a matter of minutes.

The shape of a watershed also influences its runoff characteristics. Watersheds that have a generally square or circular shape tend to have a rapid runoff; long, narrow, winding watersheds generally take longer to drain, given the same slope of terrain.

ESTIMATING RUNOFF QUANTITY

Professional hydrologists are generally called on to make estimates of future runoff from specific watersheds. They have found that the best way of estimating this runoff is to review historic records of precipitation in nearby watersheds, and to review the records of resulting stream flows measured at stream-gauging stations. Unfortunately, such records are not often available, so the projected runoff must be calculated instead, based on whatever data are available and on some assumptions. Many computer programs are available to assist hydrologists in doing this, but these programs require good comparable-area data and good operator judgment, if the results are to be reliable. These computer programs deal with such topics as:

- determining the amount and characteristics of storm water runoff from urban areas and rural drainage basins
- modelling storm water flows in a network of storm sewers
- storm water flows in open ditches, streams, and canals
- design of storm water retention basins

THE RATIONAL EQUATION METHOD OF ESTIMATING RUNOFF

A fairly simple equation was developed over a hundred years ago that provides a quick and easy means of estimating rainfall runoff;

it is known as the "rational equation method."

If rain were to fall at a constant rate with a uniform distribution on an impervious surface, the runoff from that surface would eventually reach a flow rate equal in volume to the volume of rain falling on the surface. The time required to reach this equilibrium is known as the "time of concentration" (Tc). This assumption is approximately correct for small impervious watersheds; it is not valid for large watersheds where the rainfall has neither a constant rate nor uniform distribution, and in which the rain soaks into the surface of the earth to varying degrees rather than flowing directly to the outfall of the watershed.

The basis for the rational equation is:

$$Q = C\,I\,A$$

Where:

Q = the peak rate of runoff in acre inches per hour or in cubic feet per second (cfs)[3]

C = the average runoff coefficient of the watershed

I = the intensity of rainfall in inches per hour for a duration equal to the time of concentration

A = area of the watershed in acres

The rational equation is widely used today to estimate the runoff from simple, small watersheds (with an area of no more than 320 acres) that have fairly uniform characteristics, especially if no good local data are available. Modern hydrologic studies indicate that the equation is not reliable for application to large or nonuniform watersheds, and that its use can lead to substantial errors, usually resulting in costly overinvestment in drainage facilities. Linsley and Franzini point out that in view of the high cost of urban drainage structures, the rational formula approach cannot be considered an adequate basis for the design of extensive storm sewers.

SOURCES OF HYDROLOGIC INFORMATION

Hydrologists get data on rates and amounts of precipitation, and on stream flows, from local records whenever it is available (which occurs all too rarely). A number of state agencies keep good hydrologic data, especially those agencies concerned with water resources and flood control. At the national level, the U.S. Geological Survey, the U.S. Army Corps of Engineers, and the National Weather Service are notable sources of hydrologic data.

Notes

1. Thanks are given to Laurence C. Gerckens; he prepared the first version of this chapter.

2. Adapted from the *Highway Design Manual*.

3. Since 1 acre inch per hour is equal to 1.008 cubic feet per second, the rational equation is commonly assumed to give peak flow in cubic feet per second.

Recommended Reading

Lynch, Kevin and Gary Hack. *Site Planning*. 3rd ed. Cambridge, MA: MIT Press, 1984, pp. 233-239, 461-462.

Sources of Further Information

Colley, Barbara C. *Practical Manual of Land Development*. 3rd ed. New York: McGraw-Hill, 1998, pp. 203-237.

Department of Transportation, State of California. *Highway Design Manual*. 5th ed. Sacramento, CA: the author, 1998.

Linsley and Franzini. *Water-Resources Engineering*. 4th ed. New York: McGraw-Hill, 1992.

Seelye, Elwyn E. *Design: Data Book for Civil Engineers*. 3rd ed. New York: John Wiley & Sons, Inc., 1996.

Urban Land Institute, National Association of Homebuilders, American Society of Civil Engineers. *Storm Water Management*. Washington, DC: Urban Land Institute, 1975.

7

"Other Utilities"

"Other utilities" considered here include electric power, telephone, cable TV, and natural gas. This discussion reviews only their effects on local community design. Regional transmission lines are not discussed; those facilities usually require special studies.

THE INFLUENCE OF "OTHER UTILITIES" ON URBAN FORM

None of the "other utilities" considered here has a significant impact on urban form. They all generally follow the development patterns set by other development forces such as land use and transportation, rather than being strong design influences themselves.

It should be noted that contemporary urban development does not need to have these facilities delivered from conventional public utility companies using traditional methods. Electric power, for example, can be generated by on-site generators. Telephone service can be provided by satellite relays instead of telephone cables. Bottled gas can be used in place of gas transmitted in pipelines. Water and sewer services can be supplied by recirculating systems. Roads can be eliminated if we choose to rely on helicopters and wireless communications. This means that units of urban development (such as resi-

dences, offices, and industries) can be dropped down in any part of the countryside, and we are no longer dependent upon the umbilical cords of conventional utility lines. The implications of this new freedom are tremendous: if we are willing to pay a fairly modest, increased economic cost, we can urbanize any place.

CHARACTERISTICS OF VARIOUS UTILITIES

Electric Power

Electric power lines are installed either above or below ground. In either case, a loop or grid pattern should be developed to permit uninterrupted service when a section of the power line is damaged or requires servicing. In above-grade, electric power distribution systems, wires are carried on poles set 100 to 125 feet apart. Pole-top transformers convert the power in the primary distribution lines (which typically carry 12,000 to 21,000 volts) down to residential service use levels (120 and 240 volts). This secondary run from a transformer to the point of entry at a dwelling unit should not be more than 400 feet, because transmission of power of this low-voltage current for greater distances results in uneconomical line losses. Secondary runs therefore run radially from pole-top transformers to residences within 400 feet of the transformer. These lines may be installed either aboveground or underground.

Underground electric power distribution systems are usually two to five times as expensive as above-grade installations. Underground installations reduce winter and wind damage to the transmission lines, eliminate tree-trimming maintenance costs, and remove the poles and wires from view; however, when breaks occur in these underground lines, they are expensive to repair.

Transformers for electrical service may be in underground vaults, which must be drained and vented, instead of on utility poles. Aboveground "pad-mounted" transformers are often used, however, as a compromise between the all-overhead and the all-underground systems. Underground electric service is generally not feasible where bedrock is within 5 feet of the surface of the ground, or where a high water table exists. It should also be remembered that underground service may eliminate some low-cost street lighting, because utility poles are commonly used as supports for street-lighting fixtures. Otherwise, poles must be provided along the streets solely to support the street-lighting fixtures.

Natural Gas

Gas service, like water supply, is a pressurized system. In general, it has the same system needs as the central water supply with regard to its grid (or loop) geometry. In addition, gas piping must be provided with a continuous downgrade of at least 0.1 percent to allow for drainage of condensation in the pipes. One of the problems with the installation of gas pipelines is that of electrolytic action. This is the process by which metal from the pipe is removed by the process of electrolysis and deposited elsewhere. If care is not taken, this action can eat away a pipe after a number of years, making the pipe no longer safe to carry high-pressure gas. Gas companies are very aware of this problem and usually take effective steps to counteract it.

Telephone Service

Telephone service installation requirements are not nearly as demanding as are many other utility systems, and they generally place no significant restraints on residential development. Telephone lines may be located aboveground on the same poles with electric lines, placed underground in buried conduits, or buried directly in the ground. In most cases, aboveground telephone lines are separated by at least 8 feet from electric power transmission lines, in order to reduce electrical interferences and provide safety for workers. Telephone lines carry a very low voltage; they generate virtually no heat and require relatively little insulation.

The advent of the cellular telephone, which connects users to the traditional telephone network via radio signals, is currently bringing about many changes in telephone service all over the world.

The Gas/Electric/Telephone/ Cable TV Service Interface

There appear to be no nationally accepted standards for the spatial relationships of various utility lines. However, a major utility company in California observes the following standards:

- *For aboveground wires*—Primary electric distribution lines are located at the highest level on utility poles. Secondary distribution lines (0 to 600 volts; often 240 volts) are placed lower down. Telephone lines and cable TV lines (mentioned above) are usually about 8 feet lower down.

- *For utility lines buried in a trench*—Natural gas lines are separated by at least 12 inches from primary electric distribution lines, and 4 inches from secondary electric distribution lines, telephone lines, and cable TV lines. Primary electric distribution lines are separated at least 12 inches from natural gas lines, telephone lines, and cable TV lines. A 1-inch separation is maintained between telephone lines, secondary electric distribution lines, and cable TV lines.

LOCATIONS OF RESIDENTIAL UTILITY LINES

Utility lines for residential areas are usually located in any of three different places:

1. in the street right-of-way (ROW) under the street paving
2. in the street ROW, but to one side of the street paving
3. in easements across private properties; at their front, side, or rear property lines

Sanitary sewers, water lines, and storm sewers are commonly installed in the centers of street rights-of-way under the street paving. The advantage of this location is that it results in approximately equal lengths of run from these pipes to residences at both sides of the street. Other utility lines (such as gas, electrical, and telephone) could also be installed here. There is a disadvantage to this location, however: every time a repair or modification to the utility line is required, street traffic is disrupted, and excavating and repaving is relatively expensive.

Locating gas, electrical, and telephone utilities in the street ROW, but to one side of the street paving (either in planting strips or between the sidewalk and the edge of the ROW), has the advantages of minimizing the disruption of traffic, and reducing the costs of excavation and repaving when repairs are needed. However, with this system, the cost of house runs varies considerably from one side of the street to the other, and roots of nearby plants are potentially more detrimental to the utilities than if the lines are located under the center of the street. Above-grade wires at this location definitely come in conflict with street trees and other plantings.

When utilities are located along rear or side lot lines of private properties, an easement of at least 20 feet wide (10 feet on each property) is needed; when the easement is along the front property line, only 10 feet is required. These locations have the advantage of eliminating the disruption of street traffic when utility lines are installed or serviced. When house runs are constructed, they often result in shorter house runs than when utilities are located in the street ROW. However, these easements must be policed to make sure that private property owners do not construct structures such as fences, playhouses, and patios, or plant trees in the easements that would restrict or preclude their use by utility company service vehicles.

Where telephone or electric service is provided in an easement at a side or rear lot line, the easement need not be more than 8 feet wide (4 feet on each property).

ISSUES IN URBAN DEVELOPMENT CONCERNING "OTHER UTILITIES"

There are a number of issues concerning utility installation that from time to time come to the attention of subdivision designers and developers, and city engineers and planners. The most frequent are:

1. Which utility lines should be aboveground and which should be underground?

2. How should the utility lines be located in relation to each other?

3. Should utility lines be located in the public street ROW, or in easements across private properties?

4. The underground installation of telephone and electric power lines is usually done for aesthetic reasons. Installation of these utility lines aboveground is usually far cheaper than for lines underground. How much added cost are we willing to pay for an improved aesthetic environment? Who should pay these costs?

5. Currently, a number of cellular radio-telephone ("cell phone") systems are being installed. Where is the most effective but least objectionable location for the many transmitter-receiver stations that are required for these systems?

Another factor to be considered concerning underground utility lines is the threat of the backhoe. All too often, backhoe operators snag or puncture underground lines, causing service disruption and the need for expensive emergency repairs.

Concerning the installation of utility lines in relation to each other, practices seem to be changing. Some writers on the subject say that any utility line may be in the same trench with any other line. Past practice, however, has been to keep some lines separated from each other, especially water from sewer, and electricity from gas and telephone. When a number of utility lines are in the same trench, most or all lines are uncovered and disturbed when a worker wants to get at one line to repair or splice into it; this sometimes causes problems for the other lines.

Another problem of putting all utility lines in one trench is coordinating the initial installation. It is rare when all the utility companies involved can get their scheduling worked out and agree to install their facilities in a specific sequence, in an open trench, in a short period of time. Although it costs more for each utility company to dig a separate trench, it does make the installation of utilities less complicated for each of them. In high-density urban areas (such as central business districts) where there are many utility lines, it is desirable to build underground galleries where the lines can be placed on racks, rather than burying each line in the soil. This makes maintenance and modification work far easier. Here again, problems arise concerning coordination and agreement regarding who is going to pay how much for what. Unfortunately, a lack of coordination has resulted in adherence to the old pattern in most cities, wherein each utility company digs its own trenches and buries only its own lines, even in the very busiest of urban streets.

As of 2000, there is considerable uncertainty about the future of communication lines. It is not now known what physical characteristics these lines will have: Will they use traditional copper wires, fiber optics, ground-based radio relay stations (as now used by cell phones), satellite-based relay stations, or will they take some other form? Will there be a need for only one connection to each house or place of business, or will we continue to have multiple lines (such as a line for voice telephone, a line for cable TV, and a line to connect with internet computer services)? As of this writing, it appears probable that there will be substantial changes in the means of communication that will be available to us in the near future, but it is not yet clear just what form those changes will take.

Sources of Further Information

Dewberry and Davis. *Affordable Housing Development Guidelines for State and Local Government.* Washington, DC: U.S. Department of Housing and Urban

Development, Office of Policy Development and Research, 1991.

Lynch, Kevin and Gary Hack. *Site Planning.* 3rd ed. Cambridge, MA: MIT Press, 1984, pp. 249-250.

Macaulay, David. *Underground.* Boston: Houghton Mifflin, 1976. This is an admirably illustrated book that shows underground patterns of building foundations and of underground utilities; suitable for young and old alike.

Seelye, Elwyn E. *Design: Data Book for Civil Engineers.* 3rd ed. New York: John Wiley & Sons, Inc., 1996.

Transportation

8

Introduction to Transportation Planning

THE SCOPE OF TRANSPORTATION PLANNING

The field of transportation planning is generally considered to involve the movement of people and goods. "People" includes both individuals and groups of people (e.g., busloads of commuters). "Goods" includes bulk cargo (e.g., shiploads of iron ore or flatcars loaded with lumber), and smaller units of freight (e.g., packages for local delivery or truckloads of mixed cargo being moved from one city to another).

Many different modes of transportation are considered in transportation planning. For the movement of people, these include:
- pedestrian movement
- "people movers" (moving belts)
- bicycles
- private motor vehicles (cars and motorcycles)
- car pools and van pools
- taxicabs and jitneys
- intracity buses for commuters
- intercity buses for long-distance travel
- intracity trains for commuters
- intercity trains for long-distance travel

- ferry boats
- airline transport
- ships

Among the modes of transportation for the movement of goods are:
- bicycle couriers
- parcel delivery services
- trucks carrying mixed cargo
- trucks carrying bulk cargo (e.g., liquids in tanker trucks, or dry cement in hopper-bottom trucks)
- rail lines, which may carry:
  — less-than-carload lots of mixed freight
  — carloads of bulk cargo (e.g., ores, coal, or liquids)
  — piggy-back carriage of truck trailers on flatcars
- pipelines, which transport either gases, liquids, or slurries
- barges (primarily used in inland lakes and canals)
- ocean-going ships, which may carry:
  — mixed cargo in the holds of ships
  — cargo enclosed in containers, and loaded in and on container ships

— bulk cargo (e.g., ores, wheat, or oil)
- aircraft, which may carry:
  — packaged cargo on passenger-carrying airplanes
  — general cargo on air-freight aircraft

THE MAJOR BRANCHES OF TRANSPORTATION PLANNING

Transportation Planning

Transportation planning concerns the planning, functional design, operation, and management of facilities of any mode of transportation used to provide movement of people and goods.[1]

Transportation planners are concerned with a wide variety of topics including the transportation of liquids in pipelines, parcel delivery systems, cargo handling on ocean-going ships, airline routes and terminal locations, public transit systems, as well as the flow of traffic on urban streets and rural highways.

While a variety of professionals participate in transportation planning, it is probable that the majority of them hold degrees in civil engineering.

Traffic Engineering

Traffic engineering is a branch of transportation engineering that deals with the planning, geometric design, and traffic operations of roads, streets, and highways; their networks; and their relationships with other modes of transportation.[2]

Traffic engineers are primarily concerned with planning for the flow of traffic on urban and rural streets. They investigate topics such as trip generation, the distribution of traffic flows on alternative routes, planning urban mass transit systems, and other matters such as the location and timing of traffic signals, recommendation of speed limits, location of stop signs, and traffic management, which includes "traffic calming."

Traffic engineers usually have degrees in civil engineering, with specialization in traffic engineering.

Highway Engineering

Highway engineering is a phase of traffic engineering that deals with the design and construction of roads, streets, and highways.

Highway engineers design streets, bridges, interchanges, and street drainage facilities; they prepare construction plans and specifications for them, and supervise their construction.

Highway engineering is also usually considered to be a branch of civil engineering.

DEFINITIONS OF SOME VERY BASIC TRANSPORTATION TERMS

The following definitions are used in transportation planning:

Trip—A one-way movement from an origin to a destination.

Trip origin—The location where a trip begins.

Trip destination—The location where a trip ends.

Trip purpose—The traveler's primary purpose for making a trip.[3]

Person trip—A trip made by one person.

Vehicle trip—A trip made by a vehicle. (The number of persons occupying the vehicle is not relevant.)

Mode—The means used for travel (e.g., walk, drive own car, ride as a passenger in a bus).

Modal split—The share of travelers using each mode of travel (in some communities, the modal split for the morning journey to work might be 90 percent drive own car, 5 percent riders in car pool, 4 percent public transit, and 1 percent walk to work).

AN OVERVIEW OF THE TRANSPORTATION PLANNING PROCESS

The following section of text provides an overview of the transportation planning process that is often used in urban areas. It deals primarily with planning for the movement of people in private motor vehicles and in public transit vehicles. It should be noted that this process is *not* generally used when planning for the movement of freight or other goods, which most often involves very different factors. Most freight transportation services (such as rail lines, the postal service, barge lines, package delivery services, and pipeline services) have their own transportation planning procedures which are very different from those used for planning for the movement of people in urban areas.

What follows is a simplified version of the process used to plan transportation systems in urban areas; it is intended to give you a feel for the basic concepts used. The actual practices are much more complex, and discussion of them is beyond the intended scope of this text. A more detailed description of the planning process will be found in Chapter 4 of the *Transportation Planning Handbook* by the Institute of Transportation Engineers. That chapter is recommended for those who may become professionally involved, even slightly, with transportation planning. Another source, which summarizes the process very well, is Chapter 12 of *Fundamentals of Traffic Engineering* (14th ed.), by Homburger et al.

Figure 8.1 illustrates the basic steps included in many forms of an urban transportation planning procedure.

The basic steps involved in this process are discussed below.

Identify Land Uses and Socioeconomic Conditions

Land uses vary in the amount of traffic that they generate and attract.

For example, high-density apartment developments often generate a lot of traffic; agricultural areas generate very little. Successful shopping centers attract a lot of traffic; nature preserves usually attract very little.

Socioeconomic factors influence the number of trips made. Young people tend to generate many more trips than do the elderly. Rich people usually have more cars than do poor people, and make more trips because they usually have the means, the time, and the opportunity to do so.

Knowledge of present land uses and present socioeconomic conditions are needed as input to a traffic model; they are a source of the data that is used to test the ability of the model to replicate existing traffic flows.

Predictions of *future* land uses and future socioeconomic conditions are the basis for estimating the amount of *future* traffic generation and traffic attraction. These predictions are usually based on the general plans of the communities within the transportation study area.

Most of the foregoing factors, plus some others, are usually taken into consideration when estimates are made of the number of trips that will be made within a specific urban area.

Estimate Trip Generation and Trip Attraction

In this phase of the process, the planning area is divided into a number of traffic zones; these are usually subparts of census tracts. The number of trips generated within, and attracted to, each zone is then estimated. These trips may be estimated either in *person* trips or in *vehicle* trips. The trips are tabulated

Figure 8.1. A Generalized Version of the Urban Transportation Planning Process

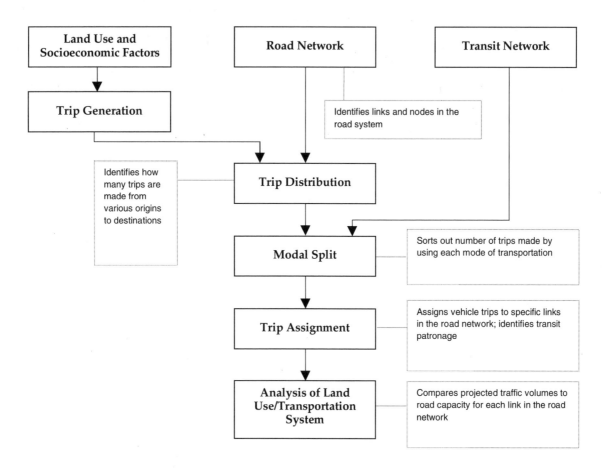

- A number of iterations are made of the model.
- The first iteration is usually based on existing land uses, existing socioeconomic conditions, and the existing road network; it is used to verify that the computed traffic flows correspond with the actual observed traffic flows. If the model replicates existing conditions, this indicates that it is probably reasonably accurate. If it does not, the model must be "calibrated" by inserting multipliers to various factors here and there, so that it does replicate current conditions.
- Subsequent iterations are made using such factors as alternative future land use patterns, economic and demographic conditions, trip-generation factors, road networks, and model splits.

by the number of trips that originate within each traffic zone and by the number of trips that are attracted to each zone. Very often, these estimates are based on surveys of trip generation that have been made of a wide variety of land uses in the U.S. by the Institute of Transportation Engineers, and published in their report, "Trip Generation." Table 8.1 presents a brief summary of trip-generation data for a small sample of land uses. It is included

Table 8.1. Sample Trip-Generation Rates By Land Use

Type of Development	Average Weekday Trip-Ends	Range	Number of Studies
RESIDENTIAL			
Single-family, detached	9.57 per DU*	4.31-21.85	348
Condo/townhouse	5.86 per DU	1.83-11.79	53
Mobile home park	4.81 per occupied DU	2.29-10.42	37
Low-rise apartment	6.59 per occupied DU	5.10-9.24	22
High-rise apartment	4.20 per DU	3.00-6.45	9
MAJOR INSTITUTIONS			
Junior/community college	1.54 per student	0.94-2.16	4
University/college	2.38 per student	2.03-3.31	7
Hospital	5.17 per employee	2.17-11.10	19
COMMERCIAL			
Fast-food restaurant with drive-thru	496.12 per 1,000 sq. ft. gross floor area	195.98-1132.92	21
Supermarket	111.51 per 1,000 sq. ft. gross floor area	68.65-168.88	2
Shopping center	49.97 per 1,000 sq. ft. gross floor area	16.70-227.50	123
General office building	3.32 per employee	1.59-7.28	62
INDUSTRIAL			
General light industrial	3.02 per employee	1.53-4.48	18
Industrial park	3.34 per employee	1.24-8.80	48
General heavy industrial	0.82 per employee	0.75-1.81	3

* DU = dwelling unit

Source: Institute of Transportation Engineers. "Trip Generation." 6th ed., Washington, DC: ITE, 1997.

here to illustrate typical generation of vehicle trips by various land uses.

Describe the Road Network

The network of roads within the planning area is mapped in a schematic manner, using "links" and "nodes." Links represent the roadways and are often shown as simple straight lines. Nodes representing the centroids of trips made from, or attracted to, traffic zones are identified. Nodes representing the junctions of links are also indicated, showing locations where trips may change direction in their travel within the planning area. For each link information on the number of travelled lanes, its capacity to carry traffic, and the average speed of travel over the link are usually tabulated.

These descriptions are made first for the existing road system and then for planned future road networks.

Describe the Transit System

The routes of existing transit services (such as bus routes and train routes) are mapped, and then a transit service network is prepared using links and nodes. Transit nodes are located at the points in the network where passengers may get on or off the transit system. Information is assembled on travel time between nodes and the capacity of the transit services.

Distribute Trips Between Origins and Destinations

These are usually person trips, not vehicle trips. This step is a quantification that indicates where people want to go. Note that it does not assign trips to the links within the transportation networks; that work is done later in the process.

This step is done by a computer program. Many computer programs use what is known as "the gravity model," which is based on the premise that the force of attraction for traffic to move from a point of trip origin to a point designating the trip destination is inversely proportional to the square of the distance between the two points.

Make a Modal Split

This distributes the anticipated trips among the various modes of travel such as "drive own car," "ride on bus," and "bicycle to work."

By applying an estimate of persons per vehicle, it is possible to transform "person trips" into "vehicle trips."

Note that sometimes the modal split is made before the trip-distribution process, rather than after it.

Make Trip Assignments

In this phase of the work, vehicle trips are assigned to the links in the road network. Many transportation planning computer programs have a "capacity constraint" feature to them. This feature assigns vehicles to alterna-tive routes once the original (usually shortest) route becomes loaded to its capacity.

This phase also involves assigning passengers to the transit network.

Calibrate the Model

It is necessary to make sure that the computer model produces valid results. This is usually done by analyzing existing conditions with existing populations, existing socioeconomic conditions, existing land uses, and existing road and transit networks, and applying the results of traffic counts and travel interviews. If the model assigns trips to the existing street and transit networks that appear to replicate current traffic flows with reasonable accuracy, it is probable that the model is working reasonably well. However, this is rarely the case the first time the model is run, so the model must be "calibrated." This is done by modifying the various factors that are built into the equations used in the computer model, so that the model will more accurately reflect reality.

After the model has been calibrated so that it appears to produce reasonable results under existing conditions, computer runs are made using projected future land uses, future socioeconomic conditions, future road and transit networks, and future modal splits.

Analyze the Results

In this step, an analysis is made of what the present conditions are and what would happen if the planned transportation networks were to be built for the use of future trip-makers. Which streets and transit facilities would be overloaded? Which would be underutilized? What new infrastructure should be built to accommodate future traffic? What changes in traffic regulations should be made in order to expedite the flows of anticipated future traffic? What measures should be taken in order to prevent the flow of through traffic in residential neighborhoods? What urban planning actions, such as channeling the location of urban growth to appropriate areas and limiting it from inappropriate areas, are called for? Are the routes used by public transit in optimal locations?

COMMENTS ON THE TRANSPORTATION PLANNING PROCESS

There are a number of limiting factors that should be kept in mind when using computer models for transportation planning. Attention should be given to the data used as input to the models, including consideration of the following:

- Trip-generation data tell the number of trips that can be expected to originate from a specific location, but provide no data on where the travelers are going or what the purposes of their trips are.
- Trip-attraction data tell the number of trips that can be expected to arrive at a destination but provide no clues about their origin.
- Traffic counts tell the number of vehicles that pass by a specific section of a roadway at a specific time of day, but provide no clues about their origin, where they're going, the purpose of their trip, or the number of persons riding in the vehicle. Also, most mechanical traffic counters don't distinguish between passenger cars, trucks, buses, and motorcycles. Traffic counts, however, are relatively easy and inexpensive to make.[4]
- Traveler interviews provide data on trip origin, trip destination, trip purpose, and (sometimes) socioeconomic factors. These interviews are very useful but are time-consuming and expensive to make; only limited sampling is affordable.

Computer models interpret the data available to them, attempt to replicate present traffic flows, and then make estimates of future traffic flows. These models do surprisingly well but they are not infallible. The accuracy of the traffic projections depends on the validity of the assumptions made concerning how, when, where, and why people make trips; on the logic of the computations used in the model itself; and on the quality of the data used.

Table 8.2 provides some general guidelines for the use of transportation planning models.

THE HIERARCHY OF STREETS

Streets provide the basic framework for the movement of people and vehicles in urban areas. There are many different types of streets; each has its own characteristics, and each is best suited for use in specific conditions.

There are two major functions of streets. The first is to provide a route for vehicles to move on a trip from an origin to a destination; in other words, streets are facilities for *through* traffic. A second function is to provide access to abutting properties.[5] This access point may be an origin such as a residence, or it may be a destination such as a place of employment.

Figure 8.2 illustrates the relationships between various types of streets and their functions of accommodating through traffic, and of providing access to adjacent properties.

As can be seen from the figure, some streets (such as cul-de-sacs and loop streets) only provide access to adjacent properties; they carry no through traffic whatsoever. At the other end of the scale, freeways provide absolutely no access to adjacent properties but are very good at carrying through traffic. There are other types of streets (such as local collector streets, collector streets, arterials, and expressways) that are compromises between the two extremes just discussed.

Table 8.2. Tips on Using Models ...

**TIPS ON USING MODELS, or Everything You Wanted to Know About
Super-Fantastic, Multipath Stochastic Whizz-Bang Transportation Planning Models**

by Jerry Lutin, Ph.D., P.E., A.I.C.P.

Used with permission of the author.

It has been a little more than 30 years since computers first appeared on the urban transportation planning scene. Since then we've evolved through several states of hardware and software. Today, we have more computing power in our desk-top micros than most of us had in our 1970's vintage IBM mainframes.

For most of our projects, our clients have come to expect us to use computers and run transportation planning models. "As the results of our computer model indicate ..." carries the aura of science and authority. Sometimes, however, we rely too much on the machine results. We feed in huge gobs of data and get ulcers when our big models don't "calibrate" and replicate the real world. We sometimes walk away disappointed in our efforts, disillusioned with the whole process. I have made a whole spectrum of computer mistakes starting with selecting a machine that was too small for a problem (which promptly grew out of my available data storage space) to creating a model that was much too detailed (and expensive) for the level of accuracy required.

On the other hand, I have had some spectacularly good experiences, accompanied by the thrill of discovery and insight into a problem gained from probing a database, as well as of achieving fame, fortune, and a view of the beautiful sunrises one gets to see after working all night.

From all this, I have extracted a few jewels of wisdom to pass along.

- **Work backwards in deciding what models to use.** Decide first exactly what information and format you want on the tables you present in your final report. Especially when using "canned" programs, you may find a big disparity between what you need to present and the output created by the program.

- **Avoid black box models.** If you don't understand (and can't explain) how a model works, you probably won't be able to convince anyone that your results are worth anything.

- **Check your input data carefully, recheck it, and check it again.** There are few things more embarrassing (and expensive) in our profession, than finding out, while presenting the results of a three-month traffic assignment exercise, that the two-lane street you said would have a future V/C ratio of 0.6 was actually coded into your model with sixteen lanes.

- **Make sure you have plenty of space,** be it in output table formats, array sizes, CPU core, disk storage, and file space for your floppies and printouts. Everything takes more room than you think.

- **Understand and document every assumption and parameter value you use.** More often than not, model results are more sensitive to your assumptions than to anything else in your data. In fact, once you understand how sensitive your model is to changes in assumptions and input variables, you can often figure out the results on your hand calculator without running the model.

- **Trust your own judgement and that of the senior professionals with whom you work.** If the model output looks wrong, it probably is. Although computers have perfect recall and can do boring tasks very fast, they are basically very stupid compared to human beings.

- **Present your results clearly and briefly.** To most audiences, model results are a crashing bore. Few decision-makers have the time or patience to sit through long-winded explanations or read more than one page. Make your major points immediately; then be prepared to elaborate on the details in answers to questions. If you are writing, place the details and supporting data in a later chapter or an appendix.

- **Maintain your professional integrity.** Models are often run to quantify the impacts of projects with ardent supporters and opponents. Modelers may feel pressure to take sides or advocate a particular position. Be prepared to defend your work professionally. Your reputation for fairness and integrity is your most valuable asset.

Figure 8.2. Hierarchy of Streets

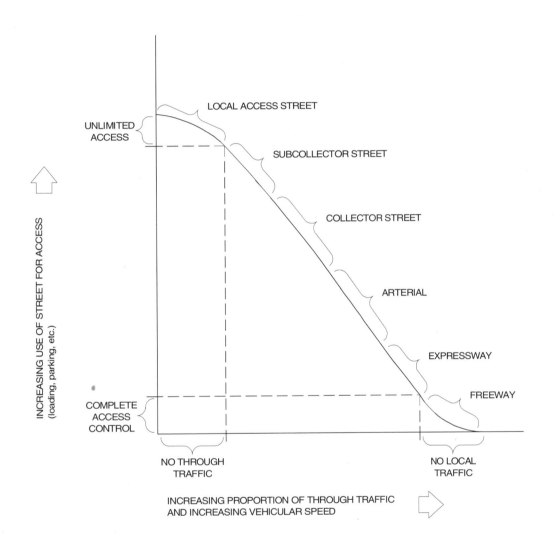

TYPES OF STREETS AND HIGHWAYS

There is considerable variation in the terminology used by laypersons to describe various types of streets. For example, in the eastern part of the U.S. there seems to be some confusion about the terms "freeway," "expressway," and "parkway." Across the nation, there is some difference of opinion (even among professionals) concerning the definitions of "expressway," "major arterial," and "minor arterial." While I have tried to use the definitions currently used by transportation planners, you may wish to review the definitions found in the *Traffic Engineering Handbook* (ITE), *Residential Streets* (ASCE-NAHB-ULI), or *A Policy on Geometric Design of Highways and Streets* (AASHTO).

Figure 8.3 illustrates various types of streets, and how they might relate to each other in a hypothetical residential development.

Freeways

Freeways are highways which are devoted entirely to the high-speed movement of traffic between major segments of metropolitan areas or between regions of the country. Direct access from the roadway to adjacent properties is prohibited. Freeways are built as divided highways (i.e., directional flows of traffic are on separate roadways). Access to freeways is provided only at grade-separated structures[6]; there are no stop signs or traffic signals on freeways.

Freeways usually carry very heavy volumes of traffic[7]; because of this, they generate considerable noise and some air pollution. It is therefore desirable to locate residential uses at least a quarter mile from freeways, even if noise barriers are erected. Typical vehicle speed on freeways is about 65 miles per hour (mph) [105 kilometers per hour (km/h)]; it is higher on uncongested freeways in the open countryside, and often substantially lower on congested, urban freeways.

Parkways

Parkways are highways located within a park or within a ribbon of park-like development. They are intended to carry recreational traffic; commercial traffic is often banned from them. Access to or from adjacent lands is permitted only at carefully selected locations.

Expressways

Expressways are streets which are designed to expedite the flow of through traffic. In metropolitan areas, this traffic flows between communities and between activity centers.

Access from expressways to adjacent properties is usually very limited. Access to major traffic generators, such as shopping centers or major institutions, is often permitted if the turning movements into and out of them are carefully engineered. Parking on expressways is generally banned. Access from expressways to individual homes should always be prohibited, not only to enhance the free flow of traffic, but also to protect the safety and tranquility of residents.

Expressways often have two, three, or even four lanes of traffic in each direction; traffic flow on them is usually heavy.[8] Traffic flowing into or across expressways from minor streets must observe either stop signs or traffic signals. Intersections with other expressways or with major arterials may be grade-separated. Vehicle speed on expressways depends on the amount of congestion and cross-traffic; it typically ranges from 40 to 50 mph [65 to 80 km/h].

Arterial Streets

Most transportation planners divide arterial streets into two categories, *major arterials* and *minor arterials*. The difference between these two seems to be largely a matter of degree (that is, differences in the amount of traffic they carry, differences in their design standards such as width and number of lanes, and differences in the degree of access to adjacent properties permitted). The traffic carried on arterials ranges from 5,000 to 25,000 vehicles per day. Vehicular speed is typically between 35 and 45 mph [55 to 75 km/h].

Arterial streets are primarily intended to carry through traffic within sections of urban areas. In rural areas, they serve as major thoroughfares. They also provide connections between communities and major traffic generators, and serve as connectors to higher order highways such as expressways and freeways. While they may provide access to some major traffic generators, they are *not*

Figure 8.3. Street Types and Subdivision Street Patterns

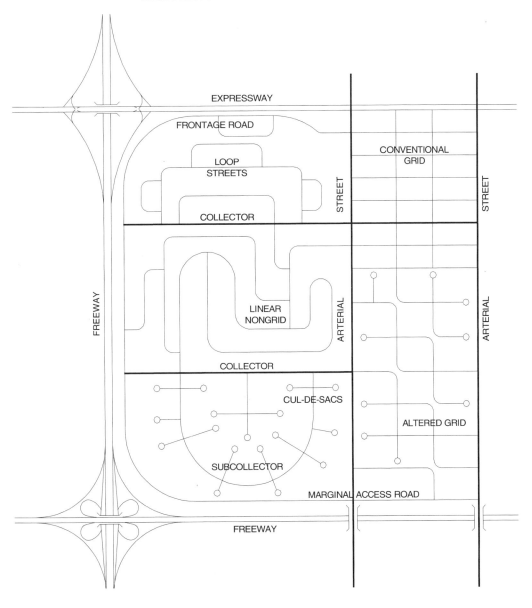

TYPICAL AVERAGE DAILY TRAFFIC (ADT)

Freeway	20,000 –	200,000
Expressway	20,000 –	50,000
Arterial street	5,000 –	25,000
Collector street	1,000 –	10,000
Subcollector street	250 –	1,000
Local access street	0 –	250

intended to provide access to numerous small traffic generators such as roadside strip commercial uses or single-family homes.

Curbside parking and loading is often restricted or banned on major arterials; it is sometimes permitted on minor arterials, even though it slows the flow of through traffic.

Major arterials commonly have two or three lanes in each direction; minor arterials are more likely to have one or two.

Note that major traffic-carrying streets (such as arterials, expressways, and freeways) should be designed to *go around residential communities, not through them.* They should also avoid dividing commercial areas and industrial districts; traffic arteries should serve these areas, not destroy them.

Collector Streets

Collector streets are the principal arteries within residential or commercial areas. Their primary function is to provide a convenient link between major arterial streets, subcollector streets, and local access streets. They typically have one or two lanes of traffic in each direction. Parking may or may not be permitted on them. Access to many adjacent nonresidential properties is usually permitted. Since collector streets carry substantial through traffic, low-density residential uses such as single-family homes should not have direct access to collector streets. Typical traffic volume on collector streets is from 1,000 to 10,000 vehicles per day, at speeds ranging from 25 to 35 mph [40 to 55 km/h]. It is desirable to keep this figure to less than 3,000 vehicles per day in residential areas.

Subcollector Streets

Subcollector streets provide a linkage between collector streets and local access streets. They also may provide access to adjacent properties.

Subcollector streets usually provide space for one lane of traffic in each direction, and may also provide space for on-street parking. These streets typically carry from 250 to 1,000 vehicles per day.[9] Vehicular speeds on these streets should be kept at less than 25 mph [40 km/h].

Local Access Streets

The primary and perhaps sole function of a local access street is to provide access to adjacent residential properties; it is not intended to carry any through traffic. These streets take the form of cul-de-sacs and loop streets. (For an illustration of these types of streets, refer to Figures 8.2 and 8.3.) They may have two narrow lanes, or one wide lane, for two-way traffic, depending on anticipated traffic flow. The amount of on-street parking that should be provided depends upon the density of the adjacent residential development. In very low-density rural areas, it may be feasible and desirable to provide no on-street parking. In low-density residential areas, perhaps parking on one side of the street would be sufficient. In medium- and high-density residential areas, it is usually appropriate to provide parking on both sides of the street.

The typical traffic volume of a local access street is approximately 0 to 200 vehicles per day.[10] Vehicular speed on these streets should never exceed 25 mph [40 km/h]; 15 to 20 mph [25 to 32 km/h] is more reasonable and prevalent.

Notes

1. This definition is adapted from the Institute of Transportation Engineers. *1995 Membership Directory.* Washington, DC.

2. *Ibid.*

3. There are many possible categories of trip purposes, such as trips related to work, home, shopping, school, recreation, social meetings, dining, medical/dental, and religious services. However, when coding

data for use in a computer model to predict future travel flows, the categories are very often condensed into these three: home-based work trips; home-based nonwork trips; and nonhome-based trips.

4. For a brief description of various traffic-counting techniques in current use, see Homburger et al., pp. 5-2, 5-3.

5. There are a number of other functions that the rights-of-way of streets provide but which are not usually considered to be of primary importance. These are: (A) space for parked vehicles, (B) walkways for pedestrians, (C) an attractive, landscaped setting for adjacent properties, and (D) a location for aboveground and underground utilities.

6. In highway design, the term "grade" refers to the elevation of the surface of the roadway. "At-grade" means that the roadway runs along the surface of the earth. "Grade-separated" means that the elevations of intersecting roadways are separated by space, as you can observe in cloverleaf interchange structures on some freeways. This separation of the roadways permits traffic on one roadway to flow freely, without interference from traffic on the other roadway.

7. Average daily traffic on a freeway ranges from 20,000 to more than 200,000 vehicles per day.

8. Average daily traffic on an expressway is often from 20,000 to 50,000 vehicles per day.

9. ASCE-NAHB-ULI, p. 28.

10. *Ibid.*

Recommended Reading

Lynch, Kevin and Gary Hack. *Site Planning.* 3rd ed. Cambridge, MA: MIT Press, 1984. See Chapter 7, "Access," pp. 193-221.

Sources of Further Information

American Association of State Highway and Transportation Officials (AASHTO). *A Policy on Geometric Design of Highways and Streets.* Washington, DC: AASHTO, 1994.

[ASCE-NAHB-ULI]—American Society of Civil Engineers, National Association of Home Builders, and the Urban Land Institute (ASCE, NAHB, and ULI). *Residential Streets.* 2nd ed. Washington, DC: Urban Land Institute, 1990.

Homburger, Hall, Loutzenheiser, and Reilly. *Fundamentals of Traffic Engineering.* 14th ed. Berkeley, CA: Institute of Transportation Studies, University of California, 1996.

Institute of Transportation Engineers. *Traffic Engineering Handbook.* 4th ed. James L. Pline, editor. Englewood Cliffs, NJ: Prentice-Hall, 1992.

Institute of Transportation Engineers. *Transportation Planning Handbook.* John D. Edwards, Jr., P.E., editor. Englewood Cliffs, NJ: Prentice-Hall, 1992.

Institute of Transportation Engineers. "Trip Generation." 6th ed. Washington, DC: ITE, 1997. Data from this report are available on a compact disc for use on desktop computers.

Transportation Research Board, National Research Council. "Highway Capacity Manual" (Special Report No. 209). Washington, DC: Transportation Research Board, 1994.

Some suggested sources of current information on computer programs for use in transportation planning and engineering are:

- **PC-TRANS:** A quarterly magazine/catalog of program applications relating to highway engineering and transportation using personal computers; has an extensive list of transportation software that it offers for sale. It is published by:

  Kansas University Transportation Center
  2011 Learned Hall
  Lawrence, KS 66045

- **McTRANS:** Similar in function to the PC-TRANS. It is published by:

  Center for Microcomputers in Transportation
  Transportation Research Center
  P.O. Box 116585
  Gainesville, FL 32611-6585

9

Street Capacity

SOME BASIC DEFINITIONS

Traffic volume—The total number of vehicles that pass over a given point or section of a lane or roadway during a given time interval; volumes may be expressed in terms of annual, daily, hourly, or subhourly periods.[1]

Highway capacity—The maximum hourly rate at which persons or vehicles can reasonably be expected to traverse a point or uniform section of a lane or roadway during a given period of time under prevailing roadway, traffic, and control conditions.[2]

Level of service (LOS)—A qualitative measure describing operational conditions within a traffic stream, generally in terms of such factors as speed and travel time, freedom to maneuver, traffic interruptions, comforts, convenience, and safety.[3] Six levels of service are used for describing highway capacity; they are given letter designations, ranging from LOS A (representing the best operating conditions) to LOS F (representing the worst).

Average daily traffic (ADT)—The total volume during a given time period (in whole days) greater than one day and less than one year, divided by the number of days in that time period.[4] ADT counts may be made for specific time periods (such as Fridays or months). They are useful for considering con-ditions found in peak problem periods (such as Fridays or Julys).

Average annual daily traffic (AADT)—The total volume of traffic at a specific location for a whole year. AADT counts are useful for considering long-term trends, such as comparing traffic flows in 1990 and 2000 with those projected for the years 2010 and 2020.

Hourly traffic volume—The volume of traffic counted during a one-hour period (such as between 5:30 and 6:30 p.m.). This is the most common measure of traffic volume used in traffic engineering studies.[5]

Peak traffic flow—Traffic counts made during a short period of time (such as 6 minutes or 15 minutes) and expanded to reflect a potential flow in one hour by multiplying by the appropriate expansion factor (such as 10 or 4, in the examples given above). Peak traffic flow is used to examine conditions such as maximum flow rates and capacity limitations.[6]

POTENTIAL STREET CAPACITIES

Under very good conditions, a street can carry about 2,000 passenger cars per hour per lane (pcphpl).[7] This is for a rather ideal street under quite ideal conditions (i.e., for a straight, wide, and level multilane street, which has no merging or crossing traffic, and has no stop signs or traffic lights).

However, under normal conditions, when there is traffic on cross streets, and when there are intersections with stop signs or traffic lights, each lane in a typical urban street may be expected to carry only about 500 vehicles per hour, as a very generalized rule of thumb. The flow of traffic may be reduced from the theoretical 2,000 vehicles per hour depending upon the factors cited below.

FACTORS THAT REDUCE STREET CAPACITY

Factors that reduce the capacity of a street to carry traffic include:
- width of the travelled traffic lane
- number of lanes in the street
- presence of opposing traffic in an adjacent lane
- lateral clearance adjacent to the travelled lane
- width of the shoulder adjacent to the travelled lane
- presence of mixed traffic types (such as trucks and buses mixed with the flow of automobiles)
- types of terrain
- weather and visibility
- stop signs
- traffic signals
- left-turning traffic
- pedestrian crossings
- driver competence

Width of the Travelled Traffic Lane

The usual width for a traffic lane on an urban arterial street is 3.3 meters [11 feet]. For freeway lanes, the desirable width is 3.6 meters [12 feet]. 3.0-meter streets [10 feet] can be used for restricted areas where there is little truck traffic.[8] Experience has shown that prudent drivers will drive at somewhat slower speeds where they encounter traffic lanes that are narrower than those identified above, but may drive somewhat faster when the lanes are wider. It has also been observed that accident rates are somewhat higher on streets that are narrower than those recommended above, perhaps because of the presence of imprudent drivers.

Number of Lanes in the Street

A two-lane street may be defined as a roadway having one lane for the use of traffic in each direction. Passing of slower vehicles requires the passing vehicle to use the opposing traffic lane where sight distance and gaps in the traffic stream permit. As traffic volumes increase and sight distances decrease, the ability to pass decreases, resulting in the formation of platoons in the traffic stream. Motorists in these platoons are subject to delay because of the inability to pass.[9]

The layperson might think, at first consideration of a two-lane highway, that under good conditions each lane might carry as many as 2,000 vehicles per hour. This does not happen, however, because of the presence of slow-moving vehicles and difficulties in passing them. In practice, it is not unusual to find that two-lane highways will carry a maximum of about 2,000 vehicles per hour *counting traffic in both directions,* rather than the 4,000 the layperson might envisage.[10] The actual traffic flow will depend upon a number of factors, including the directional split of traffic flow, the number of slow-moving trucks, and the type of road terrain.[11]

Freeways and expressways usually have two or more lanes of traffic in each direction, so the passing problem found on two-lane highways is not as serious a problem on them. However, there must be enough lanes to accommodate the anticipated traffic if congestion is to be avoided. On arterial streets, lanes must be provided not only for the through traffic but are also often needed for the left- and right-turning traffic.

The capacity of two-lane highways in rural areas can be increased by adding a third lane in selected areas which serves as a "passing lane." This is especially effective on upslopes, so that slowly moving vehicles (such as heavy trucks) can pull into the right-hand lane and let other traffic pass by. The addition of left-turn lanes at busy rural intersections can also increase the capacity of the roads.

In urban areas, the capacity of two-lane streets can be increased by adding a continuous third lane which can be used for left turns from both of the opposing lanes of traffic flow. Provision of this turning lane eliminates the delays that might otherwise be experienced by traffic cuing up behind left-turning drivers. This third lane is appropriate, of course, only in areas where a considerable number of left turns are expected.

Presence of Opposing Traffic in an Adjacent Lane

Freeways, by definition, separate the flows of traffic, so that opposing flows are never adjacent to each other. (This is done by building a separate roadway for each directional flow, or by erecting barriers in the median strip.) Expressways often have barriers in their median strips to prevent vehicles in opposing traffic flows from colliding with each other. Arterial streets usually do not have median strips or barriers to separate opposing traffic flows.

Whenever drivers are in a lane which is immediately adjacent to an opposing flow of traffic, the prudent ones tend to drive carefully; they know that head-on collisions are possible under these conditions. We can therefore conclude that on streets where opposing traffic flows are adjacent to each other, moderate vehicle speeds can be expected, and that the volume of traffic per lane will be somewhat less than that of streets which have separated traffic flows.

Lateral Clearance Adjacent to the Travelled Lane

Prudent drivers tend to shy away from obstructions that are near the travelled way. This applies to barriers or obstructions on both the right- and left-hand sides of the travelled lane. These may be in the form of lighting standards, retaining walls, traffic barriers in the median, and bridge abutments. Experience has shown that if the lateral clearance to a roadway is less than 6 feet, the traffic flow will be diminished.[12] The amount of reduction of flow depends upon how much the lateral clearance is reduced, the lane width, and what type of road is being considered. As an example, on a four-lane undivided highway, with 9-foot lanes and zero distance between the lane and the lateral obstruction, traffic flow in the right-hand lane will be reduced to about 72 percent of normal traffic flow.

Width of the Shoulder Adjacent to the Travelled Lane

The shoulders alongside a travelled lane are important to the psychological well-being of the driver. Some people consider roadside shoulders to be "breakdown lanes" because they are so useful to disabled vehicles. Some states allow the use of these shoulders by slow-moving vehicles; this frees up the regular lanes for vehicles moving at normal speeds. Most states prohibit the use of the shoulder for passing to the right of vehicles which are on the regular roadway lanes.

AASHTO states that:

"Arterials having sufficient traffic volume to justify the construction of four lanes also justify the provision of full width shoulders. The width of usable outside shoulders should preferably be at least 2.4 meters [8 feet]."[13]

Presence of Mixed Traffic Types

When the traffic stream includes both slow- and fast-moving vehicles, the capacity of the street is reduced. Heavy vehicles that have relatively low power in relation to their weight move slowly on streets that have uphill grades, frequent stop signs, or traffic signals. "Heavy vehicles" (for traffic flow analysis purposes) include trucks, recreational vehicles, and buses.

New passenger cars in 1999 typically weighed from 16 to 24 pounds per horsepower (lb/hp).

Typical trucks have an average weight-to-horsepower ratio of 200 lb/hp, although some (such as gravel trucks) have as high as 400 lb/hp.[14]

Recreational vehicles generally range from 30 to 60 lb/hp. While this is not very restrictive in itself, the drivers of these are often inexperienced, and this accentuates the performance limitations of their vehicles.

Intercity buses generally have from 70 to 100 lb/hp, and are generally capable of maintaining speed in level and rolling terrain, except on isolated, long or steep uphill grades.

Heavy vehicles take up more space on highways than do passenger cars, need more space to maneuver in traffic, and are slower on uphill sections of roadways. In calculating the capacity of a roadway, therefore, the percent of heavy vehicles in the traffic flow is taken into consideration. This is done by assigning a number that indicates how many average passenger cars each heavy vehicle is equivalent to, under specific roadway conditions. For example, trucks are considered to be the equivalent of 1.7 passenger cars on multi-

lane highways in level terrain, 4.0 cars on uphill sections in rolling terrain, and 8.0 cars in uphill sections of mountainous terrain.[15]

Types of Terrain

For the purposes of calculating highway capacity, terrains are divided into three types:[16]

1. Highways in *level terrain* have a combination of grades, and horizontal and vertical alignment, that permit heavy vehicles to maintain approximately the same speed as passenger cars; this generally includes short grades of no more than 1 or 2 percent.

2. Highways in *rolling terrain* have a combination of grades and road alignment causing heavy vehicles to reduce their speeds substantially below those of passenger cars, but *not* causing them to operate at crawl speeds for any significant length of time.

3. Highways in *mountainous terrain* have a combination of grades and road alignment causing heavy vehicles to operate at crawl speeds for significant distances or at frequent intervals.

Weather and Visibility

The "Highway Capacity Manual" [HCM-1985], published by the Transportation Research Board, discusses the effect of weather on the traffic capacity of freeways. It is probable that weather affects other types of roads in a similar manner. To quote from HCM:

"The capacity of freeway systems is also affected by weather. The most extreme case is represented by heavy snowfalls that cause multiple lane closings. However, a variety of weather conditions—rain, snow, fog, glare, and others—affect capacity without such dramatic evidence of their existence.

"Quantitative information is sparse, but some indications do exist: one study found that rain reduced capacity by 14 percent. Another found a typical figure of 8 percent for rain, although much variation was observed. Indeed, the substantial variations due to the intensity of the weather condition and the specifics of the location are entirely rational. It is most important to recognize that 10 to 20 percent reductions are typical, and higher percentages are quite possible. These effects must be considered in facility design, particularly when adverse conditions are common."[17]

Stop Signs

Stop signs bring a degree of order to intersections that might otherwise be chaotic. Nevertheless, stop signs do reduce the capacity of a street to carry traffic (given otherwise unimpeded traffic flows).

Let us take a hypothetical example: A single lane of traffic is flowing at the maximum rate of 2,000 vehicles per hour. At this speed, there is a headway of 1.8 seconds per car. Let us say that the drivers of these vehicles in this stream come up to a stop sign, and that all the drivers slow, come to a stop, and immediately start up again. Cars do not go through stop signs every 1.8 seconds; 4 to 6 seconds is closer to the time required. With headways between vehicles of this magnitude, the flow of traffic is cut back from 900 to 600 vehicles per hour per lane—a very substantial reduction in highway capacity indeed.

The foregoing example omits consideration of any cross traffic at the intersection. If the stop sign is at an intersection which has considerable traffic on a cross street, the traffic flow on the major street will be diminished substantially more.[18]

Traffic Signals

Traffic signals are used at intersections that carry more traffic than is found at intersections with stop signs. Like stop signs, traffic signals can cause a significant reduction in street capacity when compared to streets with free-flowing traffic. They do, however, promote orderly flows of traffic through intersections.

Traffic signals by themselves are not a panacea for traffic ills. Intersections where signals are proposed to be installed should be carefully reviewed to make sure that they have an adequate number of lanes to carry the through traffic, that provision is made for turning movements (often by the installation of left-turn lanes), that channelization is provided where appropriate, and that the geometric design of the intersection is well suited to the local conditions.

The "Highway Capacity Manual" is generally considered to be the basic source of information on the analysis of intersections to determine if traffic signals are warranted, and on the timing of the cycles of traffic signals. These analyses are not appropriate tasks for the well-intentioned amateur; they are best left to professional traffic engineers.

While traffic engineers can usually figure out traffic signalization programs using pencils, paper, and hand calculators, most of them prefer to use one of the many computer programs that are widely available to do that work (such as PASSER II and TRANSYT-7F).

Left-Turning Traffic

On streets with two-way traffic, any vehicles whose drivers wish to turn left must wait until there is a break in the oncoming traffic. If no left-turn lane is provided, all vehicles behind the turning vehicle must stop and wait until the driver of the first car is well into their left turn. On lightly travelled rural roads, this is not a problem; on heavily travelled urban streets, left-turn movements can cause notable delays in traffic flow.

Providing a left-turn lane is usually an effective way to reduce the delays experienced by traffic that wishes to go straight through an intersection, although these lanes do not completely eliminate those delays.

AASHTO's book, *A Policy on Geometric Design of Highways and Streets*, provides some excellent suggestions concerning left-turn movements (see pp. 536-537).

Pedestrian Crossings

Pedestrians crossing at unsignalized intersections of lightly travelled rural roads rarely cause a significant interruption to vehicular traffic. At the other end of the intensity scale, however, the impact on traffic flow by pedestrian crossings can be substantial. For example, in central business districts of large urban centers where pedestrians may outnumber vehicles two to one, when walkers stream across an intersection they severely slow, or may even completely halt, the flow of vehicular traffic. Therefore, the volume of pedestrian crossings is often considered when estimating the capacity of urban streets.

Driver Competence

Drivers have an influence on highway capacity. Competent, calm, serious drivers found in high concentrations in daily commuter traffic generally expedite traffic flow better than any other group of drivers.

Recreational drivers ("Sunday drivers") tend to create problems; some of them seem to be in no hurry to get anywhere and their driving habits are somewhat erratic (e.g., stopping suddenly to watch a bunny at the side of the road). The "Highway Capacity Manual" states that "capacity losses as high as 10 to 25 percent have been observed in rec-

reational traffic streams as compared to commuters using the same facility."[19]

It is this author's observation that some of our elderly citizens also cause traffic flow problems, especially those who drive only rarely. The behavior of some other types of drivers remains to be evaluated. They include drivers afflicted with "road rage" and drivers who keep cell phones glued to their ears.

CALCULATING HIGHWAY CAPACITY

The major factors that affect highway capacity were discussed in the preceding part of this chapter. Most of them are considered by traffic and transportation engineers when they calculate the capacity of a specific section of highway to carry traffic. They make these calculations by using the procedures described in the "Highway Capacity Manual." These procedures are technical in nature and require a good deal of judgment in their application; their use is not recommended for novices.

WHY CALCULATE HIGHWAY CAPACITY?

Figures for the calculated capacity of a section of highway are compared with counts of traffic actually using that section. If the traffic using the highway is substantially less than the calculated capacity, it is evidence that the highway is uncongested. On the other hand, if the traffic flow is near the calculated capacity, it documents that the highway is close to being overcrowded.

Of course, going out and driving in traffic flowing on a highway can tell most people whether or not the roadway is underused or overcrowded. That observation, however, is qualitative in nature, rather than quantitative. We need to have specific numbers that can be substantiated when we plan street networks and budget for improvements or additions to those networks. Comparing carefully made traffic counts with reasonably prepared calculations of highway capacity can give us those numbers.

While comparisons of traffic flow with highway capacity are useful in identifying existing traffic problems, they are also widely used to anticipate future traffic issues. Some examples:

- Given a projection of urban growth in a metropolitan area for the year 2020, which highways in the area will be underutilized and which will be overly congested if they are not improved?

- If a jurisdiction has limited funds for highway improvements, which streets should receive priority for increasing their capacity?

- If a jurisdiction finds that it cannot afford to improve its existing traffic arterials (or if it chooses to not modify them), how much urban growth can occur before intolerable traffic congestion will take place?

HOW DO WE DESCRIBE INTENSITIES OF HIGHWAY USAGE?

There are two major methods used to describe the intensity of traffic on highways. The first, which is a description of the traffic flows on highways or "level of service" (LOS) is *qualitative* in nature. The second, which is an expression of the numerical ratio of observed (or projected) traffic volumes to the calculated highway capacity, known as the "volume-to-capacity ratio" (V/C ratio), is *quantitative* in nature. There are specific relationships between these methods of describing the intensity of highway usage; these will be discussed later in this chapter.

THE LEVEL OF SERVICE CONCEPT

The concept of *level of service* (LOS) is defined as a qualitative measure describing operational conditions within a traffic stream, and their perceptions by motorists and/or passengers. The definition generally describes these conditions in terms of such factors as speed and travel time, freedom to maneuver, traffic interruptions, comfort and convenience, and safety.

Six levels of service are defined for each type of facility for which analysis procedures are available. They are given letter designations, from A to F, with LOS A representing the best operating conditions and LOS F the worst. The following are descriptions of levels of service:

1. *LOS A* represents free flow. Individual users are virtually unaffected by the presence of others in the traffic stream. Freedom to select desired speeds and to maneuver within the traffic stream is extremely high. The general level of comfort and convenience provided to the motorist or passenger is excellent.

2. *LOS B* is in the range of stable flow, but the presence of other users in the traffic stream begins to be noticeable. Freedom to select desired speeds is relatively unaffected, but there is a slight decline in the freedom to maneuver within the traffic stream from LOS A. The level of comfort and convenience is somewhat less than LOS A because the presence of others in the traffic stream begins to affect individual behavior.

3. *LOS C* is in the range of stable flow, but marks the beginning of the range of flow in which the operation of individual users becomes significantly affected by interactions with others in the traffic stream. The selection of speed is now affected by others and maneuvering

within the traffic stream requires substantial vigilance on the part of the user. The level of comfort and convenience declines noticeably at this level.

4. *LOS D* represents high-density, but stable, flow. Speed and freedom to maneuver are severely restricted, and the driver experiences a generally poor level of comfort and convenience. Small increases in traffic flow will generally cause problems at this level.

5. *LOS E* represents operating conditions at or near the capacity level. All speeds are reduced to a low, but relatively uniform, value. Freedom to maneuver within the traffic stream is extremely difficult and is generally accomplished by forcing a vehicle to "give way" to accommodate such maneuvers. Comfort and convenience levels are extremely poor, and driver frustration is generally high. Operations at this level are usually unstable because small increases in flow or minor perturbations within the traffic stream will cause breakdowns.

6. *LOS F* is used to define forced or breakdown flow. This condition exists whenever the amount of traffic approaching a point exceeds the amount that can traverse the point. Queues form behind such locations. Operations are characterized by stop-and-go waves which are extremely unstable. Vehicles may progress at reasonable speeds for several hundred feet or more, then be required to stop in a cyclic fashion.[20]

Illustrations of traffic flows at various levels of service are shown in Figure 9.1.

THE RELATIONSHIP OF "LEVEL OF SERVICE" AND THE "VOLUME-TO-CAPACITY RATIO"

Most of us are concerned about traffic congestion. We just finished a discussion of how we describe it, but how do we measure it in quantitative terms? The most common method used is to compare the actual volume of traffic flow on a highway with the calculated capacity of that highway to carry traffic. This comparison produces the "volume-to-capacity ratio," abbreviated "V/C ratio."

Let us look at some examples:

• You have a city street that has a calculated highway capacity of 1,000 vehicles per hour. You observe that the morning peak-hour traffic is pretty congested; your eyeball observation is that the LOS at this time is about D, but you want to quantify just how congested it is. You therefore make a traffic count during the morning peak hour, and you find that the street carried 850 vehicles in that period. By making a simple calculation, you find that the V/C ratio was 850/1000, or 0.85.

• You observe that the same street carries traffic with no observable congestion during midafternoon periods. Your curbside observation is that the LOS at that time is about B, but you are curious as to what its V/C ratio actually is. You therefore make another traffic count from 2:30 to 3:30 p.m., and find that only 200 cars passed your counters. Again, a simple calculation shows that during the noncongested afternoon hour, the V/C ratio was 200/1000, or 0.2.

Another way of discussing traffic flow conditions is to consider what happens as uninterrupted flows[21] run along a highway.

Take, for example, a straight, level, wide highway. If a single car is driven along this highway, there are obviously no traffic prob-

Figure 9.1. Levels of Service

Level of Service A

Level of Service B

Level of Service C

Level of Service D

Level of Service E

Level of Service F

PHOTOGRAPH BY CHAD SURMICK, *SANTA ROSA PRESS DEMOCRAT*

lems involved; there are no cars to pass and no other driving constraints. Under these conditions, we would clearly identify the LOS as A. However, as additional cars join the traffic on the highway, moderate constraints develop: drivers do not have as much freedom of movement; passing or being passed by other cars becomes of greater concern. On our hypothetical ideal highway, LOS A continues until the volume of traffic reaches approximately 35 percent of the calculated capacity of the highway.[22]

As additional traffic is loaded on the highway, the drivers' freedom of movement becomes more constrained. As an approximation, LOS B is experienced when the V/C is between .35 and .5, and LOS C is experienced with a V/C between .5 and .75.

LOS D generally occurs when the volume of traffic on a highway is between .75 and .9 of the calculated highway capacity.

Remember that these are only approximations; there are substantial exceptions to them that will be mentioned later.

When more traffic is loaded onto the hypothetical highway, drivers will start experiencing severe congestion and will have to reduce their speed. This is an example of LOS E, which occurs when the V/C lies between .9 and 1.0.

When the theoretical highway is loaded at 100 percent of its rated capacity, even one additional car is going to overfill it, and cause traffic slowdowns and stoppages. Some of these will be in the form of stop-and-go driving; others may result in longer delays caused by "fender-bender" collisions. This is known as LOS F and it occurs frequently when the V/C is 1.0 or more.

Traffic engineers have made careful studies of traffic flows and traffic congestion, and some of their findings are graphically summarized in Figure 9.2. This diagram illustrates what happens to hypothetical traffic conditions on a hypothetical highway as the hypothetical traffic flow increases. In this diagram, the horizontal scale represents traffic conditions, calibrated both in V/C and LOS.

If we examine the curve in the diagram, starting at the upper left-hand corner, we see that, with only one car on the highway, its speed, which is unconstrained by traffic, might be about 70 mph, but that the density of traffic (as read from the right-hand scale) would be very close to zero vehicles per minute. The driver of the car would obviously enjoy an LOS of A.

Following the curve down and towards the right, we note that, as more traffic is loaded onto the highway, the operational speed (marked on the left-hand scale) decreases because of moderate congestion. We also note that the number of cars on the road, measured in vehicles per minute, increases (see right-hand scale).

Traffic density increases from LOS A through LOS E as we move to the right along the curve. When the highway is filled to capacity, and traffic is still flowing (that is, when V/C = 1.0), we arrive at what is called the "critical speed." After that point, if the loading increases, both traffic speed and driver convenience are greatly diminished. Past this point, as we go around the nose of the curve, we pass from LOS E into LOS F, and observe that the volume of traffic continues to *increase*, even though it is under very unpleasant driving conditions. This increase (shown in the dashed line going down towards the left) is in the form of unstable flow (i.e., stop-and-go), until it reaches what is known as "jam density," which occurs when the highway is filled with cars, but none of them is moving.

In practice, the relationship between LOS and the V/C ratio varies somewhat from that

**Figure 9.2. Conceptual Relationship of Level of Service to Some Measures
of Quality of Flow Under Ideal, Uninterrupted Flow Conditions**

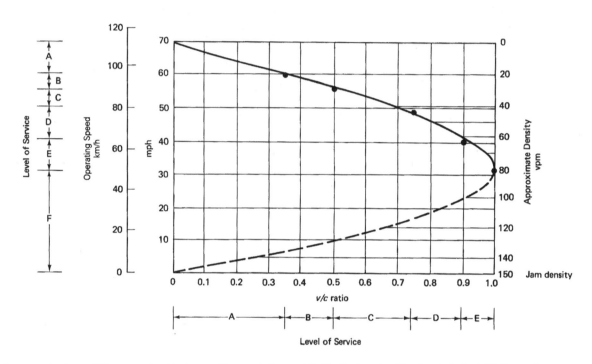

Source: Institute of Transportation Engineers, *Transportation and Traffic Engineering Handbook.* 2nd ed. Wolfgang S.
Homburger, Louis E. Keefer, and William R. McGrath, editors. Washington, DC: Prentice-Hall, 1982. Prepared for the
Institute of Transportation Engineers, p. 473. Used with permission.

in Figure 9.2. For freeways and multilane highways, the relationship varies with the design speed of the roadway and with the number of lanes. For two-lane highways, the relationship varies with the design speed, the type of terrain and, more significantly, the percent of no-passing zones of the roadway. For more information, consult the "Highway Capacity Manual."

Notes

1. HCM-1985, p. 1-5.
2. *Ibid.*, p. 1-3.
3. Homburger et al., p. 8-1.
4. AASHTO, p. 53.
5. *Traffic Engineering Handbook*, p. 392.

6. *Ibid.*
7. Freeways, under some conditions, may carry higher traffic volumes. The 1997 update of the "Highway Capacity Manual" will include consideration of capacities of 2,250 passenger cars per hour per lane (pcphpl) for a 55 mph free-flow speed, and 2,400 pcphpl for a 70 mph free-flow speed.
8. AASHTO, 1994, p. 515.
9. HCM-1985, p. 8-18.
10. A layperson might calculate the capacity of a two-lane street by multiplying the number of lanes (2) by 2,000 vehicles/hour/lane, resulting in 4,000 vehicles/hour.
11. For further discussion of this topic, see the *Transportation Planning Handbook*, pp. 418-420.
12. HCM-1985, p. 7-7. *See also* AASHTO, p. 477.
13. AASHTO, p. 497.
14. HCM-1985, p. 1-11.

15. *Ibid.*, p. 7-9.

16. *Ibid.*, p. 1-11.

17. *Ibid.*, p. 6-15.

18. The effects of stop signs on traffic flows are reviewed in detail in the "Highway Capacity Manual."

19. HCM-1985, p. 7-4.

20. The preceding LOS descriptions were adapted from HCM-1985, pp. 1-4, 1-5.

21. An uninterrupted flow is one that is not interrupted by stop signs, traffic signals, traffic from cross streets, or flows of merging or departing traffic.

22. The relationships between the V/C and LOS given in this discussion are only approximations.

Sources of Further Information

[AASHTO]—American Association of State Highway and Transportation Officials (AASHTO). *A Policy on Geometric Design of Highways and Streets.* Washington, DC: AASHTO, 1994.

Homburger, Hall, Loutzenheiser, and Reilly. *Fundamentals of Traffic Engineering.* 14th ed. Berkeley, CA: Institute of Transportation Studies, University of California, 1996.

Institute of Transportation Engineers. *Traffic Engineering Handbook.* 4th ed. James L. Pline, editor. Englewood Cliffs, NJ: Prentice-Hall, 1992.

Institute of Transportation Engineers. *Transportation Planning Handbook.* John D. Edwards, Jr., P.E., editor. Englewood Cliffs, NJ: Prentice-Hall, 1992. See Chapter 12, "Capacity in Transportation Planning," by Carlton C. Robinson, Herbert S. Levinson, and Leon Goodman.

[HCM-1985] and [HCM-1994]—Transportation Research Board, National Research Council. "Highway Capacity Manual" (Special Report No. 209). Washington, DC: Transportation Research Board, 1985 and 1994. NOTE: The first edition of the manual was published in 1965. A revised edition was published in 1985. An update to the 1985 edition was published in 1994. An additional update was scheduled for publication in 1997. A complete revision of the manual is scheduled for 2000.

10

Basic Highway Design

A NOTE ON TERMINOLOGY

The terms "highways," "streets," and "roads" are all used in this chapter to refer to public thoroughfares which are primarily intended to carry vehicular traffic.

- *Highways* are often considered to be main roadways, especially those connecting towns and cities.
- *Streets* are usually considered to be urban roadways, often with sidewalks, and which provide access to adjacent properties.
- *Roads* are similar to "streets" but are usually less urban in character; they are often found in rural areas.

In common usage, however, the terms are somewhat interchangeable. For example, the term "highway design" is generally used to refer to the design of roads, streets, and highways (as well as to the design of accompanying features such as bridges and drainage facilities).

AASHTO DESIGN STANDARDS AND PROCEDURES

Many of the geometric design standards and procedures included in this chapter are derived from *A Policy on Geometric Design of Highways and Streets*, published by the American Association of State Highway and Trans-

portation Officials (AASHTO) in 1994. This was done because, to quote from a publication by the Institute of Transportation Engineers:

"The most widely accepted design criteria in the United States are those developed by the American Association of State Highway and Transportation Officials (AASHTO). Although every state and many countries, cities, and other governmental bodies have developed their own standards, they are based largely on AASHTO standards for two reasons: (1) AASHTO design policies, standards, and guides have been developed and approved by every state; and (2) the Federal Highway Administration (FHWA) has made them applicable standards for design and construction of Federal-aid highways. AASHTO design criteria are also used as the basis for design standards used by many other countries."[1]

USE OF THE METRIC SYSTEM

Homburger et al. state that:

"Although the National Highway System Designation Act of 1995 postponed to October 2000 the requirement that federal-aid transportation facilities be designed in SI[2] (metric) units, most states have already made this change."[3]

The SI (metric) system of measurements uses units such as centimeters, meters, kilometers, grams, kilograms, etc. The system of weights and measures currently in wide use in the United States is known as "the English system," and uses units such as inches, feet, yards, rods, miles, ounces, pounds, etc.

While it is true that the design of state and federal highways in the United States is now done using the SI system, that practice is not widely used by city or county governments, nor is it used (except in rare occasions) by private land developers. In California, and a number of other states, cities and counties are required to use SI dimensions when designing new highway projects which are to receive state or federal funding. However, when designing changes to existing facilities, they may use the measurement system that was originally used for that facility.

The following text includes a number of tables that give design guidelines which were developed by their originators using the SI measurement system. In a number of cases, this author has amended those tables to add the English system equivalents, in order to provide readers who are not yet familiar with metric units with a basis for comparison.

Table 10.1 provides a table of factors that may be used to convert some measurements of distance from one system to the other. It should be noted that most of the computer programs used in highway design today make it very easy to convert from the English system of measurements to the SI system, and vice versa.

SOME BASIC ROAD DESIGN QUESTIONS

There are many questions that a road designer needs to consider when contemplating the design of a new road, or the modification of an existing one.

Table 10.1. Conversion Factors Between English Measurement Units and SI (Metric) Units

To convert from **meters** to **feet**, multiply by 3.28 (or 3.2808).
To convert from **kilometers** to **miles**, multiple by .621 (or .62137).
To convert from **feet** to **meters**, multiply by .305 (or .30480).
To convert from **miles** to **kilometers**, multiply by 1.61 (or 1.6093).

- Where is the road to go? Does it have specific points of origin and destination? Is there an already accepted general (or specific) route for it? What type of environments (natural and urban) is it to pass through?
- What will the major functions of the road be? What degree will it serve through traffic, and to what degree will it provide access to abutting properties? What type of traffic will it serve (commuters, shoppers, recreational drivers, or commercial truckers)?
- For what volume of traffic should it be designed to accommodate?
- For which level of service should the road be designed?
- For what driving speed should the road be designed?

Definitions of various measures of traffic flow were given at the beginning of the previous chapter. Table 10.2 identifies which measures are usually needed for designing various types of roads.

AVERAGE DAILY TRAFFIC

Estimates of past, present, and projected average daily traffic (ADT) on a road should always be examined. In areas of stable population and employment levels, this year's ADT may serve fairly adequately as a basis

Table 10.2. Summary of Traffic Elements Needed for Design Purposes

Type of Highway	Traffic Elements Required for Design	
Local roads and streets	ADT	current or estimated average daily traffic
Two-lane arterial highways	ADT	current and estimated (for some future year) average daily traffic
	DHV	design hourly volume for some future year
	T	percentage of trucks during design hour
Multilane arterial highways and freeways	ADT	current and estimated (for some future year) average daily traffic
	DDHV	directional design hourly volume for through lanes and turning movements
	T	percentage of trucks during design hour

Source: Institute of Transportation Engineers, *Transportation and Traffic Engineering Handbook.* 2nd ed. Wolfgang S. Homburger, Louis E. Keefer, and William R. McGrath, editors. Washington, DC: Prentice-Hall, 1982, p.589. Prepared for the Institute of Transportation Engineers. Used with permission.

for designing roads which are expected to serve for the next 30 years or so. Stability of population and employment has not been a characteristic of many of our North American metropolitan areas, however. In most of these areas, it is of critical importance to examine projected urban and suburban population growth for the next 30 years, and to consider their impacts on future daily traffic flows. Computer models are widely used to make those analyses.

DESIGN HOURLY VOLUME

While ADT (which reports 24-hour traffic volumes) is a basic data requirement for the design of many roads, it usually must be translated into peak-hour traffic, in what is called "design hourly volume" (DHV). On roads that are busy all day long (such as circumferential roads in metropolitan areas), DHV is a relatively low percentage of ADT. On the other hand, roads which primarily serve employment centers, or are radial roads in metropolitan areas, may have DHVs which are a relatively high percentage of the average daily volume.

DESIGNING FOR PEAK-HOUR FLOWS

It is desirable to design roads to accommodate peak-hour traffic flows. However, which peak hour are we talking about? Is it the highest hourly volume of the year or the highest hourly volume of a typical day? There are many roads that have extremely high peak-hour flows on a few days a year (such as roads serving sports stadia, and roads serving recreational areas which have peaks on the Fourth of July and Labor Day weekends). On the other hand, there are also many urban arterials and freeways that have consistently heavy peak-hour traffic flows five days a week, for at least 45 weeks a year. Experience has shown that it is advisable to design roads to serve the *30th highest peak hour* of the year. This practice accommodates the needs of consistent commuter flows, and avoids the high economic cost of accommodating the extreme peak-hour flows which occur only rarely.

CONSIDERING DIRECTIONAL FLOWS

On many rural roads and many urban local streets, ADT and DHV (with appropriate projections for future traffic) are suitable for estimating needed road capacity. There are, however, many arterial roads where directional flows should be considered. For example, some arterials which run between residential areas and employment centers may carry 70 percent inbound and 30 percent outbound traffic in the mornings, but this may reverse to 30 percent inbound and 70 percent outbound traffic in the evening hours. For this reason, "directional design hourly volume" (DDHV) should be analyzed and considered when designing some roads, especially multilane arterials and freeways.

DESIGN SPEED

AASHTO has this to say about design speed:

> "Design speed is the maximum safe speed that can be maintained over a specific section of highway when conditions are so favorable that the design features of the highway govern. The assumed design speed should be a logical one with respect to the topography, the adjacent land use, and the functional classification of the highway. Except for local streets where speed controls are frequently included intentionally, every effort should be made to use as high a design speed as practicable to attain a desired degree of safety, mobility, and efficiency while under the constraints of quality, economics, aesthetics, and social or political impacts. Once selected, all of the pertinent features of the highway should be related to the design speed to obtain a balanced design. … Some features, such as curvature, superelevation, and sight distance, are directly related to, and vary appreciably with, design speed …
>
> "The design speed chosen should be consistent with the speed a driver is likely to expect. Where a difficult condition is obvious, drivers are more apt to accept lower speed operation than where there is no apparent reason for it. … A low design speed … should not be assumed where the topography is such that drivers are likely to travel at high speeds. Drivers do not adjust their speeds to the importance of the highway, but to their per-

ception of the physical limitations and traffic thereon."[4]

DESIGN LEVEL OF SERVICE

We can be sure that everyone would like to have their roads designed and built to provide LOS A driving conditions, but would gladly settle for LOS B. The reason that our roads do not meet those comfortable standards, of course, is economic: it costs much more money to acquire rights-of-way and build spacious roads than it does roads with lesser design standards.

It is true that some roads which are designed to accommodate LOS D in the year 2030 will probably provide a LOS B or C soon after they are built (if that is about the year 2000), but the LOS will decline over the years as the traffic on them builds up.

The design LOS selection is a matter of policy. This policy is often established by the agency that provides a major share of the funding for the road design and construction. AASHTO discusses design service flow rates and provides a table that suggests a starting point for selection of appropriate LOSs for various types of highways. These suggestions are reproduced in Table 10.3.

BASIC ROAD DESIGN PROCEDURES

The fundamental parts of designing roads, once their basic character and general routing have been decided, consist of two phases, which are usually undertaken concurrently.

1. designing the horizontal geometry

2. designing the vertical geometry

The process of how highway engineers undertake these phases is discussed in the remainder of this chapter.

Table 10.3. Guide for Selection of Design Level of Service

Highway Type	Type of Area and Appropriate Level of Service			
	Rural Level	Rural Rolling	Rural Mountainous	Urban and Suburban
Freeway	B	B	C	C
Arterial	B	B	C	C
Collector	C	C	D	D
Local	D	D	D	D

Source: American Association of State Highway and Transportation Officials (AASHTO). *A Policy on Geometric Design of Highways and Streets*. Washington, DC: AASHTO, 1994, p. 90. Used by permission.

HORIZONTAL ALIGNMENT GEOMETRY

"Horizontal alignment geometry" refers to the geometric qualities of a road when seen from above in "plan" view.

There are three general types of horizontal road alignment patterns:

1. straight roads
2. tangent-curve roads
3. continuously curved roads

These are shown in diagrammatic form in Figure 10.1.

- *Straight roads* need little further definition. They may be straight road sections in a gridiron street pattern, or straight road sections which are tangents located between curved road sections.
- *Tangent-curve roads* consist of straight roads connected to circular curves. In this case, the curves are arcs of a circle, and each arc has a constant radius.
- *Continuously curved roads* consist of tangents and circular curves joined by *spiral curves*. A spiral curve is a curve which has an infinitely long radius at its junction with the tangent end of the curve; this radius is gradually reduced in length until it becomes the same as the radius of the circular curve with which it joins.[5] This form of road design is rarely used for local streets. About half of U.S. states

use it in the design of their freeways and major arterials; the other half use the tangent and curve procedure.

On the tangent sections of roads, which are straight as an arrow, traffic speed is primarily limited only by road surface conditions, lane width, vertical grade, passing opportunities, the capabilities of the vehicle, and the desires of the driver (that is, if there are no social constraints on vehicular speed, such as speed limits in populated areas). Such straight roads signal to the driver that "no changes in speed are needed; there are no unknowns ahead." Straight roads are appropriate where high speeds are desired and where the nature of the terrain does not put economic constraints on their construction.

The tangent-curve alignment may result in a mixed bag for the driver if the road is not carefully designed. In this pattern, the straight sections may communicate to the driver that "no changes in speed are necessary," but the following curved sections of road may require a substantial reduction in speed.

The continuously curved alignment generally clues the driver that "changes are taking place; be ready for something new." On highways which are designed for high speeds, this pattern makes driving easier and generally

Figure 10.1. Horizontal Alignment Patterns Used in Road Design

STRAIGHT (or "tangent")

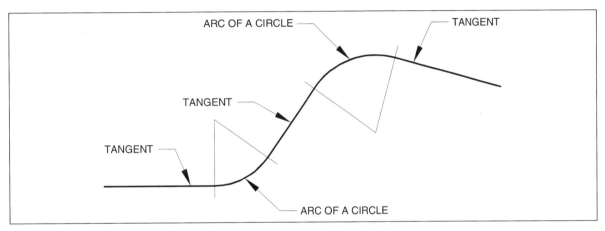

TANGENT-CURVE
(tangents combined with "circular curves")

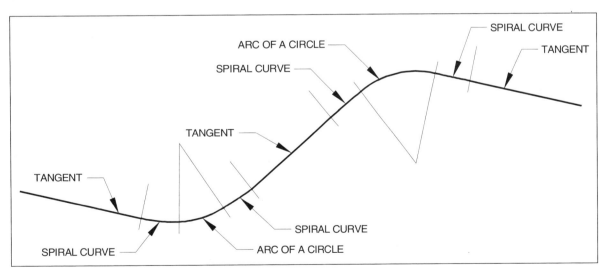

CONTINUOUSLY CURVED
(tangents and circular curves, joined by "spiral curves")

produces a road design that is visually more graceful than the tangent-curve approach.

MINIMUM SAFE RADIUS FOR CURVES

The *minimum safe radius* for a curved section of a roadway (designated "R," which may be in feet or meters) is a function of:

1. the design speed of the roadway (designated "V," the velocity in kilometers per hour (km/h), or miles per hour (mph));
2. the superelevation of the roadway (i.e., the degree to which the roadbed is tilted or "banked") at the curves (designated "e," which is the superelevation rate in feet per foot or meters per meter); and
3. the friction factor, which is a function of the relationship between the vehicle's tires and the roadbed. It is used to assure that side slipping induced by centrifugal force at curves will not be excessive (designated "f," the friction factor; it has no dimensions).

The equations for calculating a minimum safe radius are:

$$R = \frac{V^2}{127 (e + f)}$$

(where R is in meters and V is in kilometers per hour)

and

$$R = \frac{V^2}{15 (e + f)}$$

(where R is in feet and V is in miles per hour)

Factor "e" in the equation above represents the superelevation of the roadway; it varies with climate and location. In areas where there is no snow or ice, roadways can be banked up to a maximum of .12 meters per meter (or feet per foot) of road cross section. In areas that experience snow or ice, "e" should never exceed .08. A general minimum figure for "e" is .06.[6]

Factor "f" in the equation above represents the side-friction factor. Studies have developed a fairly wide range of values for this factor. An approximation of the figures recommended by AASHTO can be produced by using a value of .14 for design speeds of 80 km/h, and reducing this by .01 for each 10 km/h increase in speed. For English units, an approximation can be produced by using a value of .16 for design speeds of 30 mph and reducing it by .01 for each additional 10 mph through 50 mph, then the factor is reduced by .02 for each 10 mph increase, resulting in .08 at 80 mph.

Table 10.4 provides the recommended minimum radii for horizontal curves, when SI units are used in measurement. Table 10.5 reports the recommended minimum radii when English measurement units are used.

Example

Given a design speed of 100 km/h, calculate the minimum radius for a curve. Assume that Factor "e" = .08. We know that Factor "f" is .14 for 80 km/h, and will be .13 for 90 km/h and .12 for 100 km/h.

$$R = \frac{V^2}{127 (e+f)} = \frac{100^2}{127 (.08+.12)} =$$

$$\frac{10,000}{127 (.20)} = \frac{10,000}{25.4} = 394 \text{ meters}$$

Table 10.4 provides figures for the minimum radius of rural highways and high-speed urban streets, as recommended by AASHTO. It must be remembered, however,

Table 10.4. Minimum Radius in Meters for the Design of Horizontal Curves in Rural Highways and High-Speed Urban Streets

Maximum e	Design Speed (km/h)									
	30	**40**	**50**	**60**	**70**	**80**	**90**	**100**	**110**	**120**
.04	35	60	100	150	215	280	375	490	635	870
.06	30	55	90	135	195	250	335	435	560	755
.08	30	50	80	125	175	230	305	395	500	665
.10	25	45	75	115	160	210	275	360	455	595
.12	25	45	70	105	150	195	255	330	415	540

- Radius figures are expressed in meters.
- The figures in the table have been rounded to significant figures for use in highway design.

Source: American Association of State Highway and Transportation Officials (AASHTO). *A Policy on Geometric Design of Highways and Streets.* Washington, DC: AASHTO, 1994, p. 156. Used by permission.

Table 10.5. Minimum Radius in Feet for the Design of Horizontal Curves in Rural Highways and High-Speed Urban Streets

Maximum e	Design Speed (mph)					
	30	**40**	**50**	**60**	**70**	**80**
.04	300	560	930	1,500	2,300	3,600
.06	270	310	830	1,300	2,000	3,000
.08	250	460	760	1,200	1,800	2,700
.10	230	430	700	1,100	1,600	2,400

Source: Calculated using the equations in this book; results rounded to 2 significant figures.

that the figures in the table do *not* take sight distance into consideration.

A note of caution: Table 10.4 does not provide the readers of this text with all the skills needed to design highway curves; it illustrates how the minimum radius for turns varies with the speed of the vehicle and with the amount of superelevation of the roadbed. (Actual highway design requires more than the ability to pick numbers out of a table.) For a more comprehensive discussion of calculating minimum radii, see AASHTO-1994, pp. 141-173.

SUPERELEVATION RUNOFF AND TRANSITION CURVES

Superelevation runoff is the general term denoting the length of roadway needed to accomplish the change in road cross section when it shifts from a straight and level section to a section in an adjacent curve which has superelevation. Some distance is required for this because you can't drive along a straight road which has no superelevation and then suddenly come upon a section of superelevated road right at the beginning of a curve;

there has to be a transition from the flat section to the banked section, and this transition must be somewhat gradual (see Figures 10.2, 10.3, and 10.4).

The length of this transition section is called "superelevation runoff," and it varies in length with the design speed of the vehicles on the road, the width of the traffic lanes, and the superelevation used in the curved section of the roadway. AASHTO reports that there are a variety of methods used to determine the length of superelevation runoff, and states that:

> "Review of current practice indicates that the appearance aspect of superelevation runoff largely governs the length. Spiral lengths as determined otherwise often are shorter than determined for general appearance, so that spiral formula values give way to long empirical runoff values."[7]

SPIRAL CURVES

There appears to be no universally accepted basis for computing the optimum length of the spiral curve, but common practice is to make the length of the spiral curve the same length as is required for the superelevation runoff.[8]

SIGHT DISTANCE

Sight distance is the length of roadway ahead that is visible to the driver. Sight distance should provide the driver with adequate warning about possible hazards or obstructions in the roadway, and of changes in the alignment of the road that lies ahead. Sight distances of three kinds are considered in highway design:

1. stopping sight distance
2. decision sight distance
3. passing sight distance

Stopping sight distance is the sum of two calculated distances, which are:

A. the distance a vehicle travels between the time the driver sights an object and the time the brakes are applied; and

B. the distance the vehicle travels between the time the brakes are applied and the time the vehicle stops.

Recommended minimum distances are given in Table 10.6. This table documents an obvious truth: the faster a vehicle is moving, the greater distance it will travel during the stopping period.

Stopping sight distances are calculated using the assumption that the height of the driver's eye is 3.5 feet [1.05 meters] above the pavement, and that the object being seen is 0.5 feet [15 cm] high.

Stopping distances are calculated using the assumption that wet pavement is present, rather than dry pavement (which would have shorter stopping distances) or icy pavement (which would have far, far greater stopping distances).

Table 10.6. Minimum Stopping Sight Distances (on wet pavements)

Design Speed		Stopping Sight Distance
(mph)	(km/h)	(in feet; rounded for design)
20	30	120
30	50	200–200
40	65	275–325
50	80	375–475
60	95	525–650
70	115	625–850
80	130	750–1,100

Source: Institute of Transportation Engineers, *Transportation and Traffic Engineering Handbook.* 2nd ed. Wolfgang S. Homburger, Louis E. Keefer, and William R. McGrath, editors. Washington, DC: Prentice-Hall, 1982. Prepared for the Institute of Transportation Engineers, p. 591.

Figure 10.2. Cross Section of a Road With No Superelevation

Figure 10.3. Cross Section of a Road With Superelevation

Figure 10.4. Location of Transition Sections in Roads

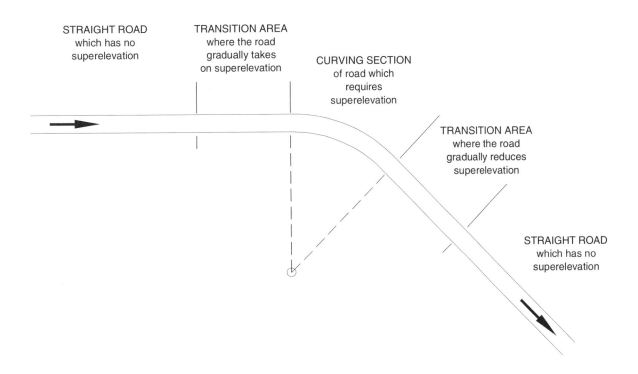

STRAIGHT ROAD
which has no
superelevation

TRANSITION AREA
where the road
gradually takes
on superelevation

CURVING SECTION
of road which
requires
superelevation

TRANSITION AREA
where the road
gradually reduces
superelevation

STRAIGHT ROAD
which has no
superelevation

Stopping distances are increased on down-hill grades and decreased on uphill grades, because vehicles tend to go faster downhill than they do uphill. For data on the effects of grade on stopping sight distance, see AASHTO-1994, p. 125.

Decision sight distance is "the distance required for a driver to detect an unexpected or otherwise difficult-to-perceive information source or hazard in a roadway environment that may be visually cluttered, recognize the hazard or its potential threat, select an appropriate speed and path, and initiate and complete the required safety maneuver safely and efficiently."[9]

Decision sight distance is important when drivers are faced with a somewhat confusing situation and must make a quick decision. These situations may arise when drivers come upon freeway interchanges that are new to them, when approaching a toll booth, or when driving along a street that has an abundance of signs which make it difficult to identify street names or direction signs. AASHTO-1994 discusses decision sight distance and provides information on the distances required for "avoidance maneuvers" under a variety of different situations (see pp. 126-127 of that text).

Passing sight distance is an important design factor for two-lane highways; it is not relevant for highways that have two or more lanes of traffic in each direction.

Passing sight distance is "the length of highway ahead necessary for one vehicle to pass another before meeting an opposing vehicle which might appear after the pass begins."[10] Minimum passing sight distances are given in Table 10.7.

Table 10.7 shows that, for a given highway design speed, it is assumed that the overtaking vehicle is going somewhat faster than the design speed, and that the vehicle being passed is going somewhat slower.

It should also be noted that sight distances required for passing on uphill grades are longer than those on level terrain because the ability of the overtaking vehicle to accelerate to a passing speed is reduced. Conversely, sight distances required on downhill grades are somewhat shorter. It has been observed, however, that occasionally the overtaken vehicle may increase its speed, thereby making it more difficult for others to pass it.

Another consideration of sight distance is found at street intersections. If the operator of a vehicle drives along a street and comes to an intersection with another street, how much sight distance does the driver need in order to cross that street in a prudent manner, or to turn onto it?

The answer to that question is not a simple one. For one thing, it depends upon what type of intersection is encountered. There are five types to be considered:

1. *no control* at the intersection, where all drivers adjust their speed based on their personal judgment
2. *yield control,* where vehicles on the minor intersecting street must yield to vehicles on the major intersecting street
3. *simple stop control,* where traffic on the minor street must stop prior to entering the major roadway
4. *four-way stop control,* where traffic from all streets must stop before entering the intersection
5. *signal control,* where movement of traffic on all legs of the intersecting roadways is controlled and sequenced by traffic signals

It is beyond the scope of this book to discuss the subject in depth, so the reader is referred to the AASHTO book (pp. 696-722), or to Stover and Koepke's good summary of

Table 10.7. Minimum Passing Sight Distances for Design of Two-Lane Highways

Assumed Speeds						Minimum Passing Sight Distance for Design	
Design Speed		Passed Vehicle		Passing Vehicle			
(km/h)	*(mph)*	(km/h)	*(mph)*	(km/h)	*(mph)*	(meters)	*(feet)*
30	*19*	29	*18*	44	*28*	217	*710*
40	*25*	36	*22*	51	*32*	285	*935*
50	*31*	44	*28*	59	*37*	345	*1,130*
60	*37*	51	*32*	66	*41*	407	*1,330*
70	*44*	59	*37*	74	*46*	482	*1,580*
80	*50*	65	*40*	80	*50*	541	*1,770*
90	*56*	73	*45*	88	*55*	605	*1,980*
100	*62*	79	*49*	94	*59*	670	*2,200*
110	*68*	85	*53*	100	*62*	728	*2,390*
120	*75*	91	*57*	106	*66*	792	*2,600*

The figures in *italics* are the author's translation of the metric units into English measurement units. These figures are included for the purpose of illustration, not for use in design.

Source: American Association of State Highway and Transportation Officials (AASHTO). *A Policy on Geometric Design of Highways and Streets.* Washington, DC: AASHTO, 1994, p. 134. Used by permission.

the subject (pp. 120-127). The topic will also be mentioned in Chapter 16 under the heading of *Clear Sight Distance.*

VERTICAL ALIGNMENT GEOMETRY

Maximum Grades

The maximum vertical grade of a road is related to its design speed. In general, the higher the design speed, the lower the maximum permissible percent of slope. Tables 10.8 and 10.9 list the maximum grades for some types of roads, as recommended by AASHTO in 1994. The increase in maximum grades in mountainous areas is caused by the economics of construction; it can be extremely costly to build roads in rugged terrain.

Vertical Curves

Crest curves occur at the crests of hills; *sag curves* occur at the bottoms of valleys. They are both long, simple *parabolas*; they are not circular arcs. Figure 10.5 illustrates several forms of crest curves and Figure 10.6 shows some forms of sag curves.

The qualities of vertical curves are primarily determined by stopping sight distance requirements; that is, their form must be such that the driver can see an object on the road surface far enough ahead and be able to come to a stop before hitting it. Insofar as the "hump" of the crest curve itself is the greatest impediment to such clear vision, and this impediment does not exist under sag curve conditions, crest curve parabolas must generally be longer and flatter than sag curves. Sag curve qualities are primarily influenced by the foreshortening effect of the sag on headlight beams illuminating objects on the roadway at night.

The basic formulas for crest and sag curve geometry are:

Table 10.8. Maximum Grades for Urban and Rural Freeways

Design Speed		Type of Terrain (percent)		
(km/h)	*(mph)*	**Level**	**Rolling**	**Mountainous**
80	*50*	4	5	6
90	*56*	4	5	6
100	*62*	3	4	6
110	*68*	3	4	5
120	*75*	3	4	—

Table 10.9. Maximum Grades for Local Roads and Streets

Design Speed		Type of Terrain (percent)		
(km/h)	*(mph)*	**Level**	**Rolling**	**Mountainous**
30	*19*	8	11	16
40	*25*	7	11	15
50	*31*	7	10	14
60	*37*	7	10	13
70	*44*	7	9	12
80	*50*	6	8	10
90	*56*	6	7	10
100	*62*	5	6	—

- Maximum grades for *rural collectors* and *urban collectors* will be found in AASHTO-1994 on p. 463.
- Maximum grades for *urban and rural arterials* will be found in AASHTO-1994 on p. 514.

The figures in *italics* are the author's translation of the metric units into English measurement units. These figures are included for the purpose of illustration, not for use in design.

Source: American Association of State Highway and Transportation Officials (AASHTO). *A Policy on Geometric Design of Highways and Streets.* Washington, DC: AASHTO, 1994, Table 10.7 (p. 559) and Table 10.8 (p. 421). Used by permission.

$L = KA$
where
L = length of the parabola in meters
K = stopping sight distance factor
A = algebraic difference in the percent of grades of the intersecting tangents to the curve

$$E = \frac{AL}{800}$$

where

E = the distance (in meters) between the intersection of the tangents and the apex of the parabola (see Figure 10.5)

(These equations may be used with either metric or English units.)

Table 10.10 provides values for the factor K when using metric measurements. Table 10.11 provides K values for use with the English measurement system.

In highway design, uphill grades are designated positive (+), and downhill grades are

Figure 10.5. Crest Vertical Curves

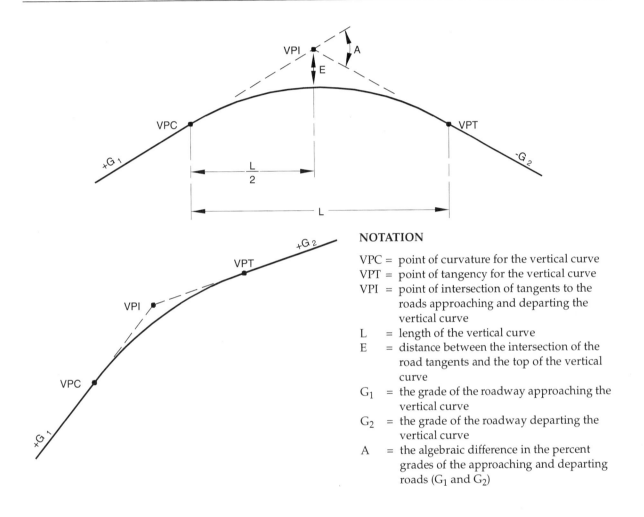

NOTATION

VPC = point of curvature for the vertical curve

VPT = point of tangency for the vertical curve

VPI = point of intersection of tangents to the roads approaching and departing the vertical curve

L = length of the vertical curve

E = distance between the intersection of the road tangents and the top of the vertical curve

G_1 = the grade of the roadway approaching the vertical curve

G_2 = the grade of the roadway departing the vertical curve

A = the algebraic difference in the percent grades of the approaching and departing roads (G_1 and G_2)

designated negative (–). The algebraic difference between a +3 percent and a –5 percent grade is 8 percent. The algebraic difference between a +3 percent grade and a +5 percent grade is 2 percent.

Following are two examples of how the dimensions of vertical curves are calculated.

Example #1

Given: V = 70 km/h

A +4 percent tangent meets a –3 percent tangent at a crest curve.

Required: Calculate the desirable length of the vertical curve and the length of dimension "E."

Solution:

L = KA

K = 31 (taken from Table 10.10, column 3)

A = 4 + 3 = 7 degrees

L = KA = 31 × 7 = 217 meters

(round to 220 meters)

Figure 10.6. Sag Vertical Curves

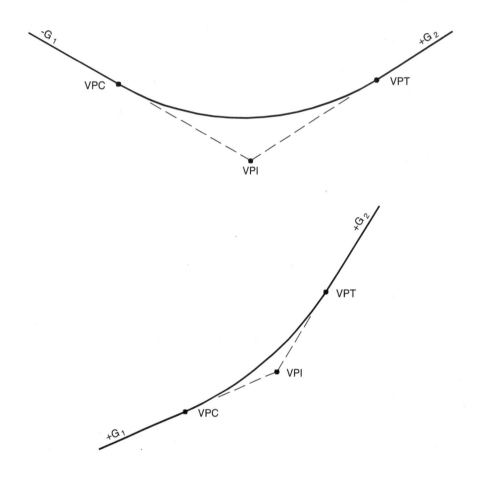

$$E = \frac{A \times L}{800} = \frac{7 \times 220}{800} = \frac{1,540}{800}$$

$$= 1.925 \text{ meters} = 1.9 \text{ meters (rounded)}$$

Example #2

Given: V = 110 km/h

A –5 percent tangent meets a +8 percent tangent at a sag curve.

Required: Calculate the desirable length of the vertical curve and the length of dimension "E."

Solution:
L = KA

K = 62 (taken from Table 10.10, column 5)
A = 5 + 8 = 13 degrees
L = KA = 62 × 13 = 806 meters
(round to 810 meters)

$$E = \frac{A \times L}{800} = \frac{13 \times 810}{800} = \frac{10,530}{800}$$

$$= 13.16 \text{ meters} = 13.2 \text{ meters (rounded)}$$

There are computer programs available that will do all the vertical curve calculations for you, and will provide you with the eleva-

Table 10.10. Values of Factor "K" for Use in Calculating Vertical Curves Using Metric System Dimensions

Design Speed	K for Crest Curves		K for Sag Curves	
(km/h)	Minimum	Recommended	Minimum	Recommended
30	3	3	4	4
40	5	5	8	8
50	9	10	11	12
60	14	18	15	18
70	22	31	20	25
80	32	49	25	32
90	43	71	30	40
100	62	105	37	51
110	80	151	43	62
120	102	202	50	73

- The units to be used in conjunction with this table are KILOMETERS PER HOUR and METERS.
- The factors in this table are for "stopping sight distance"; they are not applicable for determining "passing sight distance."

Source: American Association of State Highway and Transportation Officials (AASHTO). *A Policy on Geometric Design of Highways and Streets.* Washington, DC: AASHTO, 1994, pp. 284, 292. Used by permission.

Table 10.11. Values of Factor "K" for Use in Calculating Vertical Curves Using English System Dimensions

Design Speed	K for Crest Curves		K for Sag Curves	
(mph)	Minimum	Recommended	Minimum	Recommended
20	10	—	18	—
30	30	—	35	—
40	55	—	55	—
50	100	170	80	110
60	200	320	125	155
70	280	545	150	215
80	400	910	185	285

- The units to be used in conjunction with this table are MILES PER HOUR and FEET.
- The factors in this table are for "stopping sight distance"; they are not applicable for determining "passing sight distance."

Source: Institute of Transportation Engineers, *Transportation and Traffic Engineering Handbook.* 2nd ed. Wolfgang S. Homburger, Louis E. Keefer, and William R. McGrath, editors. Washington, DC: Prentice-Hall, 1982. Prepared for the Institute of Transportation Engineers. Used with permission.

tions along the recommended curve of the roadway. However, the shape of the parabolic curve can be easily laid out graphically in a manner which is sufficiently accurate for preliminary design review. This can be done as follows:

1. Calculate the length of the curve L.
2. Locate PC (point of curvature) and PT (point of tangency) so that they are equidistant from PI (point of intersection of the two tangents).
3. Draw a chord from PC to PT.
4. Draw a line vertically down from PI to the chord.
5. Mark the midpoint of the vertical line drawn in Step 4. (The location of this point will be about the distance "E" from point PI.)
6. Sketch in the parabolic curve, starting from PC and going to the midpoint identified in Step 5, and then proceeding to point PT. This should be a smooth curve, easing off from the straight tangent at PC, curving through the midpoint, and then easing into the tangent of the roadway at point PT. (The curve may be drawn freehand or with a French curve.)

INTERPRETING "STATIONS" SHOWN ON PLANS OF ROADS

When engineers design roads, they need to show the route of the road and identify what happens along the route (such as the start of a curve here, the end of a curve there, and the location of a culvert). They do this by identifying "stations" at regular intervals, and then relating the location of those items of interest to the stations.

In the traditional U.S. measurement system, stations are identified and marked at 100-foot intervals. The starting point is at station 0+00; 100 feet further along the route is station 1+00; the next station after that is 2+00, and so on. These stations are located exactly 100 feet apart. The number after the "+" sign indicates how much further past the station a feature to be identified is located. For instance, the mark of "17+23.5" indicates that some design feature is located 23.5 feet past station 17. (Station 17, of course, is located 1,700 feet from the beginning point.) When the time for road construction comes, surveyors place stakes to mark the locations of the stations and the intervening points which have been indicated on the plans.

The metric system is very similar to the U.S. system; the major differences are that:

A. the stations are located 100 meters apart [328 feet]; and
B. distances beyond each station are indicated in meters and decimal parts of meters. For example, "17+23.5" would indicate that the feature noted lies 23.5 meters past station 17. Station 17, in this case, lies 17 × 100 = 1,700 meters from the beginning point.

When showing station locations on plans it is desirable, whenever possible, for the stationing to run from left to right.

Figure 10.7 illustrates the plan of a highway with station locations marked on it.

GENERAL GUIDELINES FOR GEOMETRIC DESIGN

Guidelines for Horizontal Alignment

1. Consistent with topography, alignment should be as direct as possible. Two-lane road alignments should provide as many safe passing sections as reasonably possible.*
2. Minimum radius curves should be avoided wherever possible.
3. The design standards of a road should be consistent throughout its length. The driver should not be surprised by sharp

Figure 10.7. Plan of a Highway Showing Station Locations

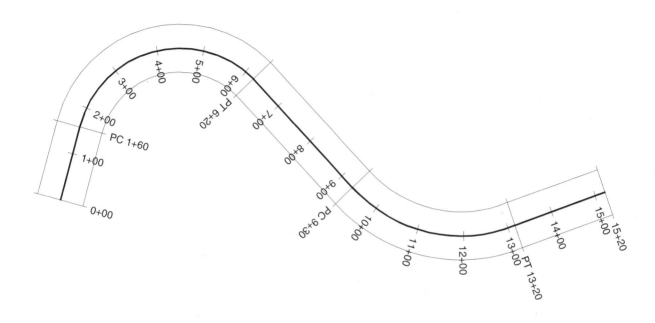

curves located at the end of long tangents. Likewise, successive curves should have the same, or similar (with 10 mph), design speeds.

4. Short lengths of curves should be avoided, even for very small deflection angles.*

5. Large radius curves are often appropriate on long fills.

6. Compound circular curves with large differences in radii should be avoided.*

7. Direct reverse curves (i.e., two connecting curves, each going in a different direction) should be avoided; a tangent (i.e., straight) road section should be used between them.

8. "Broken-back" curves (i.e., two curves in the same direction on either side of a short tangent) should be avoided.*

General Guidelines for Vertical Alignment

1. Smooth grades with gradual changes, consistent with the class of highway and the character of the terrain, should be provided.*

2. "Roller-coaster" or "hidden-dip" profiles should be avoided.*

3. "Broken-back" gradelines (two vertical curves in the same direction separated by a short tangent) should be avoided.*

4. Grades through at-grade intersections of crossing highways should be as level as possible.

5. Sag vertical curves should be avoided in cuts unless adequate drainage can be provided.**

Guidelines for Combined Horizontal and Vertical Alignment

1. Horizontal and vertical alignment should complement each other. Both

traffic operation and overall appearance of the facility should be considered in design.

2. Vertical curvature superimposed upon horizontal curvature, or vice versa, generally results in a pleasing facility, but it should be analyzed for effect on traffic. The following exceptions to these alignment combinations should be noted:**

   A. Sharp, horizontal curvature should not be introduced at or near the top of a pronounced crest vertical curve.**

   B. Only flat, horizontal curvature should be introduced at or near the low point of a pronounced sag vertical curve.

   C. On two-lane roads and streets, the need for safe passing sections at frequent intervals and for an appreciable percentage of the length of the roadway often supersedes the general desirability for combination of horizontal and vertical alignment.**

3. Horizontal curvature and road profiles should be made as flat as feasibly possible at highway intersections where sight distance is important and vehicles may have to slow or stop.**

4. On divided highways and streets, variation in the width of the median, and the use of separate profiles and horizontal alignments, should be considered to derive design and operational advantage of one-way roadways.**

5. In residential areas, the alignment should be designed to minimize nuisance factors to the neighborhood. Generally, a depressed facility makes a highway less visible and less noisy to adjacent residents.**

6. The alignment should be designed to enhance attractive scenic views of the natural and man-made environment such as rivers, rock formations, parks, outstanding buildings, and golf courses.**

PROCEDURES FOR DRAWING HORIZONTAL CURVES

Part 1: Drawing the Centerline of the Road

Given: Points A, B, and C

Required: Centerline alignment of a curve which is tangent to line AB, tangent to line BC, and has a radius of R

STEP 1

- Draw lines AB and BC.
- Draw a line parallel to AB, at a distance R from AB.
- Draw a line parallel to BC, at a distance R from BC.
- Note the point of intersection of the parallels you just drew; this point is the center point of your horizontal curve.

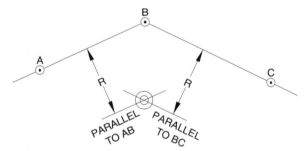

STEP 2

- Draw a line which is at right angles to AB and which passes through the center point of the horizontal curve, which was identified in Step 1. The junction of this line with AB marks the "point of curvature" (PC) of the horizontal curve.
- Draw a line which is at right angles to BC and which passes through the center point of the horizontal curve. The junc-

tion of this line and BC marks the "point of tangency" (PT) of the horizontal curve.

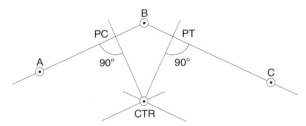

STEP 3

- With a compass set to draw a curve with a radius of R, draw in the curve from the PC to the PT, using the center point of the horizontal curve. The centerline of the road has now been constructed. It runs along a line defined by the following points: A, PC, PT, and C.

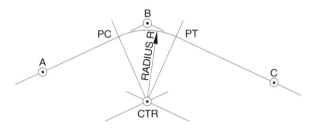

Part 2: Drawing the Edges of the Roadway

Given: The centerline of the horizontal curve of a road

Required: The edges of a roadway which has a width of W, and which follows the horizontal curve

Discussion: You know that if the roadway has a width of W, 1/2 the width W will lie on either side of the centerline of the road. If the radius of the centerline of the road is R, then the radius of the *inside* edge of the roadway will be R–W/2, and the radius of the *outside* edge of the roadway will be R+W/2.

STEP 1

- Using a compass, draw the two curves shown in the diagram below. Each curve starts at the line that connects PC and the

center, and ends at the line that connects PT and the center.

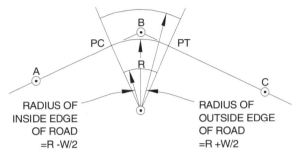

STEP 2

- Draw lines parallel to AB and BC, meeting the curves drawn in Step 1. These lines should be a distance W/2 from the centerline of the road.

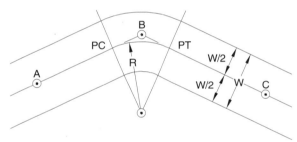

Notes

1. Institute of Transportation Engineers, *Transportation and Traffic Engineering Handbook.* 2nd ed. Wolfgang S. Homburger, Louis E. Keefer, and William R. McGrath, editors. Washington, DC: Prentice-Hall, 1982, p. 585. Prepared for the Institute of Transportation Engineers. Used with permission.

2. The abbreviation "SI" stands for "Systeme International," the French name for the expanded and modified version of the metric system, which is widely used throughout the world (except in the U.S.).

3. Homburger et al., p. iv.

4. AASHTO-1994, pp. 62-63.

5. The form of this curve is known to mathematicians and engineers as a "Euler spiral."

6. AASHTO-1994, pp. 151-153.

7. For further discussion, see ITE-1982, pp. 595-597, and AASHTO-1994, pp. 175-187.

8. For more information on spiral curves, see AASHTO-1994, pp. 174-175, or ITE-1982, p. 595.

9. American Association of State Highway and Transportation Officials (AASHTO). *A Policy on Geometric Design of Highways and Streets.* Washington, DC: AASHTO, 1994, p. 126. Used by permission.

10. ITE-1982, p. 591.

Definitions marked with * are adapted from the Institute of Transportation Engineers, 1982. Used with permission.

Those marked with ** are adapted from *A Policy on Geometric Design of Highways and Streets,* Copyright 1994, by the American Association of State Highway and Transportation Officials, Washington, DC. Used by permission.

Sources of Further Information

[AASHTO-1994]—American Association of State Highway and Transportation Officials (AASHTO). *A Policy on Geometric Design of Highways and Streets.* Washington, DC: AASHTO, 1994. See Chapter III, "Elements of Design," pp. 117-325.

Brewer, William E. and Charles P. Alter. *The Complete Manual of Land Planning and Development.* Englewood Cliffs, NJ: Prentice-Hall, 1988. See pp. 103-109 for horizontal curves, and pp. 110-127 for vertical curves.

Homburger, Hall, Loutzenheiser, and Reilly. *Fundamentals of Traffic Engineering.* 14th ed. Berkeley, CA: Institute of Transportation Studies, University of California, 1996.

[ITE-1982]—Institute of Transportation Engineers, *Transportation and Traffic Engineering Handbook.* 2nd ed. Wolfgang S. Homburger, Louis E. Keefer, and William R. McGrath, editors. Washington, DC: Prentice-Hall, 1982. Prepared for the Institute of Transportation Engineers.

[ITE-Transportation]—Institute of Transportation Engineers. *Transportation Planning Handbook.* John D. Edwards, Jr., P.E., editor. Englewood Cliffs, NJ: Prentice-Hall, 1992.

Lynch, Kevin and Gary Hack. *Site Planning.* 3rd ed. Cambridge, MA: MIT Press, 1984, pp. 212-214, 219-221.

Stover, Virgil G., and Frank J. Koepke. *Transportation and Land Development.* Englewood Cliffs, NJ: Prentice-Hall, 1988. Prepared for the Institute of Transportation Engineers.

CHAPTER

11

Parking

INTRODUCTION

The use of private vehicles by residents of the United States has been increasing ever since the introduction of automobiles and trucks. In relatively recent years (1970 to 1995), the number of automobiles increased by 52 percent, while the national population increased by only 29 percent.[1] All of these added vehicles must be stored somewhere when they are not in use; we call this storage "parking." It is not widely discussed but most vehicles require not one, but *two,* parking spaces. One of these spaces is at the point of origin of a trip; the second is at the trip destination. In many cases the trip origin is a residence, and the trip destination may be a place of employment, a shopping center, a recreation site, or some other attractive location.

The increased demand for parking space has had a substantial influence on the form of our cities and metropolitan areas. The central areas of those large American cities that do not have effective and well-patronized mass transit systems have been deluged by private automobiles and, in response, have either built a freeway system and a lot of parking spaces, or have dispersed their urban activities into areas where access is easy and parking is inexpensive to provide (such as suburban office centers, industrial parks, and shopping malls).

The form of the residential areas of American cities has also changed as more cars have appeared. The typical single-family home is no longer equipped with a one-car garage or an uncovered parking space; now, two (or even three) spaces or garages are provided. The multitude of vehicles also has had an impact on apartment design; more enclosed parking space for cars is now considered a "must."

Table 11.1 reports this trend of car ownership.

The data indicates that 30 years ago, 21 percent of American households had no vehicles; by 1995, this figure had dropped to 8 percent;

Table 11.1. Households By Number of Vehicles

Number of Vehicles	1969 (percent)	1995 (percent)
0	21	8
1	48	32
2	26	40
3 or more	5	19

Source: U.S. Department of Transportation, Federal Highway Administration. *National Personal Transportation Survey, Our Nation's Travel.* Washington, DC, 1997.

125

in 1969, only 5 percent of the households had three or more vehicles; in 1995, this number had risen to 19 percent.

These statistics document what is obvious to all of us: private cars have been coming into more widespread use in recent years. There appears, at this time, to be no apparent end or reversal of that trend. This, of course, has serious implications on the volume of vehicles that use our roads, as well as on problems related to parking.

THE SIZES OF CARS AND THEIR EFFECT ON THE DESIGN OF PARKING FACILITIES

The dimensions of three size categories of cars are given in Table 11.2. The dimensions "overall length" and "overall width" need no explanation, but it can be pointed out that "small cars" are about a foot and a half shorter than "medium cars," and about 3 inches narrower. "Large cars" tend to be about 1 foot 2 inches longer than "medium cars" (therefore 2 feet 8 inches longer than "small cars"), and about 6 inches wider (and 9 inches wider than "small cars").

Table 11.2 also reports "turning circle." This figure is significant because it is an index of how sharply cars can turn, which is a clue as

Table 11.2. Typical Sizes of 1998 Automobiles

Size Classification	Overall Length	Overall Width	Turning Circle
Small	14'6"	5'7"	36'
Medium	16'0"	5'10"	40'
Large	17'2"	6'4"	43'

Cars typical of those included in the sampling:
- Small cars (Ford Escort, Toyota Corolla)
- Medium cars (Honda Accord, Oldsmobile Cutlass)
- Large cars (Buick LeSabre, Cadillac deVille)

Source: Analysis of automobile dimensions published in the April 1998 issue of *Consumer Reports*.

to how easy it is for them to be maneuvered from a travel lane into a parking stall. Most "small cars" have a turning circle of about 36 feet; "medium cars" 40 feet; and "large cars" 43 feet.

ON-STREET PARKING

Traffic engineers are concerned with traffic congestion on city streets and with traffic safety. They point out that because cars entering and leaving curb parking spaces usually slow the flow of street traffic, and because drivers' vision is often restricted during parking and unparking maneuvers, there are many traffic accidents directly related to curb parking. A study published in 1971 reported that:

> "... it is safe to assume that curb parking is directly or indirectly responsible for at least one out of every five [traffic] accidents that occur in our cities each year."[2]

The publications of the Institute of Transportation Engineers often express the point of view set forth in the following paragraph. (In many cities local merchants, whose major concern is with the availability of parking spaces for their customers, would probably express a different view.)

> "The primary use of streets in any city is for the movement of vehicles. Parking on streets (curb parking) must be considered a secondary use of street space, as should other such uses as truck-loading zones. When parking or other secondary uses of streets conflict with the movement of traffic, those uses should be removed so that streets can best perform the function of moving traffic."[3]

FORMS OF ON-STREET PARKING

There are three basic forms of on-street parking: parallel parking, angle parking, and 90-

degree parking. These are illustrated in Figure 11.1.

Angle parking and 90-degree parking provide a greater number of parking spaces per lineal foot of curb than parallel parking, but these forms are more disruptive of the traffic flow in adjacent lanes than parallel parking.

Angle parking not only requires wider streets than parallel parking, it is also more hazardous. This is because the driver, while maneuvering into a parallel parking space, has reasonably good vision of the traffic behind; the driver of a car backing out of an angle parking space does not.

ON-STREET PARALLEL PARKING

On-street parallel parking is usually considered to require 20.0 feet of paving, measured outwards from the curb (7.0 feet for the parking space, plus at least 13.0 feet for vehicle maneuvering space). This is a minimum width; as such, it does not provide for the flow of two-way traffic while a car is entering or leaving a parking space.

The typical on-street parking stall is usually from 21 to 22 feet in length and 7.0 feet in width. "End stalls" on each block, which are easily accessible, are usually 18.0 feet in length. These end stalls should start at least 20 feet from the sidewalk edge of any cross street.

"Paired parking" is used in some jurisdictions. In this arrangement, two vehicles are parked almost bumper to bumper, and pairs of 18.0-foot stalls are separated by a clearly marked 8.0-foot long maneuvering area.

For on-street parallel parking along a curb, a clear space of at least 2 feet should be provided for opening the curb-side door of vehicles. For off-street parallel parking, as found in parking lots and parking garages, parking stalls adjacent to fences or walls should allow

at least 2 feet of clear space to make it possible to open vehicle doors.

ON-STREET ANGLE PARKING

The dimensions for on-street angle parking are somewhat more involved than are those for parallel parking, because they depend on the assumed length, width, and turning circle of the cars being parked. The space needed for on-street angle parking is essentially the same as that which is needed for off-street parking lots and in parking structures; detailed dimensions of parking layouts for these are discussed below.

DESIGN GUIDELINES FOR PARKING AISLES AND STALLS

When designing a parking area, consideration should be given to both the size of vehicles to be accommodated and the type of clientele that is to be served.

On the first point, big cars (which are long, wide, and have large turning circles) are obviously better served by parking aisles and stalls that are generously proportioned. Small cars, on the other hand, can be accommodated in stalls which are sometimes as narrow as 7.5 feet, and which are accessed by relatively narrow maneuvering aisles.

On the second point (the type of clientele to be served), the Institute of Transportation Engineers (ITE) has identified the following groups:[4]

- *Class A*—retail customers, banks, fast-food restaurants, and other very high turnover establishments
- *Class B*—retail customers and visitors (where the turnover may be high to medium)
- *Class C*—visitors, office employees, residential areas, airports, and hospitals (where the turnover may be medium to low)

Figure 11.1. Forms of On-street Parking

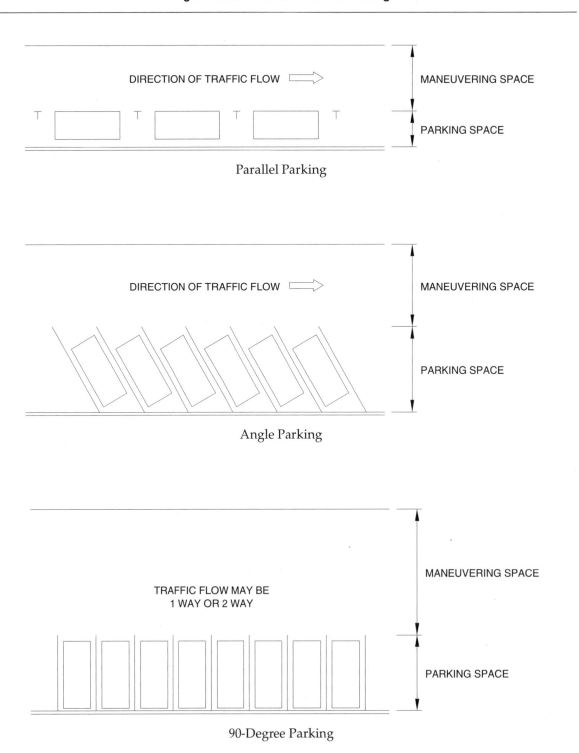

DIRECTION OF TRAFFIC FLOW

MANEUVERING SPACE

PARKING SPACE

Parallel Parking

DIRECTION OF TRAFFIC FLOW

MANEUVERING SPACE

PARKING SPACE

Angle Parking

TRAFFIC FLOW MAY BE
1 WAY OR 2 WAY

MANEUVERING SPACE

PARKING SPACE

90-Degree Parking

- *Class D*—industrial employees, commuters, and university staff and students (where turnover is generally low)

As a general rule, wide parking stalls and easy-to-maneuver-in aisles are appropriate in those areas where a high turnover of parking patrons is expected. It is also common practice for merchants and shopping center proprietors to install generously dimensioned parking facilities in order to make their areas safe, attractive, and enticing.

On the other hand, lower design standards are generally acceptable in areas where there is a low rate of parking turnover as, for example, in areas where all-day parkers are expected.

Table 11.3 provides recommended dimensions for parking stalls and aisles. The diagram below the table indicates where the dimensions apply.

OFF-STREET PARKING LOTS

Generally speaking, almost all cities of over 7,500 population need some form of off-street parking. Most cities of 7,500 to 25,000 population have plenty of curb spaces, but they are not located close enough to the destinations of the travelers to be considered reasonably convenient. In larger cities there is not enough "close-in" curb parking to satisfy the demand, so off-street parking facilities are built. In large central cities, these off-street facilities are commonly located in the very core of the central area, rather than on its fringes where land is cheaper and easier to obtain.

The maximum walking distance people will generally tolerate from parking site to place of employment is from 1,000 to 1,500 feet in large cities, and from 600 to 700 feet in small cities.[5] The maximum walking distance most often tolerated for shopping trips is 500 to 800 feet in large cities, and from 200 to 350 feet in small cities.[6]

General Locational Criteria for Off-Street Parking Lots

Off-street parking lots should be situated:
- between peripheral roads and the central core of a city, minimizing the overall travel time from outlying areas to the core
- with direct access to perimeter roads
- within walking distance of the land uses that are visited by the people using the parking lot
- with direct pedestrian access from the parking facility to the land use which is to be served, with a minimum of street crossings
- in close proximity to both daytime and nighttime uses (if possible) in order to promote greater around-the-clock usage, and thereby increase the financial return on the facility, improve the quality of the downtown urban form, and provide a greater convenience to the public
- in midblock locations (if possible) to avoid traffic congestion at intersections and the use of the high-value, corner lot locations
- on interior block locations, using a minimum of street frontages, to avoid breaking up the continuity of the development pattern facing the streets

General Site Design Criteria of Off-Street Parking Lots

- The maximum grades in a parking lot should be 3.0 percent longitudinal to the parking stall, and 5 percent for a cross slope of the stall and aisles.
- The minimum grade of a parking lot should be 1.0 percent for asphalt paving, and 0.4 percent for concrete, in order to assure proper drainage.

Table 11.3. Recommended Parking Stall and Aisle Dimensions

Parking Angle	Stall Width	Aisle Width	Length Along Curb for Each Stall	Stall Depth (Aisle to Wall)	Stall Depth (Aisle to Interlock)	Bay Width (Wall to Wall)	Bay Width (Interlock to Interlock)
P	W	A	C	S	S'	B	B'
45°	8.5	13.0	12.0	17.5	15.5	48.0	44.0
	9.0	12.0	12.7	17.5	15.5	47.0	43.0
	9.5	11.0	13.4	17.5	15.5	46.0	42.0
60°	8.5	18.0	9.8	19.0	17.5	56.0	53.0
	9.0	16.0	10.4	19.0	17.5	54.0	51.0
	9.5	15.0	11.0	19.0	17.5	53.0	50.0
75°	8.5	25.0	8.8	19.5	19.0	64.0	63.0
	9.0	23.0	9.3	19.5	19.0	62.0	61.0
	9.5	22.0	9.8	19.5	19.0	61.0	60.0
	7.5	20.0	7.5	16.0	16.0	52.0	52.0
90°	8.5	28.0	8.5	18.5	18.5	65.0	65.0
	9.0	26.0	9.0	18.5	18.5	63.0	63.0
	9.5	25.0	9.5	18.5	18.5	62.0	62.0

P = parking angle
W = stall width
A = aisle width (for one-way traffic)
C = length along curb for each stall
S = stall depth (from aisle to wall)
S' = stall depth (from aisle to interlock)
B = bay width (from wall to wall)
B' = bay width (from interlock to interlock)

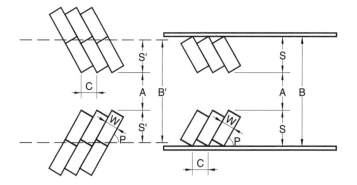

- All dimensions are given in feet.
- The 7.5-foot width stall should be used for compact cars only. Weant (1985) recommends that this width be used only for 90-degree parking of compact cars.
- Widths in excess of 9.0 feet are not recommended, except for "luxury parking."
- The dimensions given in the table were calculated on the basis of a stall length of 18.5 feet, except for compact cars, where the stall length was assumed to be 16.0 feet.
- The turns at the ends of aisles should have a minimum inside radius of 15 feet and an outside radius of 29 feet (for one-way traffic).
- Aisle width should be at least 24.0 feet wherever two-way traffic will occur.

Source: Highway Research Board, National Research Council. "Parking Principles" (Special Report No. 125). Washington, DC: National Academy of Sciences, 1971.

- The shape of off-street parking lots should be simple and easy to comprehend; preferably rectangular.
- The minimum size of an off-street parking lot should be 1.0 acre.
- The maximum size of an off-street parking lot for efficient operation should be 3.0 acres.
- If land costs appear to be expensive, an above-grade parking structure should be considered. If this is the case, it would be appropriate to make a careful analysis of current local land prices and construction costs, in order to determine the "break-point" between surface parking lots and above-grade parking structures.

Cost is not the only factor to be considered in choosing between surface lots and parking structures. If a city chooses to develop surface parking lots in its central business district, it may transform the character of the area into something like low-density, suburban shopping centers. This may or may not be desirable; it is a matter of urban design that should be seriously considered.

METHODS OF OFF-STREET PARKING

There are three different methods of off-street parking in use:

1. self-parking
2. attendant parking
3. mechanical lift parking

Each has its advantages and disadvantages.

Self-parking is usually much more convenient for the user than the other two methods because there is little or no waiting to park or unpark. It also allows patrons to lock their cars and take their keys with them; with attendant parking and mechanical lift parking, this is not possible. On the negative side, parking facilities for self-parking need relatively wide aisles and parking stalls, while attendant parking lots and garages can use

narrower aisles and stalls and can park cars in tandem; this results in a 10 to 15 percent reduction in the space required per car, which may result in considerable financial savings.

While attendant parking is economical in terms of dollars invested per parking space, it does require that parking attendants be employed, which usually more than offsets the reduced construction costs. As a result, attendant parking tends to be favored only in central urban areas where the cost of space is very high; it is not often used in areas where land costs are moderate or low.

Another distinction to be drawn is that self-parking is well suited for short-term parking; attendant parking is not.

Mechanical lift parking moves vehicles around and stacks them one above another using mechanical devices. This can result in very considerable space-saving, and the method can be used on small lots or in fairly small buildings. There are a number of drawbacks to the method, however. The first is that serious maintenance problems have been experienced with the mechanical equipment. Paul C. Box reports the finding that the equipment wears out in about seven years, which is long before it has paid for itself. A second problem is that the system can accept incoming cars only at a slow rate, and can unpark and deliver them at a slow rate, so the system is satisfactory only when the patronage takes place uniformly over the day, with no peak-hour flows. Because of these two factors, the use of mechanical lift parking systems, which has never been very substantial, has been declining.[7]

DESIGN OPTIONS FOR PARKING GARAGES

There are two basic design options for parking garages. The first is to use level floors on which to park the cars, and use ramps adjacent to the floors to provide access between floors. These ramps may be straight or helical. The second design approach is to use sloping floors, which serve the dual purpose of providing parking spaces and an internal ramp system. This second design option limits the floors to a 4 to 5 percent slope, and requires that the parking angle for the stalls be at least 60 degrees (to minimize the possibility of cars rolling backwards out of their stalls).

The choice between these design options is often based on the characteristics of the available site. The design system using external ramps may be suitable for sites which are irregular in shape, whereas the system using internal, sloping-floor ramps may not be. The sloping-floor ramp design option is usually best suited to large, regularly shaped sites.

CRITERIA FOR PARKING GARAGE SITES

- Rectangular sites are most desirable.
- Parking garages (other than those using mechanical lifts) should be at least 120 feet wide, and from 120 to 400 feet in depth (300 feet is considered the optimum length).
- Garage sites with access from two different streets, such as at a corner location, are desirable, providing that the entrance and exit locations can be located so that traffic at nearby intersections is not disrupted.
- Parking garages can often be designed to fit into sloping topography, using the natural grade of the land for ramps, and having entrances and exits on several levels.
- The general locational criteria for parking garages, and their relation to adjacent streets, are generally similar to that for surface parking lots. Parking garages usually produce more concentrated

peak-hour traffic loads than surface parking lots, however.

BELOW-GROUND PARKING GARAGES

Underground parking garages have the same general design of parking stalls, aisles, and ramps as do aboveground garages. They have no operating advantages over aboveground parking, although they are often considered to have aesthetic advantages (to outside observers, but not to users).

Underground garages cost from 1.5 to 2.0 times as much as aboveground garages because of the costs of excavation, building side walls, waterproofing, lighting, and ventilation equipment. Waterproofing underground garages can be very expensive; they need to be protected from ground-water intrusion from the bottom and the sides, and from water seeping down from above, especially if the roof of the garage is covered with vegetation. Underground parking also has relatively high operating costs for maintenance, lighting, and ventilation.

Underground parking garages are economically feasible in areas where the land cost is extremely high and a market exists for the resale of the surface rights, and in areas where the public places a high value on keeping the surface areas above them open.

AVERAGE SPACE PER PARKING STALL

The average space per parking stall can be calculated by dividing the total area of a parking facility by the number of parking stalls in it. The total area includes space used for parking stalls, aisles for circulation, landscaping, booths for collecting fees, and temporary storage lanes where incoming (or departing) cars line up to pay fees. The magnitude of this average depends on decisions made during the design process, and on such issues as:

- Are the stalls wide and long for large cars, or short and narrow for small cars?
- Are the aisles wide or narrow?
- Will angle parking or 90-degree parking be used? (90-degree parking requires slightly less space per car.)
- How much landscaping will be provided?
- How much dead (i.e., unusable) space is there?
- Will the facility be operated with self-parking or attendant parking?
- Does the site have a regular shape that poses no special design problems, or is it irregularly shaped that makes efficient use of the site difficult?

It is a general rule of thumb that "normal" parking areas require about 350 square feet of area per parking stall when self-parking is used. This figure can be reduced to about 325 square feet in some situations where space economies can be used, or increased to 375 square feet (or more) when generous design standards are used. If attendant parking, which permits storage of cars in tandem, is used, figures as low as 300 square feet per car can be achieved.

COSTS OF OFF-STREET PARKING FACILITIES

Parking lots on the surface of the ground are inexpensive to build when compared to aboveground or underground parking structures. Their cost (exclusive of the cost of the land they occupy) comes from grading the land, installing drainage facilities, paving the ground, installing lights and fences (sometimes), installing landscaping, installing wheel stops, painting stripes to identify stalls, installing signs, and occasionally providing some means of collecting parking fees.

Since construction costs vary from region to region and year to year, it is difficult to provide current and reliable figures for building lots and structures. However, in the mid-1980s, the cost of building a parking lot (exclusive of land costs) was about $800 per parking stall; in the mid-1990s, the cost was about $1,200.

Aboveground parking garages are, understandably, much more expensive to build than are surface parking lots. Most of them are built of reinforced concrete, have lighting installed, may include restrooms and elevators, and have some means of collecting parking fees. In the mid-1980s, the cost per parking stall was between $5,000 and $9,000; in the late 1990s, the cost per stall in some areas of the United States was from $10,000 to $15,000.

Below-ground parking garages, as noted above, are considerably more expensive than aboveground garages; the rule of thumb is that they cost from 1.5 to 2.0 times as much per parking stall.[8]

SPECIAL PARKING TOPICS

Incorporating Parking Facilities With Other Land Uses

In residential areas, it is standard practice to integrate parking facilities with structures such as single-family homes and apartment buildings. The amount of parking to be provided per dwelling unit will vary with the characteristics of the residents (single occupants, couples, or large families; low, moderate, or high income). It will also vary with the location of the building. Those buildings that are in locations that are well served by mass transit may be occupied by people who own fewer cars than residents in suburbia, far from transit lines.

In downtown urban areas, some commercial uses such as department stores have, in the past, built parking garages as integral parts of their main structures for the convenience of their customers. Whether or not this practice will continue is a matter of conjecture because of the apparent slowing of new construction of retail outlets in downtown areas and the rise of suburban shopping centers.

Shopping Center Parking

Modern shopping centers rely almost entirely on private automobiles to bring their customers and employees; public transit provides a very low percentage of transportation used by those people. Naturally, the cars of the employees and customers must be parked somewhere. Calculating how much parking to provide, and determining where to locate it in relation to the activities of the shopping center, take skill and judgment. Proprietors of shopping centers want to be sure that they have enough parking for their busiest days but don't have an excess amount that is expensive to build and maintain, and that, on slow days, may give the observers the impression that the shopping center is not well patronized.

Park-and-Ride in Connection With Transit

There has been a trend for transit operators to provide parking lots or garages for their transit patrons. These are usually adjacent to transit stations, or are sometimes adjacent to freeway interchanges which have convenient access for busses running along the freeways. These park-and-ride lots appear to be well utilized; they seem to provide a means of getting people to leave their cars in suburbia instead of congesting the regional road system.

Satellite Parking With Shuttle Bus Service

At least two types of land use have established parking lots (usually in areas of low land value) some distance away from their major operations, and provided shuttle bus service between the remote parking area and

their centers of activity; these include airports and universities.

The systems appear to be well patronized by people who require long-term parking but are not privileged to have parking permits for close-in parking. At universities, this usually includes staff and faculty, and students who will be on campus at least half a day. At airports, it includes employees who work all day (or night) and travelers who will be away for a day or more.

Zoning Regulations

Most cities and counties in the United States have zoning regulations that limit how private properties may be used. A section usually found in these regulations deals with the requirement for off-street parking. Most jurisdictions are interested in enacting fair and reasonable parking requirements; while they want to make sure that present and foreseeable future parking needs will be met, they do not wish to require private builders to invest in parking facilities that will not be needed. Determining how much off-street parking is reasonable to require for each type of land use takes good judgment, and should be based on careful studies of current local needs and trends in automobile ownership and usage.

Notes

1. Calculated from data provided by the U.S. Bureau of Transportation Statistics.
2. "Parking Principles," p. 163.
3. Institute of Transportation Engineers. *Transportation and Traffic Engineering Handbook.* 1st ed. Washington, DC, 1976, Chapter 15, p. 712. Used with permission.
4. ITE Committee 5D-8, "Guidelines for Parking Facility and Design," May 1990, as cited on p. 209 of the *Traffic Engineering Handbook*, 4th ed., by the Institute of Transportation Engineers, 1992.
5. Weant. *Parking Garage Planning and Operation,* 1978, p. 55.
6. *Ibid.,* p. 40, quoting the works of Levinson and Whitlock.

7. Paul C. Box, in ITE's *Traffic Engineering Handbook,* 1992, p. 220.
8. *Ibid.*

Recommended Reading

Lynch, Kevin and Gary Hack. *Site Planning.* 3rd ed. Cambridge, MA: MIT Press, 1984, pp. 216, 263-266.

Suggested Sources of Further Information

Highway Research Board, National Research Council. "Parking Principles" (Special Report No. 125). Washington, DC: National Academy of Sciences, 1971.

Institute of Transportation Engineers. *Guidelines for Parking Facility Location and Design.* 1992.

Institute of Transportation Engineers. *Parking Generation.* 2nd ed., 1987.

Institute of Transportation Engineers. *Traffic Engineering Handbook.* 4th ed. James L. Pline, editor. Englewood Cliffs, NJ: Prentice-Hall, 1992. See Chapter 7, "Parking and Terminals," by Paul C. Box.

Institute of Transportation Engineers, *Transportation and Traffic Engineering Handbook.* 2nd ed. Wolfgang S. Homburger, Louis E. Keefer, and William R. McGrath, editors. Washington, DC: Prentice-Hall, 1982. Prepared for the Institute of Transportation Engineers. See Chapter 21, "Parking, Loading, and Terminal Facilities," by James M. Hunnicutt.

Institute of Transportation Engineers. *Transportation Planning Handbook.* John D. Edwards, Jr., P.E., editor. Englewood Cliffs, NJ: Prentice-Hall, 1992. See Chapter 6, "Parking Systems and Loading Facilities," by Paul C. Box, and pp. 399-407 of Chapter 11, "Transportation Planning Studies," by James H. Kell.

National Parking Association and the Urban Land Institute. *The Dimensions of Parking.* 3rd ed. Washington, DC: Urban Land Institute, 1993.

Stover, Virgil G., and Frank J. Koepke. *Transportation and Land Development.* Englewood Cliffs, NJ: Prentice-Hall, 1988. Prepared for the Institute of Transportation Engineers. See Chapter 7, "Parking and Service Facilities."

Weant, Robert A. *Parking Garage Planning and Operation.* Westport, CT: Eno Foundation, 1978.

Weant, Robert A. "The Influence of Smaller Cars on Parking Geometry." *Transportation Quarterly,* July 1985.

Whitlock, Edward M. *Parking for Institutions and Special Events.* Westport, CT: Eno Foundation, 1982. See section on parking demand.

12

Transit Planning

PURPOSE

The purpose of this chapter is to provide the reader with a basic description of contemporary public mass transit, and a discussion of its strengths and weaknesses. It is hoped that some of the readers will be able to make a future contribution to improving the effectiveness and desirability of the urban transportation modes available to us today.

INTRODUCTION

Public transit is in direct competition with private cars. Cars provide door-to-door, no-transfer, comfortable, demand responsive, flexible route transportation at any hour of the day or night, and their cost is often compatible (when two or more people ride in the car) with fares charged by public transit. While there are many forms of public transit (some of them are very satisfactory), most still compete with the private car.

Often the strongest factors influencing a traveler's decision on mode of travel are time en route and convenience. In these days of widespread economic well being, cost is a less important factor (except for those people who cannot afford a car). There are also many people who are considered "captive transit riders" because they are too young, too infirm to

drive, or too poor to have access to a private car.

In many ways, the use of a private car is not a completely satisfactory solution for personal transportation. It loses its attractiveness as traffic congestion intensifies and clogs our streets; when downtown parking is hard to find or expensive; and when the cost of buying, insuring, and operating a private car goes up and up.

COMPARING TRANSIT SERVICE WITH THE USE OF PRIVATE CARS

It is possible to measure the "level of service" for mass transit systems, but it is reported to be far more complex a process than it is for highways, so we won't go into it here.[1]

It is, however, quite easy to compare the time required to make a trip via one mode of transportation with the time required using a different mode. When this comparison is made in relation to the time of the "drive-own-car" mode, it produces an important clue on the relative satisfaction that various modes of transportation produce. This is true when the speed of travel is the only criterion, and other factors (such as passenger comfort, frequency of service, and cost) are disregarded. Let us call this comparison "relative travel time."

When relative travel time is less than 1.0 (that is, when the travel time on a competing mode is less than that of the private car mode), that mode is often considered superior or equal to the "drive-own-car" mode.

When the relative travel time is between 1.0 and 2.0, the competing mode is considered to be generally satisfactory but somewhat less attractive than the use of a private car. Factors other than speed (such as the availability of a car in a one-car family, economic cost, comfort, or parking problems) may induce public transit patrons to keep using public transit.

As the relative travel time rises, the competing mode of travel becomes less and less attractive. When the travel time on some mode of transit is 3.0 times or more than the travel time by private car, it is quite likely that only "captive transit riders" will use transit, and do so only because they have no alternative.

RELATIVE TRAVEL TIMES FOR SOME HYPOTHETICAL SITUATIONS

Given: A resident of a suburban community travels to her job that is located in a low-density employment area about 17 miles away. She lives 1 mile away from a rail rapid-transit station. The transit line runs northerly 15 miles to a station which is 1 mile from her place of employment. A freeway parallels the transit line and has interchanges close to the transit stations.

To be calculated: Relative travel times for the following four modes of transportation:

1. Employee walks from home to the bus stop; takes feeder bus to the transit station; rides rail transit northward; takes feeder bus to the general vicinity of her job location; walks to her job.
2. Van-pool vehicle picks up employee at her doorstep; meanders through the

nearby subdivision area to pick up five more riders; drives to the freeway; drives northerly on the freeway; leaves the freeway and drives on local streets to the place of employment of the van riders.
3. Employee drives her own car (alone) directly to her place of employment via local streets, the freeway, and then local streets again.
4. Employee changes her place of residence to within a 4-minute walk of the transit station, and is assigned to a job location which is also a 4-minute walk from the northern transit station. She walks from her home to the transit station, rides the rail transit, and walks to work from the northern transit station.

Table 12.1 provides calculations of the travel times that would result from the foregoing scenarios.

Based on the travel times indicated in Table 12.1, the relative travel times are:

1. Conventional transit = 60/22 = 2.7
2. Van pool = 37/22 = 1.7
3. Drive own car (22 min.) = 1.0
4. Relocate; use rail = 42/22 = 1.9

An interpretation of the effects of "relative travel times" indicates that:

1. "Drive own car" is the fastest mode of making the trip.
2. The van pool is second fastest.
3. The relocation of residence and job, and the use of rail transit, is a bit slower than the van pool and takes almost twice as long as "drive own car."
4. Conventional transit, with the use of feeder buses and transfers to rail transit, is slow in comparison to the alternative modes of transportation and might require the payment of three fares. It probably would not be the mode of choice for most people.

AN ALTERNATIVE SCENARIO

Suppose that, in our hypothetical situation, the "drive-own-car" mode of transportation is so attractive that it lures many more people to use it. And suppose that, with this added traffic load, the freeway becomes so congested that the average speed of vehicles on it during peak hours drops from 55 to 25 mph. This would increase the driving times of the van pool and the "drive own car" from 16 minutes to 36 minutes, making their total trip times 57 minutes and 42 minutes, respectively.

The relative travel times under this condition would be:

1. Conventional transit = 60/42 = 1.4
2. Van pool = 57/42 = 1.4
3. Drive own car (42 min.) = 1.0
4. Relocate; use rail = 42/42 = 1.0

Under these conditions, "drive-own-car" and "home-and-job relocation" modes yield the same travel times, and might be equally convenient. Use of the rail transit system would probably be more economical, however, if the private car carried only one person. It may be noted that with today's urban patterns, it is often difficult to find attractive residences within a 4-minute walk of a suburban transit station.[2]

Conventional transit and van pools take about the same travel time, and both of them might well be competitive with the "drive-own-car" option, especially if economic cost is a major consideration. Conventional transit would probably not be very popular because it entails three waiting periods and two transfers for the trip from origin to destination; these would be quite vexing to some travelers.

THE USE OF PUBLIC TRANSIT

Public transit in the United States plays two major roles. First, it provides a means of transportation to those people who do not have ready and convenient access to a private car, or for some reason (such as age or physical impairment) cannot operate one. Without public transit, many of these people would be somewhat stranded; they would have to rely on friends, neighbors, relatives, car pools, or taxicabs for rides, or else they would have to walk, bicycle, or stay at home.

Table 12.1. Calculation of Travel Times of Hypothetical Trips

1. Traditional transit movement	
Walk 0.2 miles @ 3 mph to bus stop	4 minutes
Wait for feeder bus	4 minutes
Ride bus to station 1 mile @ 12 mph	5 minutes
Wait for transit train	4 minutes
Ride train 15 miles @ 30 mph	30 minutes
Wait for feeder bus	4 minutes
Ride bus 1 mile @ 12 mph	5 minutes
Walk to job 0.2 miles @ 3 mph	4 minutes
TOTAL TIME FOR TRIP	**60 minutes**
2. Trip made by van pool	
Wait for van to arrive	3 minutes
Ride van 3 miles @ 12 mph to pick up 5 more riders, then go to freeway	15 minutes
Drive freeway 15 miles @ 55 mph	16 minutes
Drive local streets 1 mile @ 20 mph	3 minutes
TOTAL TIME FOR TRIP	**37 minutes**
3. Trip by "drive own car"	
Drive to freeway 1 mile @ 20 mph	3 minutes
Drive freeway 15 miles @ 55 mph	16 minutes
Drive local streets 1 mile @ 20 mph	3 minutes
TOTAL TIME FOR TRIP	**22 minutes**
4. Trip by rail transit from new home to new job location	
Walk to transit station	4 minutes
Wait for train	4 minutes
Ride rail transit 15 miles @ 30 mph	30 minutes
Walk to workplace	4 minutes
TOTAL TIME FOR TRIP	**42 minutes**

Secondly, transit carries many people between their homes and places of work, thereby reducing the number of people who drive their own cars on the public streets during morning and evening peak hours. Inducing these people to leave their cars at home does much to keep our traffic congestion problems from growing worse.

In 1980 (which is the latest year for which data from comprehensive traffic surveys for metropolitan areas are available), it was reported that public transit carried about 50 percent of the peak-hour person trips made to the central business districts (CBDs) of those large American cities that have well-defined, concentrated employment centers (e.g., New York, Boston, Chicago, and Washington, DC).[3] It can be presumed that the percent of work trips made by transit to areas outside the CBDs were substantially lower.

In 1980, transit carried a relatively small share of peak-hour work trips in those cities that do not have concentrated CBDs, and which had a low overall density of development. In those cities, the share of person trips that transit carried on the journey to work was often in the range of 5 to 10 percent.[4]

When consideration is given to the total number of trips made in this country in 1994, only 1.4 percent of the passenger miles travelled were made by public transit.[5] The remainder of the passenger miles were made using private cars, taxicabs, motorcycles, and intercity transportation modes. Many of these trips made were for nonwork-related travel such as shopping, social contacts, and recreation.

SOME BASIC DEFINITIONS

Public transit—Passenger transportation service, usually local, that is provided to any person who pays a prescribed fare; it operates on established schedules along designated routes with specific stops.*

Captive transit rider—A person who does not have immediate access to private transportation or who otherwise must use public transportation in order to travel.

Headway—The spatial distance or the time interval between the front ends of vehicles moving along the same lane or track in the same direction.*

Level of service (as applied to transit)—A measure of the quality and quantity of transportation service provided. It includes characteristics that are quantifiable (such as travel time, travel cost, and number of transfers), and those that are difficult to quantify (such as comfort, convenience, cleanliness, and reliability).

Major activity center—A distinct geographical area characterized by a large transient population and heavy traffic volumes (for example, a central business district, a large shopping center, an industrial park, a sports arena, and a large university).*

Mode—A means of travel (such as by private car, taxicab, bus, and commuter train, or walking).

Modal split—The proportion of total person trips that uses each of various modes of transportation; the process of separating total person trips into modes of travel used.*

Trip-end density—The number of transit patrons per unit of land area (e.g., per square mile, per hectare, per acre).

DEFINITIONS OF VARIOUS FORMS OF TRANSIT SERVICE

Commuter rail—Regional passenger service for commuters provided on the urban sections of railroad networks.

Demand-responsive transit—A transportation service characterized by flexible routing of relatively small vehicles to provide door-to-door or point-to-point transportation, scheduled to serve in response to users' needs (sometimes known as *Dial-A-Ride*).*

Express service—Transit service that provides higher speeds and fewer stops than are generally found on other portions of the transit system, or on the same route in local service.

Feeder service—Local transit service that picks up and delivers passengers to a rail rapid-transit station, or to an express bus stop or terminal.

Jitney service—A nonscheduled paratransit system in which small vehicles operate much like taxicabs, except that passengers do not command exclusive use of the vehicle; the vehicles generally follow a specific route but may occasionally deviate from it to pick up or discharge passengers.*

Kiss and ride—The procedure in which transit passengers are driven to their first transit terminal point in a private vehicle by another person, who then drives the vehicle away from the terminal to another destination.

Light-rail transit—An urban transportation system that uses electrically powered rail cars operating singly or in short trains on fixed rails. Many sections of the route may be grade-separated and operate on exclusive rights-of-way.

Local service—A type of service which delivers and picks up transit passengers as close to their destinations or origins as possible; consequently, it often involves circuitous routes and frequent stops, which result in low overall speeds.

Many-to-many service—A transit service that collects passengers from many origins and delivers them to many destinations.

One-to-many service—A transit service that distributes passengers from one point of origin to many destinations. (Note that the return flow of passengers results in a *many-to-one* pattern of service.)

Paratransit—Forms of public transportation service that are more flexible and personalized than conventional, fixed-schedule, fixed-route service, usually serving special groups of people (e.g., airport shuttle passengers, handicapped persons, and retirement community residents).*

People movers—Automated systems designed to move large volumes of passengers short distances within or between major activity centers (for example, between satellite airport terminals, within amusement parks, and within central business districts; may utilize vehicles on rails, rubber-tired vehicles on guideways, moving walkways, escalators, or other forms of transit.[6]

Rapid transit—A high-speed rail or bus service that operates on exclusive rights-of-way over long distances with few stops.*

Streetcars—Vehicles which are very similar to light-rail transit vehicles, but usually operate on city streets (rather than on exclusive rights-of-way), are manually controlled (rather than computer controlled), and usually travel at low speeds (often averaging less than 10 mph).

Trolley bus—A large, rubber-tired bus which runs on city streets and is powered by electricity from overhead wires.

Van pool—A prearranged ride-sharing service in which a number of people travel together on a regular basis in a van, which may be a company-sponsored van that has a volunteer driver.*

MAJOR TYPES OF TRANSIT VEHICLES

The major forms of transit vehicles in use in North America today are:

- jitneys (not widely used in the U.S.)
- van pools
- Dial-a-Ride van service

Table 12.2. Characteristics of Some Widely Used Transit Vehicles

Type of Vehicle	Length (feet)	Width (feet)	Typical Passenger Capacity		
			Seated	Standees	Total
BUSES					
20' bus	20	8	18	12	30
30' bus	30	8	36	19	55
40' bus	40	8.5	45	25	80
Articulated bus	60	8.5	73	37	110
RAIL CARS					
Streetcar	46	8.5	42	83	125
Light-rail car	75	9	68	122	190
Rapid-transit car	75	10	72	153	225
Commuter-rail car	85	10.5	120	—	120

- Streetcars often run with several cars joined together.
- Light-rail trains often run with about 3 or 4 cars.
- Rapid-transit trains often run with about 8 cars.
- Commuter-rail trains often run with about 10 cars.

Sources: Adapted by the author from:
- Institute of Transportation Engineers. *Transportation Planning Handbook.* John D. Edwards, Jr., P.E., editor. Englewood Cliffs, NJ: Prentice-Hall, 1992, pp. 135, 397.
- Homburger, Hall, Loutzenheiser, and Reilly. *Fundamentals of Traffic Engineering.* 14th ed. Berkeley, CA: Institute of Transportation Studies, University of California, 1996, p. 11-8.
- Carter, Everett C. and Wolfgang S. Homburger. *Introduction to Transportation Engineering.* Reston, VA: Reston Publishing Co., 1978, p. 199.

- buses
  — small buses (20-30 passengers)
  — medium buses (40-80 passengers)
  — large buses (60-110 passengers)[7]
- trolley buses
- fixed-rail transit vehicles
  — streetcars
  — light-rail transit
  — commuter trains
- people movers

It should be noted that while single-occupant private cars, ride-sharing private cars, and taxicabs provide a major share of urban transportation, they are generally not classified as forms of "public transit."

The characteristics of some transit vehicles are reported in Table 12.2.

SPEEDS OF VARIOUS MODES OF TRANSIT

There are two types of speed to be considered for transit vehicles. The first is the typical speed of the vehicle when it is rolling along the street or private right of way, without interruptions to pick up or drop off passengers. This is known as "performance speed."

The second type of speed is known as "platform speed," and represents the average speed of the transit vehicle, taking into consideration the time needed to load passengers, accelerate, run at performance speed, wait in traffic delays, decelerate, and offload passengers. Platform speed is notably slower than performance speed. Performance speeds and platform speeds of typical transit vehicles are reported in Table 12.3.

The speed of a transit vehicle when it is accelerating or decelerating is limited by the tolerance of the passengers. If all passengers are seated, a transit vehicle can speed up or slow down quite rapidly. However, if there are standing passengers (especially those who have no hand grips), accelerating and decelerating is usually limited to 3.0 to 3.5 mph per second.[8] Moreover, the rate of change of acceleration or deceleration, which is known as "jerk rate," is very important,

and should generally be limited to 2.0 mph per second.[9] The concept of jerk rate can be visualized by considering a transit vehicle starting from a dead stop; to start its forward motion it must accelerate, but it should not start up so rapidly that all the passengers experience a sudden and unpleasant backwards jerk.

THE ECONOMIC COSTS OF BUILDING TRANSIT SYSTEMS

The cost of building transit systems consists of three major categories:
1. the cost of land for rights-of-way, when separate guideways are required;
2. the cost of constructing guideways (such as rail lines, tunnels, and bridges); and
3. the cost of rolling stock (such as buses and trains).

The planning and engineering costs for designing the overall system are not included in the items above; these can be substantial.

The cost figures in the following tables are reported in 1989 dollars. Although costs have risen since 1989, the figures below should give the reader a feeling for the order of magnitude of current costs.

Land costs in the U.S. and Canada for conventional rail systems were reported to average about $6.3 million (U.S.) per mile, and about $3.0 million (U.S.) for light-rail transit systems.[10]

Construction costs of guideways were reported to be:[11]

At grade................$14 to 48 million per mile
Elevated..............$38 to 108 million per mile
Underground.....$86 to 292 million per mile

Vehicle costs were reported to be:[12]
Articulated light-rail car
  (75 feet)......................................$1.5 million
Rail rapid-transit car
  (75 feet)...........................$1.5 to 1.7 million

Table 12.3. Performance Speeds and Platform Speeds of Transit Vehicles

Transit Vehicle and Type of Service	Maximum Performance Speeds (mph)	Platform Speeds (mph)
Urban bus		
Local	50-65	8-14
Limited stop	50-65	12-18
Express	50-65	16-32
Streetcar, local	40-60	8-15
Light-rail transit	50-65	15-35
Heavy-rail transit	50-70	15-35
Regional rapid transit	70-85	35-55
Commuter railroad	70-100	25-65

Typical bus platform speeds are also reported as:
- In central areas: 6-8 mph
- In urban areas: 10-12 mph
- In suburban areas: 14-20 mph

Source: Institute of Transportation Engineers. *Transportation Planning Handbook.* John D. Edwards, Jr., P.E., editor. Englewood Cliffs, NJ: Prentice-Hall, 1992, Table 5.23 on p. 147 and Table 5.30 on p. 154.

Rail rapid-transit car
(50 feet) ....$0.7 to 1.2 million
Articulated bus
(with air conditioning) $400,000
Standard bus
(with air conditioning) $200,000
Minibus $125,000

THE ADVANTAGES
AND DISADVANTAGES
OF PUBLIC TRANSIT

Advantages of Public Transit

- Public transit provides mobility for those people who do not have access to private transportation.
- Transit diverts drivers from using their cars on streets and highways, thereby reducing traffic congestion.
- The use of public transit reduces the demand for parking spaces at trip destinations.
- At current prices, the fare per mile per person for riding public transit is generally lower than the cost per person per mile of operating a single-occupant private car.
- Substitution of well-patronized public transit for the operation of private cars reduces air pollution, noise pollution, and water pollution.
- Under some circumstances, public rapid transit provides faster transportation than does the use of private cars.
- Public transit appears to be the most (perhaps only) workable method of transporting people in established, high-density urban areas.
- Under some circumstances, the patrons of public transit can use their time in transit for working, relaxing, or other activities of their choice.

- In some situations, the provision of public transit may slow or prevent the development of low-density suburban sprawl.
- Under some circumstances, the location and quality of transit service may have a beneficial influence on patterns of metropolitan growth.

Disadvantages of Public Transit

- Travel time on public transit routes is often substantially longer than the driving time in private cars.
- While the availability of public transit may be satisfactory for many routine trips (such as the journey to work), it is not nearly as convenient as are private cars for special-purpose trips such as multi-destination shopping, special appointments, or recreational trips.
- Transit vehicles have a low overall speed when they travel routes which require frequent stops, and which are long and circuitous.
- It is not feasible to provide public transit to areas with low densities of trip ends (such as low-density residential subdivisions) without incurring excessively long travel times and/or excessively high operating costs per passenger.
- Public transit almost always requires substantial financial subsidies for operating expenses in order to keep fares at an acceptable level.
- Public transit operations usually receive substantial public subsidies for the purchase of rolling stock.
- When transit routes require exclusive rights-of-way, substantial public subsidies are often required for land acquisition and facility construction.
- Some potential transit patrons consider that the services available to them have one or more of the following characteristics:

— inconvenient route locations
— unsatisfactory frequency of service
— too limited hours of operation
— overcrowded vehicles
— too slow an overall speed in transit
— threats to personal safety

THE FEASIBILITY OF TRANSIT IN RELATION TO TRIP-END DENSITY

It is usually not practical to provide public transit services to areas which have very low trip-end densities, regardless of the size of the total population to be served. Conversely, it is often practical to provide public transit services when:

A. The total population to be served is large enough to generate enough trips to warrant reasonably frequent transit vehicle trips (i.e., short headways between vehicles); *and*

B. The location of transit patrons is relatively concentrated at both the places of origin and destination, so transit vehicles (such as buses) do not spend a long time travelling great distances to collect or offload passengers.

When there is a good number of potential transit patrons with trip origins that are clustered fairly close together, and these people can be transported to trip destinations that are also clustered fairly close together, this usually makes it possible to provide a satisfactory transit service at an acceptable economic cost. This is sometimes referred to as a FEW [origins] to FEW [destinations] pattern of transit.

On the other hand, when the trip origins of potential transit patrons are scattered far and wide in many locations, and their trip destinations are also widely dispersed, this results in long travel times for the transit riders, and it also results in high operating costs for the transit provider. This is sometimes referred to

as a MANY [origins] to MANY [destinations] pattern of transit; it is generally unsatisfactory to both transit patrons and to the transit provider.

There are two middle cases to be considered: the "many-to-few" mode of transit service and its reciprocal, "few-to-many." Whether or not either of these situations can provide satisfactory transit service at an affordable cost depends largely on the trip-end densities at the "many" areas of the transit service. For example, if a city has an area in which there are several hundred potential transit riders in the morning peak hour, and their residences are all within a 1-square-mile area, it may be feasible to provide satisfactory transit service to them. But suppose the potential riders are evenly dispersed throughout an area of 5 or 10 square miles: would conventional transit still be feasible?[13]

The four cases discussed above are schematically illustrated in Figure 12.1.

In the United States, many of the suburban subdivisions that were built after 1948 are at such low residential densities (in terms of dwelling units per acre) that they have very low potential trip-end densities, and therefore cannot be served effectively by conventional public transit. This situation becomes even more extreme when most of the residents of these subdivisions choose to use their private cars for making all of their trips. The transit patronage in such areas often dips to perhaps 2 percent (or fewer) of the potential riders. When you have an area of dispersed trip origins, and only 2 percent of the population chooses to ride public transit, you end up with very few riders indeed.

In these low-density suburban areas, there are some alternatives to providing them with conventional bus transit:

1. Provide only express bus service on widely spaced major arterials; or pro-

Figure 12.1. Patterns of Transit Trip Ends

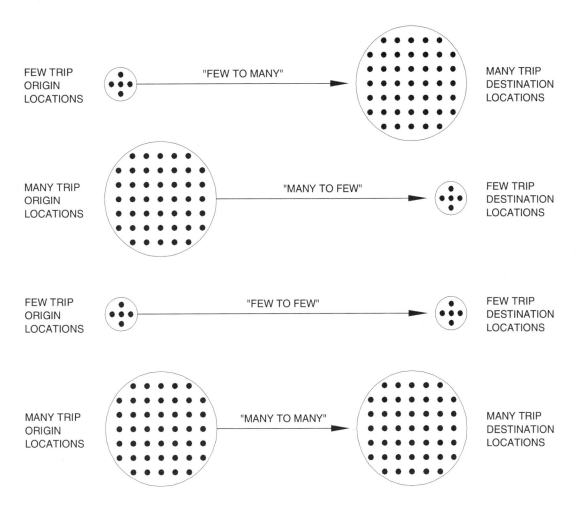

vide light-rail transit and rely on potential transit riders to drive their cars to large parking facilities at the transit stops; or else use the "kiss-and-ride" system of getting to the transit stop.

2. Provide "demand-responsive transit service" using vans to carry patrons from their homes to the transit stops described in the preceding paragraph. (A similar service may be required on the destination end of the transit run, if it also has a low density of trip-end desti-

nations.) This local, demand-responsive service might be limited to those patrons who are "captive riders," or to others, in an attempt to keep their cars from congesting the roads.

3. Provide subsidized taxi service to "captive riders" between their homes and the regional transit stops. Some people may be offended by the idea of subsidizing taxi services, but perhaps they do not realize that almost all other public transit services are also substantially subsi-

dized. If a community has a policy of providing transportation services to the transportation disadvantaged, in some cases a cost analysis will show that when trip-end densities are low, subsidized taxis are a least-cost solution.

GOALS IN TRANSIT PLANNING

When planning transit systems, one should keep in mind the goals of the program. It should be noted, however, that the goals of some groups may differ substantially from the goals of others. When this is the case, some accommodations or compromises are usually necessary. Listed below are some of the general goals often held by transit users, transit providers, and sponsoring local communities.

Goals of Transit Users

- Have available forms of transportation that:
  — are convenient, both in their route locations and their operating schedules
  — have affordable fare rates
  — provide safe vehicle operation and protection of personal safety
  — are comfortable (uncrowded, air conditioned, quiet, and provide a smooth ride)
  — are reliable (sticks to schedules)
  — serve areas where people want to go (work, shopping, and school)
  — are competitive in overall travel time with the "drive-own-car" option

Goals of Transit Providers

- To make a service available to the public that:
  — attracts substantial patronage by fulfilling the goals of travelers
  — is convenient, economical, efficient, safe, comfortable, attractive, and reliable

  — is affordable by the sponsoring governmental agency (which will usually require the use of state or federal subsidies)
  — serves a wide range of citizens (not just the poor and disadvantaged, not just the handicapped, and not just well-to-do suburbanites)

Goals of the Community

- provide a convenient and affordable alternative to the private automobile, one which will reduce the flow of private cars on public streets
- provide an affordable means of transportation for those citizens who do not own or cannot operate private cars
- provide a transit service which does not require an excessive financial subsidy from local sources
- encourage high-density urban development in selected corridors where transit service is provided, and thereby reduce the pressures for building sprawling, low-density developments over wide areas

ISSUES IN TRANSIT PLANNING

When planning transit systems, one should identify the issues that need to be considered and resolved. Listed below are some very general policy issues, and some operational issues, that are often appropriate to consider.

Policy Issues

- In which geographic areas should we provide transit?
- How low should trip-end densities be before we decline to provide areas with public transit?
- To which subgroups of our population should we give priority in the provision of transit service?

- To what degree should transit riders pay the full cost of transit service, and to what degree should the general public subsidize the service?

- Which subgroups of the general public should benefit from special subsidies for transit service? (We now provide special subsidies for schoolchildren, the elderly, and the handicapped).

- Should we continue to build sprawling suburban developments that have very low trip-end densities, and which we know can never be served economically by transit? Should local (or regional, or state, or federal) government place restrictions on such low-density development, or should we rely on the economic forces of the marketplace to determine urban patterns?

- What measures (if any) can we take to assure that place-of-work is close to place-of-residence, thereby reducing the required journey to work? Can this be accomplished when we have many households with two wage earners, each of whom may be employed in a different location within a large metropolitan area?

- If we were to cease to provide and support public transit, what would happen to the living patterns of the residents of those high-density areas of our cities that now rely on transit, and which cannot function effectively when the only transportation available is by private automobiles?

- Is traditional public transit doomed to extinction in a society in which the vast majority of people can afford to own and choose to operate a private car?

Operational Issues

- How can we minimize time lost in transferring from one mode of transit to another (or from one transit line to another) in a single trip?

- How can we spread out the transit load during the day so that it is not concentrated in morning and evening peak hours?

- How can we apply and utilize forms of transit which are innovative and cost-effective, although nontraditional?

- How can we transport residents who live in dense urban areas to job locations which are scattered in low-density suburban areas (i.e., transport central city residents to their jobs in the suburbs; a "few-origins-to-many-destinations" pattern)?

ALTERNATIVE FORMS OF TRANSIT

Many types of transit vehicles and transit services have been suggested as alternatives for the future. These include:

- vehicles elevated above a right-of-way (ROW) by air pressure (such as hovercraft)

- vehicles elevated above an ROW by electromagnetic induction

- vehicles propelled by linear induction electric motors

- monorail trains
  — suspended from a structure by wheels which are above the vehicle
  — supported on a structure by wheels which are beneath the vehicle

- moving belts similar to horizontal escalators (one concept would have low-speed belts adjacent to medium-speed belts which would be adjacent to high-speed belts; with this arrangement, passengers would walk from one belt to another to attain a reasonably high speed of travel)

- personal rapid-transit (PRT) vehicles, which are defined as "an automated guideway transit system that uses small vehicles (two to six passengers) operating under computer control between off-line stations to provide demand-responsive service (except, perhaps during peak periods), with headways of 3 seconds or less."[14]

- dual-mode PRT systems, where small individual vehicles would be operated under manual control on local streets, but would be computer controlled when running on a guideway
- small, battery-powered "loaner cars" for high-density urban areas
- "loaner bicycles"
- high-speed ferry boats
- free (no-fare) transit service for all

WHY SOME NEW FORMS OF TRANSIT MAY HAVE BEEN PASSED BY

Alternative forms of transit, as well as currently used conventional systems, must be evaluated for their costs and benefits. If the new forms turn out to have more benefits and fewer costs than existing forms, they will be used; if they don't, they will be filed in the "interesting but impractical" category.

Costs may include:

- initial investment in engineering, rolling stock, ROW, and construction
- operating costs (such as labor and fuel)
- administrative overhead costs
- time spent by patrons while in transit
- decreased land values of some properties near transit facilities
- costs of acquiring, installing, and debugging computer programs used to control the flow of transit vehicles
- environmental damages
- possible safety hazards

Benefits may include:

- increased availability of transportation for those without private cars
- time saved by transit patrons

- economic savings in transportation costs, when compared to the use of private cars
- increased land values of properties served by transit facilities
- reduced adverse environmental impacts
- possible increases in personal safety
- probability that the new form of transit will make possible or promote superior forms for future urban development; those that are more efficient, more aesthetically pleasing, and more socially beneficial than the forms we are now utilizing

Any future transit system must compete, on a cost/benefit basis, with all existing forms of public transit, and with private forms of transportation (such as cars, bicycles, and walking).

While a number of very interesting technological developments have been considered in the field of transit, at the present time few of them appear to be competitive with the existing conventional forms of transit.

TRANSIT PLANNING PROCEDURES

Chapter 8 provides an overview of the transportation planning process. Transit planning is an integral part of that process.

Transportation planning, as described in Chapter 8, includes these three phases: "Describe the Transit System," "Make a Modal Split," and "Make Trip Assignments."

In the phase "Describe the Transit System," maps and descriptions of links in the existing and proposed transit networks are prepared.

In the "Make a Modal Split" phase, an analysis is made of the number of persons who are projected to travel by each mode of transportation. Various forms of public transit may be considered here.

In the "Make Trip Assignments" phase, projections are made of the number of person trips that will be made on each link of the transit network.

The foregoing is a simplified description of the process. More detailed descriptions can be found in many of the books on transit planning. A good description can be found in Levinson's chapter in the ITE book, *Transportation Planning Handbook,* pp. 160-166. Levinson clearly considers transit planning as an integral part of the general transportation planning process. He includes a flow chart of the transit planning section in which a modal split is made early in the transportation planning process, and a separation at that time of those travelers who have a choice of transportation mode from those who do not (i.e., the captive transit riders). His diagram, which is reproduced as Figure 12.2, is well worth close examination.

Notes

1. The subject is discussed in ITE's *Transportation Planning Handbook,* pp. 427-430, and treated at some length in the HCM-1994.

2. It is true that some designers, such as Peter Calthorpe, have proposed that residential centers be built in such a pattern, but few of them exist today. See Calthorpe's book, *The Next American Metropolis.*

3. ITE, *Transportation Planning Handbook,* Table 2.40.

4. *Ibid.,* Table 2.49.

5. U.S. Department of Transportation, Bureau of Transportation Statistics, *National Transportation Statistics—1997,* Table 1-7.

6. For further information, see the chapter by Herbert S. Levinson in ITE's *Transportation Planning Handbook,* pp. 284-290.

7. Many of the largest buses are articulated; that is, they consist of two-passenger compartments which are joined by a swivel that allows the bus to bend in the middle as it goes over a hump or around a corner.

8. Levinson, p. 140.

9. *Ibid.*

10. *Ibid.,* p. 166. Levinson cites his source as: Reno and Bixby, *Characteristics of Urban Transportation System,* prepared for Urban Mass Transportation Administration, 1985.

Figure 12.2. The Transit Planning Phase of the Transportation Planning Process

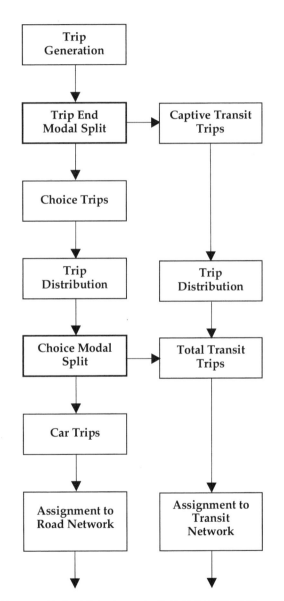

Source: Herbert S. Levinson, Institute of Transportation Engineers. *Transportation Planning Handbook.* John D. Edwards, Jr., P.E., editor. Englewood Cliffs, NJ: Prentice-Hall, 1992, p. 166.

11. *Ibid.*

12. *Ibid.*, p. 166. Levinson quotes from a report by Allen D. Biehler, prepared for the Transportation Research Board, National Academy of Science (Special Report No. 221).

13. For a more detailed discussion of the population sizes and densities that make transit services feasible, see pp. 160-161 in the Levinson reference.

14. Transportation Research Board, National Academy of Sciences. "Glossary of Urban Transportation Terms (Special Report No. 79). Washington, DC: the authors, 1978. Used by permission.

Definitions marked with * are adapted from the Transportation Research Board, National Research Council. *Glossary of Urban Transportation Terms* (Special Report No. 179). Washington, DC, 1978. Used with permission.

Sources of Further Information

American Public Transit Association. *Transit Fact Book.* Washington, DC: the authors; published annually.

Downs, Anthony. *Stuck in Traffic.* Washington, DC: The Brookings Institution and the Lincoln Institute of Land Policy, 1992.

Homburger, Hall, Loutzenheiser, and Reilly. *Fundamentals of Traffic Engineering.* 14th ed. Berkeley, CA: Institute of Transportation Studies, University of California, 1996.

[ITE]—Institute of Transportation Engineers. *Transportation Planning Handbook.* John D. Edwards, Jr., P.E., editor. Englewood Cliffs, NJ: Prentice-Hall, 1992. See "Urban Mass Transit Systems," by Herbert S. Levinson, which is Chapter 5 the ITE book noted above.

[HCM-1994]—Transportation Research Board, National Research Council. "Highway Capacity Manual" (Special Report No. 209). Washington, DC: Transportation Research Board, 1994.

Other References Cited in the Text

Calthorpe, Peter. *The Next American Metropolis.* New York: Princeton Architectural Press, 1993.

Carter, Everett C. and Wolfgang S. Homburger. *Introduction to Transportation Engineering.* Reston, VA: Reston Publishing Co., 1978.

Institute of Transportation Engineers, *Transportation and Traffic Engineering Handbook.* 2nd ed. Wolfgang S. Homburger, Louis E. Keefer, and William R. McGrath, editors. Washington, DC: Prentice-Hall, 1982. Prepared for the Institute of Transportation Engineers. See Chapter 7, "Urban Transit," by Wolfgang S. Homburger and Henry D. Quinby.

Mumford, Lewis. *The City in History.* New York: Harcourt, Brace & World, 1961.

Residential Areas

13

Introduction to Housing

There are many aspects to the field of housing. The major ones are: physical, economic, social, and environmental. These major aspects of housing are all closely interrelated. When we plan for housing, as a part of the physical environment, we may be making substantial impacts on local social, economic, and environmental conditions.

A GENERAL HOUSING GOAL

About 50 years ago, federal legislation[1] declared that it is a national goal to attain:

> "... a decent home and a suitable living environment for every American family"

What constitutes "a decent home"? What is "a suitable living environment"? Those of us who are involved with planning and building urban environments are still struggling with these questions. There seem to be no simple answers to these questions that are universally true.

SOME SPECIFIC HOUSING GOALS

In an attempt to be more specific than the national housing goal quoted above, consider the following:

Housing Requirements for Families and Individuals

1. an adequate amount of interior space, conveniently arranged (the amount of space needed will vary with the number of occupants and their level of activity; the space should be measured both in terms of floor area and cubic volume of the dwelling)
2. provision of adequate services (such as water supply, garbage collection, mail delivery, and sewage disposal) at an affordable cost
3. adequate light and air
4. adequate heating, cooling, and ventilation
5. personal safety from violent crime (burglary, robbery, and rape)[2]
   A. security within the dwelling
   B. safety in adjacent halls, corridors, elevators, etc.
   C. safety in private yards adjacent to the building
   D. safety in the general neighborhood of the building
6. protection from fire
7. protection from man-induced accidents (such as structural hazards)
8. protection from natural hazards (such as flooding, earthquakes, and hurricanes)

9. an acceptably low noise level
   A. in interior spaces
   B. in outdoor living areas
10. an adequate amount of accessible and usable outdoor living area
11. affordable economic rent, when calculated in relation to personal or family income
12. a convenient spatial relationship between the dwelling and:
    A. place of employment
    B. schools
    C. shopping areas
    D. places of social contact (such as homes of friends and churches)
13. an ownership or tenancy position that provides the occupants with a sense of stability and permanence, and yet does not burden them with a sense of being held captive by financial obligations caused by the dwelling
14. an affordable choice of housing size, price, location, and style
15. absence of social discrimination based on factors that have nothing to do with the match between the characteristics of housing, and the needs and desires of its occupants

SOME HOUSING ISSUES

The following important issues should be considered by those who become involved with planning or building housing. Space does not permit us to discuss these issues at length in this text, however.

1. What minimum standards (such as for floor area, building volume, materials, construction techniques, lot area, and side yards) are essential for the protection of public health, safety, welfare, or morals? Are not many of our housing standards really based on tradition, or on a financial institution's desire to protect its investment, rather than on a true public need?
2. What responsibility, if any, does society in general have to provide housing (or a financial subsidy for housing) for persons or families of low or moderate incomes?
3. What social impacts occur when we group housing by its economic price (that is, what happens to society when most of the high-priced housing is in one part of town, the midpriced housing in another, and the low-cost housing in another)?
4. What impact does racial or social discrimination have on our housing occupancy patterns? How does this affect the lives of those who are discriminated against, and of those who do the discriminating?
5. What effect does rent control have on housing construction, housing maintenance, and housing occupancy?
6. What is the relative economic cost of rehabilitating old housing when compared to tearing it down and building new housing in its place? What are the social costs and benefits to be considered here?

PARTICIPANTS IN HOUSING

There are a number of groups in society who are involved with housing. These include:
- users of housing
  - renters
  - home purchasers
- builders of housing
  - construction workers
  - builders who build on contract for others
  - builders who build on speculation
  - builders who build and retain as a long-term investment

- investors in housing
  - people who buy housing for their own use
  - private investors who buy existing housing, or have new housing built, and rent it to tenants
  - banks that loan money in return for mortgages
  - Real Estate Investment Trusts (REITs) that invest in housing
  - public agencies that build and manage public housing
  - public agencies that administer rent subsidy programs
- manufacturers and distributors of building materials
- regulators of housing
  - federal agencies that establish minimum standards for housing that is to receive federal mortgage insurance (i.e., FHA and VA)
  - state and local agencies that adopt building codes and housing codes
  - local agencies that adopt and administer building codes, housing codes, zoning codes, and subdivision codes

Each of these participant groups has its own objectives, priorities, and resources. Very often the objectives of one group are in conflict with those of another group.

SOME HOUSING DEFINITIONS

Dwelling unit—A room or group of rooms providing living quarters for one family, usually (in the U.S.) including space for sleeping, cooking, eating, recreation, and sanitation.

Family—One or more persons related by blood or marriage, living together and sharing one kitchen.[3]

Group quarters—Residential accommodations for persons not related by blood or marriage (such as rooming houses, dormitories, fraternities, barracks, jails, and hotels and motels for long-term occupancy).

Acre—An area containing 43,560 square feet. An acre, when laid out as a square, has sides measuring about 208 feet. The acre is an old and well-established term. It seems improbable that it will be widely replaced in the foreseeable future by metric terms, because so many properties in this country have legal descriptions using the term.

Hectare—A metric measurement of area, containing 10,000 square meters. A hectare, when in the form of a square, measures 100 meters on a side [about 328 feet on a side]. 1 hectare = 2.47 acres.

FORMS OF HOUSING

Many forms of housing have been designed and built in the United States. A number of them are described and illustrated in the text that follows. Be aware that the terminology used to identify and describe the various forms of housing is by no means standardized. This is especially true for structures with two dwelling units in them and the many forms of row housing. Remember that mobile homes are almost never mobile.

It is convenient to categorize the various forms of housing in the manner shown in Table 13.1.

Detached, Single-Family Houses

Detached, single-family house—A structure intended for occupancy by one family, and constructed on a separate building lot, which is owned in fee simple.[4] Each building has a front yard, a rear yard, and two side yards.

These houses are usually one, two, or three stories in height.

This form of housing is one of the most expensive to build because it requires so much land, and requires longer streets and utility lines than most other forms of housing.

Nevertheless, it is clearly the most popular form of housing in the United States.

The lot size for each house usually ranges from 5,000 square feet to 1 acre [43,560 square feet], although the lot may be as small as 2,500 square feet, or as large as 50 acres.

The net residential density[5] of subdivisions for detached, single-family houses typically ranges from 2.0 to 8.0 dwelling units per acre (DU/ac), with an average of about 5.0 DU/ac. There is considerable regional variation in this figure.

Table 13.1. Forms of Housing

CONVENTIONALLY CONSTRUCTED HOUSING
1. Detached, single-family houses
2. Attached, single-family houses
A. Row houses
B. Townhouses
C. Duplexes
D. Triplexes, fourplexes
3. Apartment buildings
A. Low-rise apartment buildings (1, 2, or 3 stories)
B. Medium-rise apartment buildings (4 to 6 stories)
C. High-rise apartment buildings (7 stories or more; often over 12 stories)
FACTORY-BUILT HOUSING
1. Manufactured homes
2. Modular housing
3. Panelized housing
GROUP QUARTERS (housing occupied by nonrelated individuals)
1. Dormitories
2. Rooming houses
3. Fraternities and sororities
4. Hotels and motels
5. Military barracks
6. Jails

Attached, Single-Family Houses

Row Houses

Row houses—A series of three or more dwelling units placed side by side, with no side yards between them. Each dwelling unit has a separate entry and is located on a separate building lot.

Row houses usually have a party wall separating them (that is, a solid wall that is a shared structural part of the adjacent houses). In some parts of the country, however, each dwelling unit has its own two side walls, and there may be about an inch of airspace or insulation between the houses.

Row houses may be one, two, or three stories in height.

The width of each house may be from 25 feet to 40 feet, although some as narrow as 12 feet have been built.

The lot size for each house is usually 2,500 to 3,500 square feet.

The net residential density of subdivisions composed of row houses is typically between 10 and 20 DU/ac.

Townhouses

Townhouses—A form of row housing that may utilize a combination of fee-simple and condominium land ownership.

The basic meaning of the term "townhouse" is a house that is built in a town or a city. In earlier years, it was not unusual for wealthy families to have townhouses as well as country estates. Their townhouses were often quite elegant, and many of them are still considered to be prestigious housing.

In contemporary usage, the term "townhouse" is sometimes used by real estate promoters for almost any form of row house, thereby taking advantage of the prestige of housing from an earlier era.

On the other hand, some land developers use the term to describe a structure which is

Figure 13.1. A Detached, Single-Family House

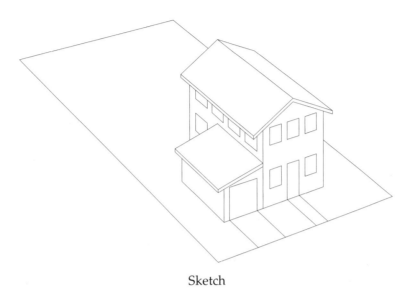

Sketch

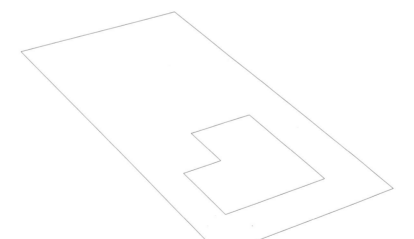

Plot Plan

Figure 13.2. Row Houses (in the San Francisco style)

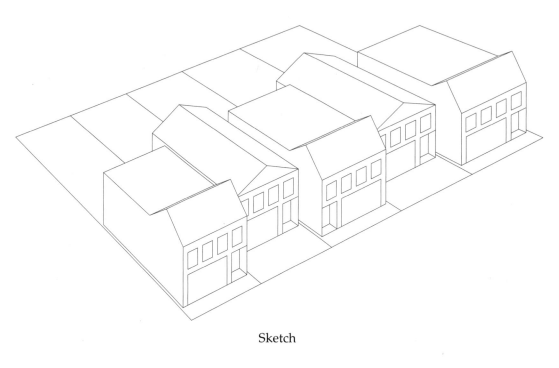

Sketch

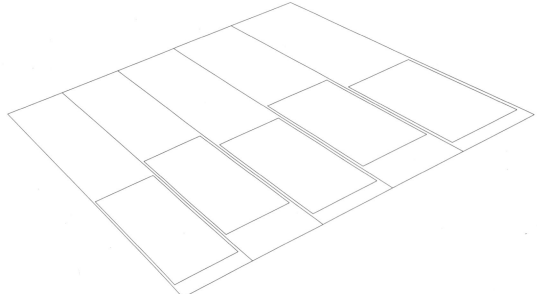

Plot Plan

similar to a conventional row house, in which the owner of each has fee-simple ownership of only that land on which the structure is situated (i.e., the "footprint" of the building), plus a small amount of land for a private patio or yard. The remainder of the land surrounding the structures is used for attractively landscaped areas and recreational facilities. This land which surrounds the private building sites is jointly owned by the owners of all the buildings, usually in condominium ownership. It is maintained by a homeowners' association with funds from monthly dues assessed to the property owners.

The lot size of the individually owned building sites is usually quite small, perhaps ranging from 1,000 to 3,000 square feet. However, because of the land held and used in common, the net residential density of these developments tends to be quite low, often in the range of from 10 to 20 DU/ac, although the range can be from 5 to 30.

Duplexes

Duplex—A structure containing two dwelling units located on one building lot.

The most prevalent form of duplex has two dwelling units placed side by side, with a solid party wall between them. In some areas, duplexes are built with one unit over the other. Another pattern of duplexes that is found from time to time is the front-and-back design, in which one unit occupies the front half of the building lot, and the second unit occupies the rear. Duplexes have front, back, and side yards.

Access to each dwelling unit is usually by way of separate entry doors, although in some cases it is from a jointly used entry hall.

Duplexes may be one, two, or three stories in height.

The lot size for duplexes ranges from 5,000 to 10,000 square feet, with an average of about 6,000 square feet. The typical net density of duplex developments is from 10 to 12 DU/ac.

Triplexes and Fourplexes

Triplex—A residential structure that contains three dwelling units and is located on one building lot.

Fourplex (also known as a *quadruplex* or *quadplex*)—A residential structure that contains four dwelling units and is located on one building lot.

A triplex is often similar in form and character to a duplex, except it has three dwelling units in it instead of two.

A triplex may have separate entrances to each of the three dwelling units, or it may have one common entryway.

In low-density urban areas, it is usual practice to design the structure so that it appears quite "residential" in style, rather than in the form of a small apartment building.

Fourplexes often have characteristics that are similar to those of duplexes and triplexes.

The lot area for a triplex generally depends on the character of the neighborhood in which it is built. It might be about 10,000 to 12,000 square feet, which would result in a net residential density of 11 to 13 DU/ac.

Low-Rise Apartment Buildings

Low-rise apartment building—A structure containing apartments, with one, two, or three stories devoted to residential use.

Low-rise apartment buildings are usually distinguished from mid- or high-rise apartment buildings by their height and method of construction. The Uniform Building Code and a number of other building codes allow low-rise apartments to be built using wood-frame construction, but require taller buildings to be built with a more fire-resistant method of construction (such as masonry or

Figure 13.3. Townhouses

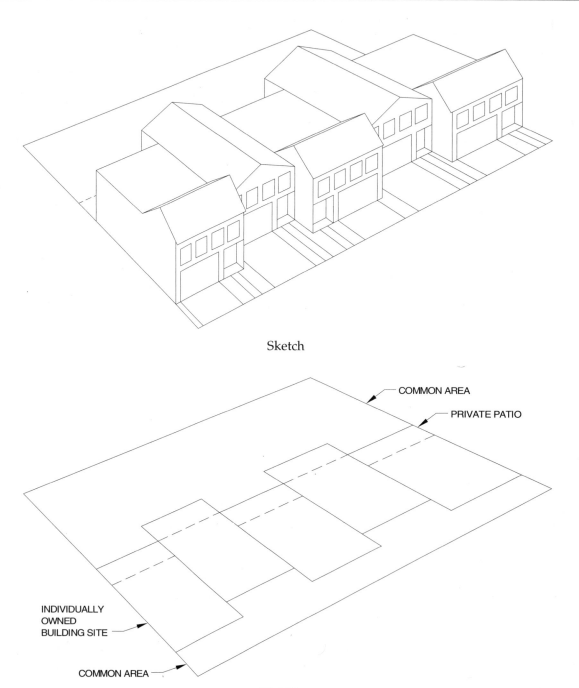

Sketch

Plot Plan

Figure 13.4. A Duplex

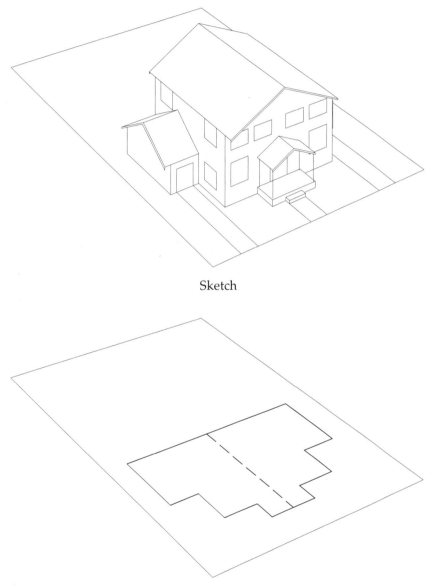

Sketch

Plot Plan

reinforced concrete), which is substantially more expensive.

One- and two-story, low-rise apartments are often built in suburban areas, and may have attractive landscaping and some recreational features (such as a swimming pool); when these are present, the developments are often called "garden apartments."

Three-story apartment buildings tend to crowd their building sites more than one- or two-story buildings; they tend to be found in medium-density urban areas.

Providing parking space for the cars of the apartment occupants becomes more of a problem as residential density increases. Parking at ground level can usually be easily developed for one- or two-story apartment developments, but it becomes a challenge for three-story buildings. In urban areas, it is not uncommon for the ground level (or basement) to be entirely devoted to parking under three stories of residential uses.

The lot area per dwelling unit for two-story, low-rise apartments is typically 1,200 to 2,000 square feet of land area per dwelling unit, which yields a net residential density of from 20 to 30 DU/ac. The density of one-story apartment buildings can be expected to be somewhat less than these figures, and that of three-story buildings somewhat greater.

Midrise and High-Rise Apartment Buildings

Midrise apartment building—A structure containing apartments, and having more than three but less than seven stories of residential use.

High-rise apartment building—A structure containing apartments, and having seven or more stories of residential use.

The design of apartment buildings that have more than three stories of residential use depends very much on elevators. There are two types of elevators in use in North America:

- *hydraulic elevators*, which employ a long, hydraulic piston to push up and lower down the cab of the elevator; and
- *electric traction elevators*, which employ electric motors and cables to hoist and lower the elevator cab.

Hydraulic elevators are generally not used in buildings over six stories in height because of the required length of the hydraulic piston; electric traction elevators are used for taller buildings. Hydraulic elevators are slow; they rise at speeds of 50 to 150 feet per minute. Electric traction elevators are much faster; they rise at speeds of 700 to 1,200 feet per minute. Hydraulic elevators are much cheaper than electric traction elevators; therefore they are used whenever their height limitation and slow speed are not serious drawbacks (often found in midrise apartment buildings).

Elevators also strongly influence the floor plans of mid- and high-rise apartment buildings. This is because most building codes place a limit on the distance from the entry of individual apartments to the location of an elevator.

Figure 13.5 illustrates how the floor plan of a building is affected by a requirement that the distance from the elevator to the farthest apartment entry is no more than 50 feet. In this case, the resulting building would be a rectangle measuring 60 to 70 feet in width, and 160 to 180 feet in length.

It is possible, of course, to have more complex shapes of buildings than the slab building illustrated in Figure 13.5. One of the ways this can be done is by having banks of elevators located in several places, and corridors radiate from the elevator locations rather than using just one linear corridor.

As mentioned previously, most building codes require a fire-resistant form of construction in buildings having more than three stories of residential use. This type of construction is substantially more expensive than the wood-frame construction permitted in lower structures. In many suburban areas, land costs per apartment unit are so low that it is economically feasible to spread out low-rise apartment buildings over a relatively large building site. In some highly urbanized areas, however, land costs are so high that it is important to minimize the land cost per apartment unit, even if the building construction costs are relatively high. Under these conditions, it is economically preferable to go to midrise or highrise apartment construction.

For families with children, mid- and highrise apartments are generally considered to be less desirable forms of housing than lower structures. This is because access to the ground level, where outdoor play and adventure areas are located, is usually very inconvenient for children. In tall apartment buildings, small children always need an adult to accompany and watch over them when they wish to play on the ground level.

The residential density of mid- and highrise apartment buildings varies greatly. Lynch and Hack report a net density of from 65 to 75 DU/ac for 6-story apartment buildings, and from 85 to 95 DU/ac for 13-story apartments. This is equivalent to about 650 to 450 square feet of lot area per dwelling unit.

Factory-Built Housing

A distinction can be drawn between the "conventional" and the "factory-built" method of building housing. Conventional construction, often referred to as "stick building," involves transporting many individual bits of building materials to a site and assembling them there. Factory building, on the other hand, assembles the building materials within a factory to form entire buildings or large modules of buildings. The buildings, or the modules, are then transported to the housing site, where the building (or assembled building components) is set on a foundation and connected to standard utilities.

The advantages of factory building are that it can take place in any kind of weather, the quality control is usually better than is found in field construction and, when large volumes are involved, it is more economical.

Factory construction originated some years ago with the manufacture of "mobile homes." The earlier mobile home construction industry is now divided into two distinct phases:

1. construction of "recreational vehicles" which, as the name implies, are used primarily for recreational use; and

Figure 13.5. Typical Floor of an Apartment Building Having One Bank of Elevators

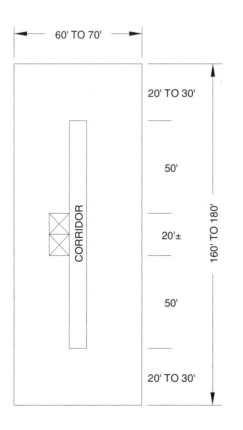

2. "manufactured housing" which is used primarily for long-term occupancy.

There are two building codes which govern construction standards for factory-built housing. The first of these is known as "the HUD code," because it is a federal code administered by the U.S. Department of Housing and Urban Development.[6] This code sets standards for the construction of some factory-built homes.

The second is known as "the UBC code" (Uniform Building Code), which has been adopted by many (but not all) cities, counties, and states. It sets standards for conventional housing and for some factory-built housing that has permanent foundations.

Manufactured housing (built under the HUD code)

Manufactured home—A residential structure, intended for use as a single dwelling, which is manufactured in a factory and then transported to a site, where it is placed on a foundation and connected to local utility systems.

Manufactured homes are built in modules which are often 14 or 16 feet wide, from 24 to 66 feet in length, and one story in height. They are also built in 10-, 12-, and even 20-foot widths. The width of the selected module depends on the design of the housing, and on regulations that set the maximum width which may be transported on state highways. In some cases, a single module is a complete dwelling unit; in other cases, two modules are joined together, side by side, to form a "double-wide" dwelling unit; sometimes three are joined together to form a "triple-wide" dwelling; and sometimes they are stacked to make a two-story structure.

Once the home is delivered to its intended site and placed on its foundation, the wheels used for its over-the-road transportation are removed and the home takes on the appearance of conventional housing.

Manufactured homes built under the HUD code may or may not be permanently fastened to foundations (that is, "permanently sited"). When they are permanently sited, they become subject to the same local regulations as is conventional housing, and they are considered "real property" for financing and tax purposes.

When the homes are placed on top of concrete foundation piers, but *not permanently fastened to them,* many local jurisdictions consider them to be in the same category as mobile homes, and usually restrict their location to mobile home parks[7] or rural areas. They are then also considered as "personal property" for financing and tax purposes because they are not permanently fixed to the ground.

The distinction between "personal property" and "real property" is that personal property is considered to be portable, whereas real property is considered to be a piece of immovable real estate. "Personal property" (such as automobiles, trucks, boats, and recreational vehicles) are taxed by state and local governments at a different rate than "real property." When loans are made on personal property, they are often at higher rates and for shorter terms than are loans on real property.

Modular housing (built under the UBC code)

Modular housing unit—A residential structure which is manufactured in a factory and then transported to a site, where it is fastened to a permanent foundation and connected to local utility systems.

Modular housing built under the UBC code is very similar in size and character to manufactured housing built under the HUD code. The major distinction, however, is that this type of housing is *always permanently fastened to a substantial foundation.* Its location is regulated by local jurisdictions in the same way as is conventionally built housing. It is also financed and taxed in the same manner as conventional housing.

Although they are frequently used as single-family homes, modular units are occasionally combined to form multifamily housing. Sometimes the modular units are stacked one above another to form multistoried buildings. Because this form of housing, when completed, is often indistinguishable from conventional housing, it is usually built in conventional subdivisions and very rarely in mobile home parks.

Panelized housing (built under the UBC code)

Panelized housing consists of housing constructed from building components such as factory-built wall panels, roof trusses, and floor trusses. These building components are trucked to the building site where they are assembled and the building is completed. The resulting structure is usually similar in appearance to conventionally built structures.

Panelized housing is used to build single-family homes, multifamily structures, offices and other commercial buildings, and some industrial construction. It is used in both single- and multistory buildings.

The location of structures built of panelized components is subject to the same local zoning codes as is conventional construction. It is also treated in the same manner as conventional construction for financing and tax purposes.

THE NEED FOR A VARIETY OF HOUSING FORMS

As we pass through various ages—from infancy to childhood to adolescence to early adulthood to middle age to old age—we have differing housing needs. No one type of housing suits all. Table 13.2 identifies what may be the most desired forms of housing for each of the major phases of aging.

This table is presented to emphasize the need for a wide variety of housing forms. The single-family, detached suburban home, priced for the traditional middle-income family, appears to be far from a complete answer to America's housing needs.

Notes

1. The National Housing Act of 1949.

2. See *Defensible Space* by Oscar Newman.

3. This definition of "family" is often used in zoning ordinances. It has shortcomings in that: (A) it does not indicate how close a blood relationship is required (is a second cousin twice removed still a member of the family?); and (B) it does not recognize that some men and women live together as families, outside the bonds of marriage.

4. "Owned in fee simple" means, in this case, that the owner of the house also owns all rights to the land on which the house is situated. This differs from condominium ownership or leasing the land. For a very good discussion of the forms of land ownership, see Lynch and Hack, pp. 253-260.

5. The definitions of various forms of residential density will be discussed in Chapter 15.

6. Its exact title is the National Manufactured Construction and Safety Standards Act of 1974 (24 CFR 3280).

7. Mobile home parks usually have building sites which are substantially smaller than typical subdivision lots. These sites are most often rented or leased rather than sold. The roads, utility systems, and recreation facilities are generally owned and maintained by the park proprietors. In other words, mobile home parks are not typical subdivisions.

Recommended Reading

Levy, John M. *Contemporary Urban Planning.* 4th ed. Upper Saddle River, NJ: Prentice-Hall, 1997, pp. 198-203.

Lynch, Kevin and Gary Hack. *Site Planning.* 3rd ed. Cambridge, MA: MIT Press, 1984. See Chapter 9, "Housing."

Table 13.2. Preferences for Dwelling Types By People in Various Stages of the Family Life Cycle

Stage	Need	Possible Housing Types
Young single person	Bachelor housing, at a modest cost, close to adult activity centers	High-rise or midrise apartment building, or an apartment in a converted house, perhaps shared with other young singles
Young married couple	A small dwelling, at a modest cost	Apartment or townhouse
Young couple with young children	A ground-oriented building, close to children's facilities; probably at a modest cost	Garden apartment, townhouse, or single-family dwelling
Middle-aged couple with teen-aged children	A large dwelling, with good access to transit services and to facilities used by teenagers	Single-family dwelling or townhouse
Middle-aged couple with grown children	A smaller dwelling with good transportation facilities, close to adult facilities	Apartment, townhouse, or single-family dwelling
Elderly couple	A small dwelling unit designed for senior citizens that is close to health care and community facilities	Apartment, townhouse, or special housing for seniors
Elderly single person	A small dwelling unit; characteristics depend on the health and mobility of the person, and on care available from nearby friends and relatives	Apartment or special housing for seniors

Source: Adapted from *Residential Site Development Advisory Document.* Canada Mortgage and Housing Corporation, Ottawa, Canada, circa 1980.

Sources of Further Information on Housing In General

Kaiser, Edward J., David R. Godschalk, and F. Stuart Chapin, Jr. *Urban Land Use Planning.* 4th ed. Urbana, IL: University of Illinois Press, 1995. See Chapter 14, "Residential Areas."

Newman, Oscar. *Defensible Space.* New York: Collier Books, 1973.

Sanders, Welford. "Manufactured Housing Site Development Guide" (Planning Advisory Service Report No. 445). Chicago: American Planning Association, 1993.

So, Frank S., and Judith Getzels, editors. The Practice of Local Government Planning. 2nd ed. Washington, DC: International City Management Association, 1988. See Chapter 12, "Planning for Housing" by Constance Lieder. The first half of this chapter, which deals with federal housing programs of the 1980s, is now out of date. The second half, which deals with housing programs in general, is still relevant.

Sources of Additional Information on Forms of Housing

Bookout, Lloyd W., Jr. *Residential Development Handbook.* 2nd ed. Washington, DC: Urban Land Institute, 1990. See especially pp. 155-172.

Kone, D. Linda. *Land Development.* 8th ed. Washington, DC: Home Builder Press (National Association of Home Builders), 1994. See Chapter 9, "Selecting Housing Types."

CHAPTER

14

Residential Density

CONCEPTS OF RESIDENTIAL DENSITY

"Residential density" is a technical term that is very useful when planning the development lands for residential use.

For those who are working for a land developer, the concept of residential density can be used to estimate the "yield" of a specific piece of property; that is, the number of houses or apartments that can be built on it. It is also a good tool for examining development alternatives, such as comparing the yields from one type of housing versus another.

For those who are working for a public planning or engineering agency, the concept of residential density can be used to prepare a plan for some sector of the jurisdiction that is to be developed (or redeveloped) for residential use; it will give an indication of the future character of the area. Calculations of residential density will produce the number of dwelling units that may be built in the area; this can then be used for calculations such as the probable number of vehicle trips the area will generate, the number of schoolchildren who will live in the area, and the amount of wastewater that can be expected to flow from the area.

For those in urban design, it will be found that residential density is perhaps the most important factor known that sets the basic character of a residential area.

The following definitions are used to describe various applications of the term "residential density."

SOME DEFINITIONS

DU—An abbreviation for the term "dwelling unit."

Residential density—An expression of the compactness of residential development, usually expressed in terms of items per unit area (such as persons, rooms, or dwelling units). The units of area may be floor area, net lot area, gross lot area, acres, hectares, or square miles.

Net residential density—The number of dwelling units per unit area (such as acres or hectares) of land devoted to a residential building site.

Gross residential density—The number of dwelling units per unit area of land devoted to residential building sites plus the area of streets serving those building sites.

Neighborhood residential density—The number of dwelling units per unit area of land devoted to residential building sites, local streets, and facilities serving the local population (such as local schools, local parks, and local shopping facilities). The area specifically excludes land uses serving populations outside of the area being analyzed (such as state universities, regional shopping centers, and regional airports). The land area may or may not include vacant land.

Jurisdiction-wide residential density—The number of dwelling units per unit area (such as square miles or square kilometers) of land within the political boundaries of a jurisdiction. (The area usually includes residential, commercial, industrial, recreational, and institutional land uses, as well as vacant land, military bases, airports, and bodies of water.)

Residential density is most often expressed in terms of dwelling units (DU) per acre (ac). Sometimes, however, the inverse of this term, lot area per dwelling unit, is used.

USING RESIDENTIAL DENSITY AS A DESIGN TOOL

Residential density, expressed in *dwelling units per acre* (DU/ac) is used as an overview planning tool.

Residential density, expressed in *lot area per dwelling unit*, is used as a regulatory tool (e.g., in specific zoning regulations).

- When calculating the yield for single building sites, density figures (expressed in terms of square feet of lot area per DU) are used.
- For a site that is to be subdivided (with streets to be subtracted from the gross area) the number of gross acres in each land use is multiplied by the gross residential density of that land use which results in an approximate yield in number of dwelling units.
- For a site that is to be subdivided (with streets, parks, shopping centers, and schools), the gross area of the tract in

acres is multiplied by the neighborhood density figure which is closest to the typical type of dwelling that will be built on the property; this will produce an approximation of the number of dwelling units that the area will produce.

It must be noted that the above calculations will give approximations only. For more precise figures, one must specify how many units of each building type will be built, the average lot area per dwelling unit for each building type, the percent of the area that will be used for streets, and the percent of the area that will be used for community facilities. This detailed analysis can usually be made only after a fairly detailed site plan has been developed.

Table 14.1 reports typical residential densities. Note that these are generalized approximations only, and that the values reported in the table are not standards that apply everywhere.

COVERAGE AND FLOOR AREA RATIO

Some additional terms are used when describing or calculating residential density:

Coverage—The area of a building lot that is covered by a structure, expressed in square feet; the proportion of a building lot that is covered by a structure, expressed in percent or in decimal parts.

Floor area ratio (FAR)—The ratio between the total gross floor area on all stories of a structure to the gross area of the building lot on which the structure is located.

Floor area ratios are often used in regulating the density of development of commercial and industrial properties; they are rarely used in regulating residential properties. This is because experience has shown that when a FAR is the primary regulation in apartment zoning, property owners tend to crowd their properties with many small apartment units

Table 14.1. Typical Residential Densities

Residential Use	Lot Area (sq. ft./DU)	Net Residential Density (DU/acre)	Gross Residential Density (DU/ac)	Neighborhood Residential Density (DU/ac)
Rural estates	20 acres	.05	.05	.05
Rural residential	5 acres	.20	.16	.15
Low-density, single family	20,000	2.2	1.7	1.5
Medium-density, single family	8,000	5.5	4.0	3.5
High-density, single family	5,000	8.7	6.5	5.2
Duplexes	4,000	11	8	6
Low-density row house	3,500	12	8	6
High-density row house	2,500	17	12	10
Low-density townhouse	5,400	8	6	5
High-density townhouse	2,700	16	12	10
1-story apartments	2,400	18	13	10
3-story apartments	1,200	36	25	20
6-story apartments	600	72	50	35
12-story apartments	300	145	100	60

- DU/ac = dwelling units per acre
- sq. ft./DU = area in the building site in square feet per dwelling unit

rather than fewer moderate-sized units. (In some instances, this may be a desired effect; in others, it may be considered an adverse impact.)

Figure 14.1 illustrates a variety of building coverages. It may be noted that very low coverage figures are usually found only in low-density suburban and rural areas, and that very high coverage figures are usually found only in dense urban areas. A coverage of 100 percent is extreme and is almost never found.

Figure 14.2 illustrates three sites, each of which is developed to a FAR of 1.0 (that is, each site has a structure on it which is equal in floor area to the land area of the site). The figure on the left shows development when the building coverage is 100 percent; the figure in the middle shows development with a coverage of 50 percent; the one on the right has a coverage of 25 percent.

Figure 14.3 illustrates the same three sites, but this time each of them is developed to a FAR of 0.5. Since it is impossible to develop a site at 100 percent coverage while having a FAR of 0.5, no structure is shown in the left-hand diagram.

Figure 14.4 again illustrates the three sites, but this time each one is developed to a FAR of 4.0.

RELATIONSHIPS AMONG BUILDING TYPE, RESIDENTIAL DENSITY, AND FLOOR AREA RATIO

Table 14.2 presents a number of examples of residential buildings that might be built under a variety of assumed conditions.

Figure 14.1. Examples of Building Coverage

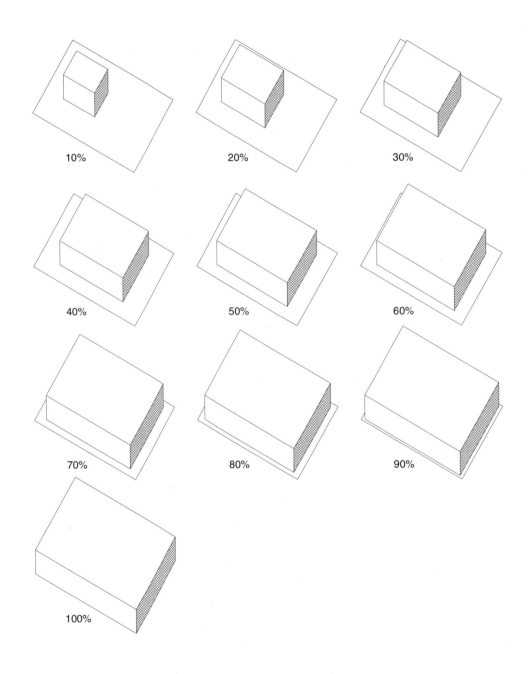

Figure 14.2. Sites Developed With a Floor Area Ratio of 1.0

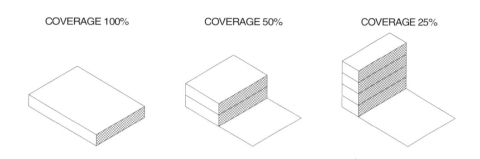

Figure 14.3. Sites Developed With a Floor Area Ratio of 0.5

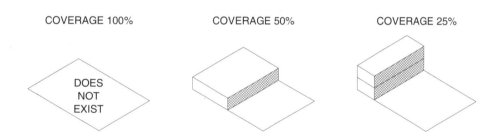

Figure 14.4. Sites Developed With a Floor Area Ratio of 4.0

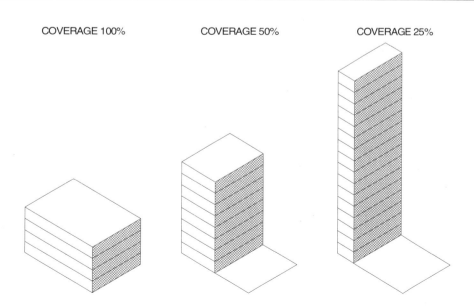

Table 14.2. Relationships Among Building Type, Residential Density, and Floor Area Ratio

| Figure | Type of Structure | ASSUMED SPECIFICATIONS | | | | RESULTING PATTERN | | | |
| | | Lot Size (sq. ft.) | Floor Area per DU (sq. ft.) | Parking Spaces per DU | Number of Stories | Residential Density | | Floor Area Ratio (FAR) | Coverage (percent) |
						Lot Area per DU (sq. ft.)	DUs per Net Acre		
A	Detached, single-family house	40,000	2,000	not shown	1	40,000	1.1	0.05	5
B	Detached, single-family house	10,000	2,000	not shown	2	10,000	4.4	0.2	10
C	Detached, single-family house	5,000	2,000	not shown	2	5,000	8.7	0.4	20
D	Row house	2,500	2,000	not shown	2	2,500	17.4	0.8	40
E	Fourplex	10,000	1,000	1.0	2	2,500	17.4	0.4	20
F	2-story garden apartment	20,000	1,000	1.0	2	1,650	26	0.6	30
G	3-story garden apartment	20,000	1,000	1.0	3	1,100	40	0.9	30
H	3-story apartment over parking	20,000	1,000	1.0	3 res 1 pkg	690	63	1.4 1.9*	48
I	6-story apartment over 2-story parking	20,000	1,000	1.0	6 res 2 pkg	350	125	2.9 3.8*	48
J	6-story apartment over 1-story parking	40,000	1,000	1.0	6 res 1 pkg	400	109	2.5 3.5*	42 res 100 pkg
K	12-story apartment over 1-story parking	40,000	1,000	1.0	12 res 1 pkg	400	109	2.5 3.5*	21 res 100 pkg
L	12-story apartment over 3-story parking	40,000	1,000	1.0	12 res 3 pkg	214	200	4.7 6.6*	39 res 64 pkg

- DU = dwelling unit
* This FAR counts floor area in the structure devoted to both residential and parking uses. Other FARs, not marked by an asterisk, are calculated on the basis of residential floor area only.

Figure 14.5 illustrates what the buildings from Table 14.2 would look like if they were to be built.

The left-hand row in Figure 14.5 contains only single-family homes, ranging in density from a low-density suburban home with a density of 1.1 DU/ac, to urban row houses at a density of 17.4 DU/ac. It has been assumed in our calculations that each dwelling unit has a floor area of 2,000 square feet. The space for parking cars has not been shown in these illustrations because off-street parking presents no serious problems at these residential densities.

The central row in Figure 14.5 contains low-rise apartment houses, ranging in den-

Figure 14.5. Relationships Among Building Type, Residential Density, and Floor Area Ratio

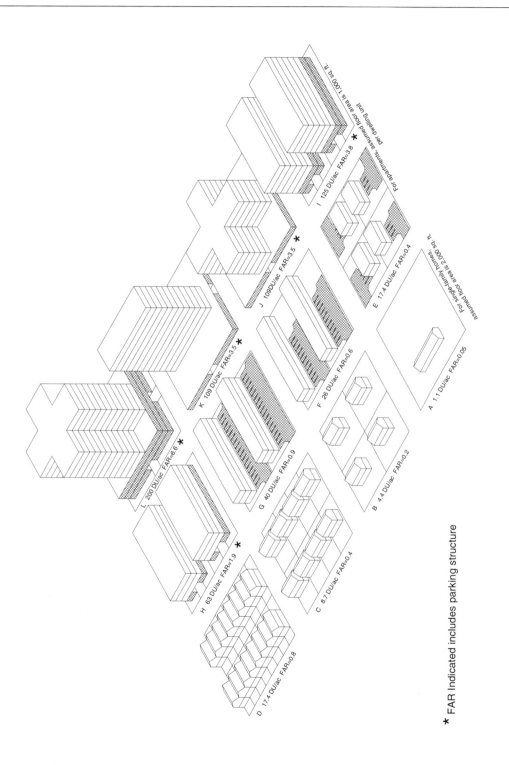

A. 1.1 DU/ac FAR=0.05

B. 4.4 DU/ac FAR=0.2

C. 8.7 DU/ac FAR=0.4

D. 17.4 DU/ac FAR=0.8

E. 17.4 DU/ac FAR=0.4

F. 26 DU/ac FAR=0.6

G. 40 DU/ac FAR=0.9

H. 63 DU/ac FAR=1.9 *

I. 125 DU/ac FAR=3.8 *

J. 109 DU/ac FAR=3.5 *

K. 109 DU/ac FAR=3.5 *

L. 200 DU/ac FAR=6.6 *

For single-family homes, assumed floor area is 2,000 sq. ft.

For apartments, assumed floor area is 1,000 sq. ft. per dwelling unit

* FAR Indicated includes parking structure

sity from 17.4 to 63 DU/ac. For these structures, it has been assumed that each apartment has a floor area of 1,000 square feet, and that one off-street parking space (of an area of about 325 square feet) will be provided for each apartment. It will be noted that as the residential density increases, the buildings become more massive and the problem of how to accommodate the parking becomes more severe. In fact, at a density of 63 DU/ac, it becomes necessary to place the parking under the residential structure.

The right-hand row in Figure 14.5 illustrates higher density apartments, ranging in density from 125 to 200 DU/ac. (Again, we have assumed a floor area of 1,000 square feet per apartment, and one parking space for each apartment.) It will be noted that as the density increases, the building mass becomes substantially greater, and off-street parking becomes more of a problem (While the illustrations show the parking on floors above the ground, in real life parking might be placed underground.)

Studying Table 14.2 and Figure 14.5 should give the reader some feeling for what happens as residential density is increased (or decreased). One can, of course, make one's own set of assumptions concerning building size and residential density, and then prepare similar tables and draw similar illustrations to show the character of development that would result.

Table 14.2 and Figure 14.5 were prepared by making some detailed calculations for each separate building example. There is an easier way to examine the relationship between residential density, building coverage, and building height: an equation.

Some years ago, when I was a young planner making an analysis for the City of Berkeley of the effects of zoning regulations on apartment building form and mass, I developed the following equation:

Number of stories =

$$\frac{(\text{floor area sq. ft. per DU}) \times (\text{DU/ac}) \times 100}{(43{,}560 \text{ sq. ft. per acre}) \times (\text{coverage in percent})}$$

In this equation, the floor area per DU is the gross floor area; it includes living areas, halls, and utility spaces. It represents an average figure for all DUs in the building. It is assumed that each story in the structure has the same gross floor area.

Appendix C indicates how this equation was derived.

Example of the Application of the Equation

Assumed density = 135 DU/ac

Assumed gross floor area per DU = 1,200 square feet

Assumed parking area provided per DU = 350 square feet (note that floor area plus parking area = 1,550 square feet)

Assumed building coverage = 40 percent

Building height in stories =

$$\frac{1{,}550 \times 135 \times 100}{43{,}560 \times 40} = 12.0$$

This equation can be used to examine the effects on building mass of various zoning regulations concerning lot coverage, floor area per apartment, building height, and number of parking spaces required per dwelling unit.

Table 14.3 indicates the building heights that would result as coverage ranges from 10 to 100 percent, and as density ranges from 10 to 120 DU/ac.

Figure 14.6 illustrates the height and form of buildings that would result from the assumptions used to calculate the contents of Table 14.3.

Table 14.3. Building Heights in Relation to Residential Density and Building Coverage

Density (DU/acre)	Building Coverage (percent)									
	100	90	80	70	60	50	40	30	20	10
120	2.8	3.1	3.4	3.9	4.6	5.5	6.9	9.2	13.8	27.6
110	2.6	2.8	3.2	3.6	4.2	5.0	6.3	8.4	12.6	25.3
100	2.3	2.6	2.9	3.3	3.8	4.6	5.7	7.6	11.4	22.9
90	2.1	2.3	2.6	2.9	3.4	4.1	5.2	6.9	10.3	20.6
80	1.8	2.0	2.3	2.6	3.1	3.7	4.6	6.1	9.2	18.4
70	1.6	1.8	2.0	2.3	2.7	3.2	4.0	5.3	8.0	16.0
60	1.4	1.5	1.7	2.0	2.3	2.8	3.4	4.6	6.9	13.8
50	1.1	1.3	1.4	1.6	1.9	2.3	2.9	3.8	5.7	11.5
40	0.9	1.0	1.2	1.3	1.5	1.8	2.3	3.1	4.6	9.2
30	0.7	0.8	0.9	1.0	1.2	1.4	1.7	2.3	3.4	6.9
20	0.5	0.5	0.6	0.7	0.8	0.9	1.2	1.5	2.3	4.6
10	0.2	0.3	0.3	0.3	0.4	0.5	0.6	0.8	1.2	2.3

- DU/acre = dwelling units per acre
- Building heights are reported in number of stories.
- Building heights were calculated on the basis of 1,000 sq. ft. of area per DU.

Figure 14.6. Building Heights in Relation to Residential Density and Building Coverage

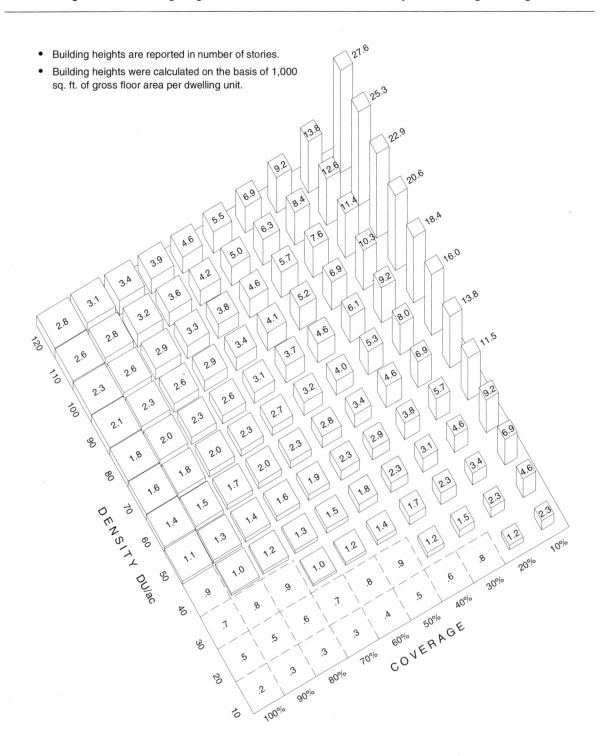

- Building heights are reported in number of stories.
- Building heights were calculated on the basis of 1,000 sq. ft. of gross floor area per dwelling unit.

CHAPTER

15

Neighborhood Planning

HISTORY

The concept of planning neighborhoods as identifiable segments of cities is not new. A notable pioneer advocate of this idea was Ebenezer Howard, who presented the idea in his book, *Garden Cities of Tomorrow*, published in England in 1898.

Under Howard's guidance, the town of Letchworth (England) was designed and built in 1903, followed by Welwyn in 1919. Both of them were "new towns," consisting of a town center with adjacent residential neighborhoods.

One of the first discussions of the neighborhood unit concept in American planning literature was written by Clarence Arthur Perry; it appeared in 1929, published as a part of *The New York Regional Plan*.

During the depression years in the United States three new towns were built which also utilized the neighborhood concept in their design. These were Greenbelt (Maryland), Greenhills (Ohio), and Greendale (Wisconsin).

A publication focussing on the neighborhood unit concept was published in 1948 ("Planning the Neighborhood," prepared by Anatole Solow and Ann Copperman). This report attracted considerable attention by American planners, because it described what an urban neighborhood might be, and recommended some specific design guidelines for planning it.

THE TRADITIONAL DEFINITION OF THE NEIGHBORHOOD UNIT

A neighborhood unit is generally defined as a residential area in which:

1. An elementary school, with an adjacent park area, serves as the focus for the neighborhood. The school is used as a community center as well as for educational purposes.

2. The size of the neighborhood is limited in population to that which will produce an appropriate enrollment for the elementary school. The school may have one, two, three, or four classes per grade.

3. The physical size of the neighborhood is determined by walking distance from residences to the elementary school. No child should be required to walk more than 1/2 mile. (This results in neighborhoods having gross areas of about 160 acres.)

4. Boundaries of the neighborhood are clearly identified, and are often natural barriers (such as rivers and unbuildable areas) or man-made barriers (such as

arterial streets, railroads, regional parks, or other large areas of nonresidential land uses).

5. A variety of housing types may be present.
6. No major flows of traffic pass through the neighborhood.
7. Stores are located on the perimeter streets, and not within the area itself.
8. There are no large centers of employment within the neighborhood that attract workers from outside.

Figure 15.1 illustrates in a schematic manner the concept used to establish the physical size of a neighborhood, and an indication of how its boundaries might be delineated.

The concept of "neighborhood design" does not imply that all neighborhoods need to have a standardized composition of housing and other land uses. There can be neighborhoods in which the residential areas are

Figure 15.1. Schematic Diagram of a Neighborhood

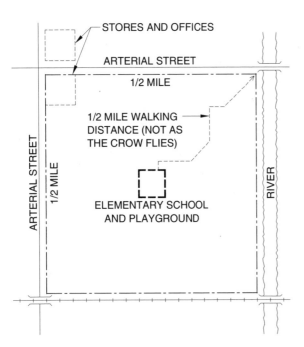

composed primarily of single-family homes; others may have a mix of single-family detached and townhouses; others may add some apartments; there may even be other mixes of housing types.

Nonresidential uses within a neighborhood are generally intended for the use and convenience of the neighborhood residents. It is important that they not generate significant traffic that will flow into the neighborhood from outside areas.

Table 15.1 provides some sample assumptions and calculations for four alternative types of neighborhoods. The table is for illustrative purposes only. Any table of actually proposed land uses would, of course, depend upon the design objectives of neighborhood development, appropriate assumptions of population characteristics, and location and features of the actual site.

REASONS FOR USING THE NEIGHBORHOOD CONCEPT

The major reason for advocating the neighborhood concept as a pattern for urban development in the past was that the design would provide a physical environment superior to that which would otherwise be built. (It appears that this goal has been attained, even though there is still room for substantial improvement in the design of neighborhoods.)

Some sociologists and urban planners have suggested that the residential pattern of the neighborhood would foster an increase in social contacts ("neighboring"). This, they said, would reduce the impersonal atmosphere that is found in many of our cities. (The degree to which this has come about in newly developed neighborhoods can be argued. It appears that increased *localized* "neighboring" does occur to some degree in sections of planned neighborhoods, but that this does not spread over wide areas.)

Table 15.1. Calculations for Prototype Neighborhoods

	Low Density	Medium Density	High Density	Very High Density
POPULATION				
Grades in K-6 school	7	7	7	7
Classes per grade	1	2	3	4
Children per class	30	30	30	30
Resulting school enrollment	210	420	630	840
Assumed % of children in school (percent)	90	90	90	90
Assumed children of age 5-11 per family	.50	.45	.40	.35
Resulting number of families	466	1,038	1,750	2,666
Assumed average family size	3.6	3.4	3.2	3.0
Resulting total population	1,678	3,529	5,600	7,998
AREAS REQUIRED				
Total area of neighborhood (acres)	160	160	160	160
Area for school (acres)	5	7	10	12
Area for parks (acres)	3	5	5	9
Area for commercial (acres)	3	3	4	5
Area for roads (25% of gross area) (acres)	40	40	40	40
SUBTOTAL nonresidential (acres)	51	55	61	66
Remaining residential lands (acres)	109	105	99	94
Average area per family (sq. ft.)	10,188	4,406	2,464	1,536
POSSIBLE HOUSING MIX (lot size per DU)				
0.459 acre (20,000 sq. ft.)	10 DU = 4.6 acre			
0.230 acre (10,000 sq. ft.)	456 DU = 104.9 acre			
0.115 acre (5,000 sq. ft.)		800 DU = 92.0 acre	150 DU = 17.3 acre	60 DU = 6.9 acre
0.0574 acre (2,500 sq. ft.)		238 DU = 13.7 acre	1,300 DU = 74.6 acre	1,000 DU = 57.4 acre
0.0230 acre (1,000 sq. ft.)			300 DU = 6.9 acre	1,000 DU = 23.0 acre
0.0115 acre (500 sq. ft.)				600 DU = 6.9 acre
Total residential area (acres)	109.5	105.7	98.8	94.2
Dwelling units per gross acre	2.9	6.5	10.9	16.7

• DU = dwelling units

POSITIVE FEATURES OF THE NEIGHBORHOOD UNIT CONCEPT

- Prior to the application of the neighborhood unit concept, a great many residential sections in American cities were being developed on the gridiron pattern. All of the streets in them were about equal in width and many carried quite a bit of through traffic; this created traffic and pedestrian hazards, and was also detrimental to the quality of the environment.

- In earlier times, perhaps not enough consideration was given to the relationship between schools and the location of the residence of their pupils. The neighborhood unit concept focussed public attention on this issue in the United States in the 1930s and, as a result, school planning markedly improved.

- Planned neighborhoods have included a variety of housing types in them to suit a variety of family sizes and life styles. This is in contrast to the spread of single-family subdivisions which are sometimes found flowing mile after mile in suburbia.

- Urban planners have found that the neighborhood serves as a convenient and usable building block for the development of new urban areas. It is possible to use neighborhood units to plan school locations as well as other public facilities such as parks, libraries, utilities, stores, and transit service.

- Residential neighborhoods, when planned, built, and established, provide their residents with a degree of certainty about the future of the area (they know that there will be no through traffic; they know where their children will go to school). This certainty appears to have engendered stability in residential areas.

- The neighborhood, when well planned, can be a safe and attractive place. It can do much to promote walking (or bicycling) from home to school, or to other locations in the neighborhood. This has potential benefits, among them environmental and energy conservation.

- The neighborhood concept is saleable in the real estate market; the public buys it.

- The neighborhood, when clearly defined on the ground, does give its residents the feeling that they have something in common with their neighbors. This "sense of neighborhood" is often expressed in the affairs of local government by spokespeople for neighborhood homeowners' associations. These neighborhood-based political activities do foster participation in local government, and this is generally regarded to be very beneficial.

- Neighborhood units form useful and easily comprehensible "building blocks" within general plans of cities and counties. Four or five neighborhoods may constitute a "community," and a number of communities may then constitute a city.

- Neighborhood plans are fairly easy to implement using Planned-Unit Development (PUD) sections of zoning ordinances.

- Advance planning of neighborhoods promotes the orderly development of a community. A jurisdiction can use its general plan, in which there may be a number of integral neighborhood plans, to budget the timing and location of public improvements (such as arterial streets and sewer line extensions), and thereby assure that the jurisdiction's development will be relatively compact and efficient, rather than in a leap-frog pattern which promotes urban sprawl and is less cost-effective.

CRITICISMS OF THE NEIGHBORHOOD UNIT CONCEPT

- The age composition of the population of urban areas fluctuates very markedly over the years. A neighborhood that may produce enough children to provide the enrollment for an elementary school in one year may yield many more (or far fewer) children 10 or 15 years hence. The neighborhood school concept will work if the size of the school can be made flexible; often, this is sometimes difficult to achieve, but not always impossible.

- There are other functions besides schools that have "service areas" such as libraries, shopping centers, parks, and churches. The size of the service areas for these is usually quite different than that of the elementary school. Therefore, what works for planning schools may not be appropriate for functions such as churches, libraries, and stores.

- In some cases, the neighborhood concept appears to have been used for populations composed primarily of families with school-aged children. When this has occurred, little consideration was given to the needs and desires of other segments of the population such as single people, childless couples, and retired persons.

- Low-density residential areas (such as those found in many neighborhood plans) are not conducive to the establishment or operation of metropolitan transit systems. As discussed in Chapter 12, mass transit systems are most feasible when they serve concentrated locations of passenger origins which are to be linked to compact clusters of destinations. Dispersed passenger origins, which are found in low-density residential areas, are usually served more conveniently by private automobiles than they are by transit.

- It is highly questionable whether the neighborhood unit, as defined in the traditional manner, with a population of between 1,500 and 8,000 people, actually does foster "neighboring." This concept may be an ideal that is fine in theory but may not take place in practice in areas as large as an entire neighborhood. It appears quite likely that small units of development (such as 20 houses clustered around a cul-de-sac) produce much more "neighboring" than do large neighborhood-sized developments, which may include a thousand or more dwelling units.

- In previous years, some neighborhoods built by private developers often had only one type of housing in them, which was then marketed within a narrow price range. This produced economic segregation and may well have contributed substantially to social and racial segregation.

- Neighborhood homeowners' associations, when representing the interests of a neighborhood in local governmental affairs, have frequently tended to be primarily oriented towards protecting the property values of the local homeowners. This viewpoint has often been quite conservative, and frequently overlooked the broader interests of residents, especially those of renters.

- The traditional definition of the neighborhood unit, described above, was developed more than 50 years ago. Times have changed since then, our urban and suburban life styles have changed, and the widespread availability of automobiles has modified our travel patterns. Furthermore, the advent of computers and telecommuting is bringing impacts which are as yet unknown to us. While it appears appropriate to retain the general concept of neighborhood units, we should not close our minds to possible changes in their design which would make them more suitable to our present and future ways of life.

NEIGHBORHOODS IN ESTABLISHED URBAN AREAS

It is recognized that neighborhoods do exist in already built-up urban areas, although they usually were not consciously planned as such in older cities (such as those built before World War II).

Neighborhood identity does occur in sections of established American cities, but neighborhood boundaries are often difficult to define because they are different for each topic of common concern (i.e., neighborhood boundaries drawn on the basis of bonds between the parents of elementary school-children may be quite different from those drawn on the basis of attendance at a particular church, or of some other common interest).

In older cities, neighborhoods may be defined on the basis of the ethnic background of the residents (e.g., "Chinatown," or "the Italian section"). It is probably true that the residents of these areas do have a number of interests in common, do have many close social ties, and do what is considered "neighboring" to some extent. One should enquire, however, how much of this ethnic segregation is by choice (and perhaps may be supported) and how much is based on past or present discrimination against the ethnic groups (and clearly should not be supported).

GENERAL PROCEDURES USED FOR NEIGHBORHOOD PLANNING

Planners usually design the city-wide framework within which residential areas are to be built (such as the location of arterial streets, schools, shopping centers, and employment centers). This design is then officially adopted by the local jurisdiction as its "General Plan."

Planners identify existing or planned future neighborhoods and identify their boundaries. This is not a trivial job to be undertaken with the stroke of a felt-tip marker pen; it requires careful review of existing social relationships, physical conditions, and goals for the future.

Planners, working with property owners and other interested citizens, prepare a *generalized* plan for each neighborhood. This plan indicates, in general terms, proposed land uses, and the location of major streets and transit routes. The plan also indicates the types and quantities of housing, and the general size and approximate location of nonresidential uses. It should be stressed that this type of neighborhood plan does *not* consider or specify the design of individual buildings, or provide site planning recommendations concerning them.

Private landowners have the design of the neighborhood (or a portion of it) in which they are interested prepared for them by qualified professionals (usually architects and landscape architects) working with civil engineers and planners, and done within the framework of the neighborhood plan.

Sometimes a public planning agency will prepare a plan for a "problem area." For example, the preparation of a neighborhood plan is appropriate when the stability of a residential area is threatened by the intrusion of nonresidential uses or vehicular traffic. Neighborhood plans are usually considered to be essential for urban renewal programs if residential areas are involved.

There is usually little urgency for the preparation of neighborhood plans for stable residential areas, especially when there are no issues concerning proposed changes in land use or circulation patterns in them.

NEIGHBORHOODS AND THE NEW URBANISM

During the 1990s, a new school of thinking about the design of metropolitan areas, cities, and neighborhoods developed, known as the "New Urbanism." Adherents of this school believe that American cities and their suburbs should be designed and built in a far better manner than they have been in the past. Their criticisms of the way these areas have been developed include these points:

- "Contemporary cities are built for the convenience of automobiles, rather than for pedestrians."
- "Most of our suburban areas are built with only a single type of housing (such as the detached, single-family home), rather than offering a choice."
- "The design of many of our suburbs results in sprawl, which isolates residents rather than promoting social contact. Suburbia lacks centers (such as schools, shops, and parks) where people can meet and interact."
- "There is a glaring lack of 'sense of design' in individual structures in our cities, and in the relationships among structures."

I wish to respond briefly to those four criticisms, speaking as an urban planner.

First of all, I generally concur with them; the statements appear to be quite justifiable, when applied to the forms of suburban development that we have witnessed during the past 40 years.

While it is true that we have seen many suburban areas develop in an unfortunate sprawling manner, not all of the urban and suburban development in the recent past has had those characteristics. There have been some bright spots, especially in the "new towns" that have been built. For example, Columbia (Maryland) and Reston (Virginia) are recognized as being both attractive and good places to live, as are a number of other more recent new towns such as Irvine (California), Foster City (California), and Waipio (Hawaii). The relevant point to be made here is that these cities were designed and built using the *neighborhood unit concept*, rather than as just large subdivisions.

"Cars vs. Pedestrians"

Concerning the observation that cities and suburbs are built for automobiles rather than for pedestrians, "New Urbanists" have said that urban planners, working with traffic engineers, have allowed the automobile to become dominant, and have given short shrift to pedestrians. It is true that automobiles are a dominant force in our current metropolitan areas. However, as long as we have many homes with two wage earners, as long as the place of employment of each of these wage earners may be anywhere in the metropolitan area, and as long as our metropolitan areas have low densities of housing and job locations, we are going to have to rely on automobiles for the vast majority of journey-to-work transportation. This means we are going to have a great many cars around.[1]

Cars cause many *metropolitan* transportation problems and problems in poorly designed suburbs, but they need not cause troublesome problems in well-designed *neighborhoods*. Yes, there will be a problem of storing cars, but they need not cause moving-traffic problems.

"Suburbs Composed of a Single Type of Housing"

Concerning the note that most of our suburbs have been built with only one type of housing (detached, single-family homes, for the most part), it must be admitted that this was quite true in the 1950s and '60s. The pattern that was set in that era will probably stay on the ground for at least the next 50 years. More recently, low-density apartments have appeared in suburbia, but we can't say that there has been much integration of various building types in a meaningful manner. To a great extent, land developers have targeted a single market (such as middle-income families with young children, or elderly people) and built for that group alone. Some of us hope that, with a new focus on neighborhood design, designers will develop plans which include a wider variety of housing types that are well related, and that are done in a manner which will earn the support of the general public.

"There Is Little Social Contact in Suburbia"

Concerning the statement that many of our suburbs tend to isolate their residents, it does seem to be true that many urban and suburban residents don't mingle with their neighbors as much as our parents and grandparents did.

A good part of their seclusion may be attributable to the changes in our life styles which have been made possible by "modern conveniences." To be more specific, people who have air-conditioned homes usually prefer to stay inside on hot days, rather than sit on their front porches and wave to their neighbors who stroll by. Our shopping habits have changed; we will often choose to drive 5 miles to a large, impersonal supermarket instead of going to a neighborhood store; neighborhood grocery stores, neighborhood butcher shops, and neighborhood bakeries are now virtually extinct, forced out of business by supermarkets.

Television has also affected our way of life. How many people stay indoors and rely on TV for their entertainment and distraction? Are we not becoming a nation of couch potatoes? (This is by no means an endorsement of that way of life; it is, rather, an observation that many people choose to stay inside their comfortable homes rather than go outside to exercise and socialize.)

Another point to be made is that telephones, automobiles, and e-mail have made it possible for us to keep in close contact with friends near and far. In the "olden days," our grandparents' circle of friends were primarily those with whom they had face-to-face contact; most of these people lived within a 5-mile radius. Today, our friends are those we choose; some of them may be nearby neighbors, but many of them may live far away.

It is true that some meeting places in neighborhoods (especially schools, churches, parks, and sports fields) do make possible (or even foster) social contact. This opportunity to meet people is certainly greater in places where these physical facilities exist (such as in well-planned neighborhoods) than it is where the facilities do not exist. However, we should not expect that just providing meeting places will automatically convert residents into sociable, communicative neighbors. Many people may still choose to leave the neighborhood in which they live to meet with friends who live elsewhere, go to church elsewhere, or participate in school activities that take place outside the neighborhood; this doesn't mean that they are socially isolated.

"There Is a Lack of a Sense of Design"

Concerning the comment that there is a lack of a "sense of design" in our cities and suburbs, much of this criticism can be attributed to a difference in the design philosophies of urban planners and architects. Most local jurisdictions (acting on the advice of urban planners) have adopted subdivision regulations and zoning ordinances which establish "building envelopes" within which landowners may build. These ordinances typically establish minimum lot sizes; minimum front, rear, and side yard requirements; maximum heights; and put limits on the intensities of use of the properties. Within these prescribed limits, there are usually no design restrictions. Urban planners are generally concerned with the large-scale, overall design of urban areas, but are not involved with the design or siting of individual buildings. (It is true that some planners, who have had training in architecture, do specialize in urban design, but they constitute a small minority of the profession.)

Architects, in contrast to urban planners, are directly involved with the design of individual buildings and groups of buildings. Because of this, some "New Urbanists" urge that the current building regulations (such as zoning and building codes) be repealed, and replaced by "design codes," which would include specific design guidelines and regulations, rather than relying on the "building-envelope" approach found in many municipal codes.

There is clearly a significant difference in the philosophy of design regulation between the two approaches described here. The urban planner's approach provides a great deal of freedom of design (within the building envelope, that is) for property owners. It must be admitted, however, that the resulting urban development has not generally produced buildings of great design quality and, in most urban areas, little or no attention appears to have been given to relationships among buildings, or between buildings and open spaces.

The approach suggested by some of the "New Urbanism" architects (i.e., establishing "design codes") would limit individual freedom to design and build structures to that which is preapproved in the design code or, perhaps, that which meets with the approval of a design review board. It is probable that the design-code approach would produce urban areas with more attractive buildings and superior site planning, but the trade-off would be a reduction in design freedom available to property owners.

NEW URBANISTS USE THE NEIGHBORHOOD CONCEPT

"New Urbanists" have incorporated the basic neighborhood concept as an organizing principle in their designs. One example of this can be found in the recommendation by the Duany/Plater-Zyberk firm for the use of a "traditional neighborhood development" (TND) pattern, with neighborhoods ranging in size from 40 to 200 acres. Another example is the Calthorpe firm's variation of neighborhood design in their "transit-oriented development" (TOD) pattern. This consists of a neighborhood of 120 acres, which is located on a transit route, and has high-intensity land uses (such as offices, retail centers, and high-density housing) at its center.

CONCLUSIONS

Old as it is, the neighborhood planning concept is still being used to good effect when planning large, new residential areas. It has been consistently used when planning new towns over the past 30 years and is currently being used, with some modifications, in a number of "New Urbanism" designs. If it were to be applied in its original form, it would present some problems, especially in the area of school planning. However, the basic concept does appear to be adaptable for use in many contemporary situations when planning new towns or planning large residential subdivisions.

Note

1. A review of Table 11.1 on page 125 will indicate how significant the growth of two- and three-car households has been between the years 1969 and 1995.

Recommended Reading

Kaiser, Edward J., David R. Godschalk, and F. Stuart Chapin, Jr. *Urban Land Use Planning*. 4th ed. Urbana, IL: University of Illinois Press, 1995. See Chapter 14, "Residential Areas," pp. 341-367.

Levy, John M. *Contemporary Urban Planning*. 4th ed. Upper Saddle River, NJ: Prentice-Hall, 1997, pp. 158-163.

Sources of Further Information

American Public Health Association, Committee on the Hygiene of Housing. *Planning the Neighborhood*. Chicago: Public Administration Service, 1948. This early work really defined the concept of neighborhood, as used in urban planning, for many years. The statistics used in the book are now very out of date, but the basic ideas in the text are worth reviewing.

Bookout, Lloyd W., Jr. *Residential Development Handbook*. 2nd ed. Washington, DC: Urban Land Institute, 1990, pp. 141-152.

Calthorpe, Peter. *The Next American Metropolis*. New York: Princeton Architectural Press, 1993.

Downs, Anthony. *Neighborhoods and Urban Development*. Washington, DC: The Brookings Institution, 1981. This excellent book focuses on established urban neighborhoods. It discusses the causes of neighborhood decline, as well as factors that add to their stability and their revitalization.

Jarvis, Frederick D. *Site Planning and Community Design for Great Neighborhoods*. Washington, DC: Homebuilder's Press, 1993.

Jones, Bernie. *Neighborhood Planning*. Chicago: APA Planners Press, 1990.

Katz, Peter. *The New Urbanism*. New York: McGraw-Hill, 1994.

Keller, Suzanne. *The Urban Neighborhood: A Sociological Perspective*. New York: Random House, 1968.

16

Street Design in Residential Areas

INTRODUCTION[1]

In urban development we observe a wide range of lanes, roads, streets, and highways. Most prominent are the freeways, which criss-cross the United States, and provide essential transportation links to our many metropolitan centers. Within our metropolitan areas we have freeways, expressways, and major arterials that provide access to the many subparts of each urban region. This section of the text is not going to talk about that regional ("macro") scale structure; it is going to deal with local ("micro") scale streets which serve local residential areas. These streets often occupy 25 to 30 percent of the land area in those residential districts and have, throughout history, had the greatest durability of all the components of the city.

BASIC RESIDENTIAL STREET SYSTEMS

There are four basic residential street systems which are used to serve residential areas in the United States:

1. the grid system
2. the altered grid system
3. the radial system
4. the linear system

The Grid System

The grid pattern of streets is probably familiar to everyone who has seen an American city. It consists of a series of parallel streets which are crossed at right angles by another series of parallel streets (see Figure 16.1).

Figure 16.1. The Grid System of Streets

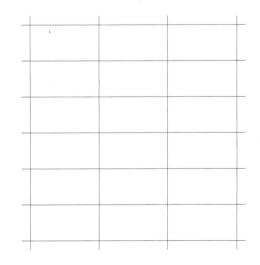

This has resulted in the creation of many rectangular blocks of land. In some cities, these blocks are very large; in some others, they are quite small.

The grid system of dividing property was used as the basis of "public land surveys" by the U.S. government, starting in 1812. This system divided public lands by defining "parallels" running east and west, spaced 24 miles apart, and "meridians" running north and south, also spaced 24 miles apart. The resulting blocks of land were further divided into "townships," which were grids measuring 6 miles by 6 miles. These were further divided into "sections," which were grids measuring 1 mile by 1 mile. In many parts of the country, roads have been built along these section boundaries, creating a basic grid pattern of roads. Many sections of land have been further divided, continuing on with the grid pattern.

The grid system of roads has been continued, sometimes based on the old public land survey boundaries, and sometimes independently from it.

The grid system has some advantages when it is used in urban areas at the *macro* scale. When a grid of major roads is established, it provides a clearly visible (and easy to comprehend) organizing framework. (This is truer for metropolitan areas that are built on gently sloping lands than it is for areas that are disrupted by a scattering of mountains and valleys.) This clearly apparent framework makes it relatively easy for people to navigate between major sections of metropolitan areas. Many communities have adopted the grid system for their macro transportation framework, often with the distance between major grid streets measured in miles.

The grid system has also been widely used at the *micro* scale for locating local streets and establishing city blocks, but the effects have not been as satisfactory as they are at the macro scale.

When applied to the micro residential scale, the grid pattern presents some problems. Among these are:

- The system allows vehicular traffic to use any and all of the streets in it for direct through passage; none of the streets in a gridded city is immune from the impacts of this traffic.
- It is difficult to apply in terrain with grades over 5 percent.
- It is quite wasteful of land area.
- It is visually monotonous.
- The four-way intersections, which are always present in the grid pattern, have a relatively high accident potential. (Four-way intersections have demonstrated a substantially higher accident rate than do three-way "T" intersections.)

If the streets in a grid system are undifferentiated, each one has the potential of becoming a high-volume traffic carrier in the future. Additionally, if all streets are built to accommodate high traffic volumes, logic leads us to believe that they all must have a wide paving width and right-of-way (ROW). This could be very wasteful.

The grid system does have a few advantages when applied to the micro residential scale:

- It is easy to approach a residential area from any direction.
- It is easy to orient yourself in a grid system (that is, it is difficult to become lost).
- It is easy for land developers and surveyors to lay out.

Even with these advantages, the disadvantages of the grid system are now considered to significantly outweigh its advantages. Although the grid system was the most common street system used at the beginning of

Figure 16.2. The Curved Grid System	Figure 16.3. The Blocked Grid System
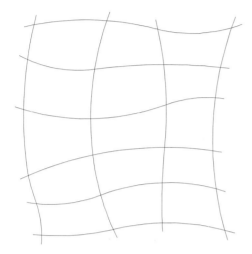	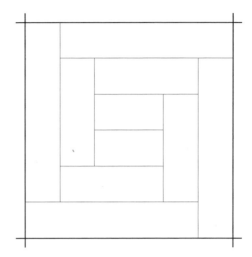

the 20th century, few residential areas have been developed with this street system since the late 1930s.

Some of the "New Urbanists" (see Chapter 15) advocate that the grid pattern of roads be used in some neighborhood designs, but with the following modifications:

- The size of blocks in the gridiron pattern of streets should have a minimum length of 250 feet, and a maximum length of 600 feet.

- Streets that carry heavy volumes of traffic should not pass through neighborhoods.

- Grid streets should be designed for the convenience of pedestrians. While these streets may also be used by automobile drivers to provide access to sites within the neighborhoods, they should be designed to minimize and slow the movement of motor vehicles.[2]

The Altered Grid System

The altered grid system consists of three sub-systems:

1. the curved grid system
2. the blocked grid system
3. the "curved and blocked" grid system

The altered grid plans shown in Figures 16.2, 16.3, and 16.4 tend to relieve the visual monotony of the pure grid system.

The curved grid system has most of the advantages and disadvantages of the conventional grid system. Its one advantage is that it does not have built-in visual monotony.

Both the blocked grid and the "curved and blocked" grid patterns not only relieve the visual monotony, but also result in some specialization of streets. It is usually difficult for traffic to pass through the center of neighborhoods in a city that has developed in this pattern, so it travels on the perimeter arterial streets, leaving the residential uses in the interior undisturbed. These patterns also slightly reduce the amount of land required for streets. Both the blocked grid and the "curved and blocked" grid systems also greatly reduce the number of four-way intersections, because they generally use three-way "T" intersections inside the macro-grid framework.

Figure 16.4. The "Curved and Blocked" System

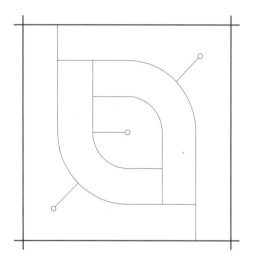

A number of cities have transformed their traditional grid street patterns into a blocked grid pattern by installing various types of impediments to traffic flow along selected streets or at selected intersections. Some of these are illustrated in Figure 16.5. The report, "Traffic Calming" by Cynthia L. Hoyle, deals with this general topic and appears to be the definitive work on the subject at this time.

Methods that are sometimes used to reduce the amount and speed of traffic in established residential areas include the following:

- install diagonal traffic diverters
- install traffic circles
- install right-turn-only traffic diverters
- convert selected streets to cul-de-sacs
- install speed bumps (humps in the roadway that are uncomfortable and dangerous to pass over at high speeds)
- install rumble strips (raised dots in the roadway that produce a loud noise in a car as it drives over them)
- install chicanes (curved sections of a roadway created by building partial bar-

riers or parking bays on alternate sides of the street)[3]
- narrow the entrances to selected streets at intersections
- convert streets to "woonerfs"[4]
- designate selected sections of a street for 60- or 90-degree, on-street parking, often on alternating sides of the street

These measures have been very effective in reducing the flow of traffic through the middle of some residential neighborhoods. They have, however, often made it difficult for visitors to navigate to their destinations within a neighborhood.

The Radial System

The radial street system, in its theoretical form, consists of a number of access streets radiating from the head of a collector street; the foot of the collector street connects with an arterial street. This is illustrated in a schematic manner in Figure 16.6.

When using the radial system, the access streets branch off from the collector street at various locations rather than at one central point, thus avoiding a concentration of turning movements. There are often branches off the branches in the radial street system (see Figure 16.7).

With the trunk of the branching system terminating at an exterior arterial street, and with no through traffic on the branches, street components can be sized to accommodate relatively low volumes of traffic. The result is that area developed for streets can be reduced considerably below that of the grid or the altered grid systems. The radial street system described above has a drawback: it creates many long dead-end streets. For safety reasons,[5] it is desirable to limit the distance from the tip of the furthest local access street to the point where the trunk empties onto a perimeter arterial street. Some jurisdictions limit this

Figure 16.5. Traffic Diverters in a Grid Pattern of Streets

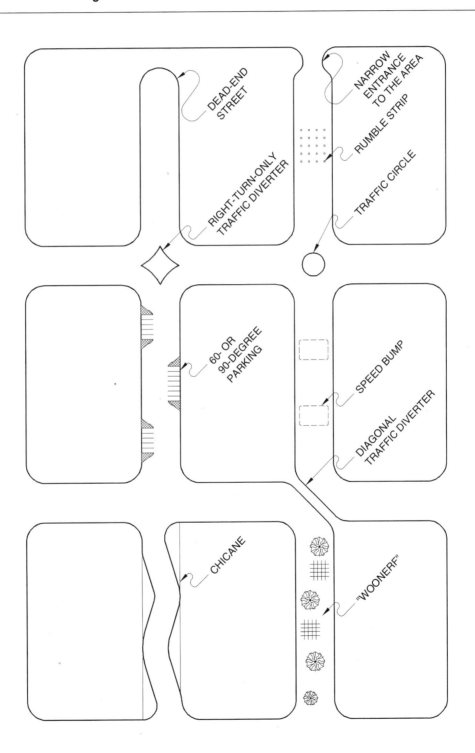

DEAD-END STREET

NARROW ENTRANCE TO THE AREA

RUMBLE STRIP

RIGHT-TURN-ONLY TRAFFIC DIVERTER

TRAFFIC CIRCLE

60- OR 90-DEGREE PARKING

SPEED BUMP

DIAGONAL TRAFFIC DIVERTER

CHICANE

"WOONERF"

to 1,000 feet [300 meters]; many others limit it to 500 feet [150 meters].

In their book, *Residential Streets*, ASCE-NAHB-ULI state that, in general, the length of a cul-de-sac should be determined by traffic volume and the number of housing units. They point out that, assuming traffic on a cul-de-sac should not exceed 200 vehicle trips per day and each dwelling unit generates 10 trips per day, a cul-de-sac should accommodate a maximum of 20 to 25 houses.[6]

Limitations on the length of cul-de-sacs have led to a further variation of the radial street pattern: the end of a selected street in one radial development is connected by way of an emergency access road to a street in an adjacent development. (See Figure 16.8.) This access road is for the use of emergency vehicles only, and is not available for use by the general public, so residents are not bothered by through traffic on their streets.

The radial street patterns described above are generally used only for low-density, single-family home subdivisions.

**Figure 16.6. Theoretical Form
of the Radial Street System**

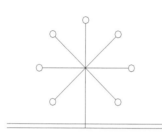

**Figure 16.7. Radial Street System
With Branching Access Roads**

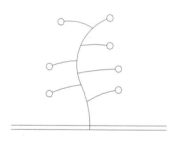

**Figure 16.8. Variation on the Radial Street System:
Use of an Interconnecting Emergency Route**

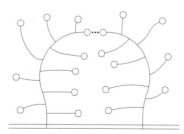

The Linear System

We can identify three types of linear street systems:

1. the "City Beautiful" system with meandering streets and a park-like setting
2. hillside streets which generally follow the contours of the terrain
3. a linear collector street which serves as a spine of the circulation system and has access streets feeding into it

The City Beautiful system of residential streets was strongly influenced by the designs of Frederick Law Olmsted, perhaps starting with his design for Central Park (New York City) in 1858. Subdivisions following that design approach were intended to create a park-like setting with graceful, curving streets (with spiral curves) and, more importantly, with a clear separation between local residential traffic and through traffic. This design approach is still used occasionally for very low-density, single-family subdivisions which are intended for wealthy families.

A second form of the linear street pattern is found in hillside areas, where the grid pattern just won't work satisfactorily. Here, the street locations are very strongly influenced by the topography, and their grades rarely exceed 15 percent. It is important to have a framework

Figure 16.9. Linear Street Pattern in the Hills of Northern Berkeley (California)

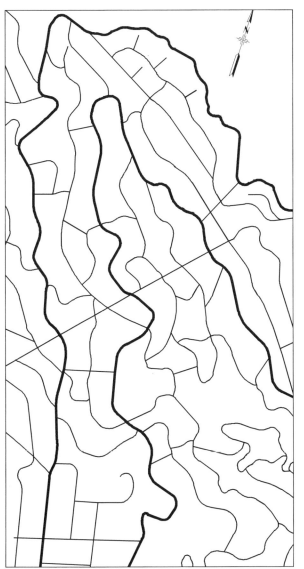

of arterial and collector streets so that the access streets will carry only small volumes of traffic. Because of the economic cost of road construction in hillside areas, street standards are often modified there. Hillside subdivisions are generally designed for low- to low-medium density, single-family homes. This street system generally precludes the construction of higher residential densities which would generate excessive traffic loads on narrow access streets.

Figure 16.9 is an illustration of hillside development in Berkeley (California). Note the presence of arterial streets. (The east-west straight line in the center of the map is Marin Avenue, which was intended as the site for a cable car line; it has a very steep grade indeed; the cable car was never installed.)

Another form of the linear street system is perhaps best described as a theoretical concept in which a spine (consisting of a collector street) has traffic fed into it from ribs, which are in the form of local access streets. These access streets may be loop streets or cul-de-sacs. The collector streets may feed into arterial streets on the perimeter of the development. This pattern is shown schematically in Figure 16.10.

This general pattern is suitable for relatively level land rather than steep hillside areas. It is generally desirable to have curves in the collector streets so that traffic on them won't travel at excessive speeds. The perimeter arterials may be straight or curved. The pattern is adaptable to single-family homes and even low-density apartment developments, if care is taken in the sizing of the streets.

Figure 16.10. Schematic Diagrams of Possible Linear Street Subdivision Patterns

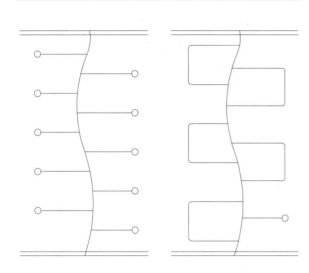

Figure 16.11. Shapes of Conventional Blocks

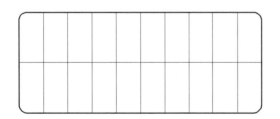

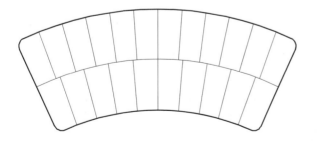

BLOCK TYPES

There are two basic types of residential blocks:

1. the linear block
2. the superblock

Linear Blocks

The typical linear block results from the application of the grid street system or the altered grid street system. It is usually characterized by having a uniform block depth, which is equal to the depth of two lots placed back to back.[7] There are no specific limits on block length, but the usual practice is to limit them to about 1,000 feet [300 meters]. The blocks can be rectangular, curved, or irregular in shape (see Figure 16.11).

Superblocks

The superblock is usually a large tract of land which has the following characteristics:

- It is bounded by arterial streets.
- Access to the lands within the block is by way of loop streets or cul-de-sacs.
- No streets pass directly though the superblock.
- It has an internal pathway system which provides convenient pedestrian access to most of the areas within the block.
- The primary land use within the block is residential; these uses may be in a variety of building types.
- Nonresidential uses (such as schools, parks, libraries, and convenience shopping facilities) are often included in the block for the convenience of the residents.
- Nonresidential uses (such as office buildings, institutions, and regional shopping centers) that attract residents from outside the superblock are generally not permitted.

Figure 16.12 is a sketch of a superblock in Radburn (New Jersey).

Figure 16.12. A Superblock in Radburn, New Jersey

This design, by Clarence Stein and Henry Wright, was a pioneering effort undertaken in 1928; it was the first superblock development built in the United States. Even today, superblocks still apply the general guidelines (outlined above) that were set forth at that time.

A word of caution concerning superblocks that incorporate residential areas which directly abut parks or common greens that are accessible to the general public: In three California communities that have used this design feature, most of the adjacent residents strongly dislike it. They point out that when any and all members of the general public have access to the open spaces, not all of them are well behaved. They also point out that these semienclosed open spaces are usually difficult for the police to patrol. In consequence, most of the adjacent property owners have erected substantial fences (without gates) between their properties and the common greens. This problem does not appear to be prevalent in "planned-unit developments" (PUDs) which include privately owned common greens from which the general public may be excluded.

Superblocks probably range in size from 20 acres [8 hectares] to as much as 160 acres [65 hectares]. The superblock pattern has been used extensively in new towns and in PUDs.

TYPES OF RESIDENTIAL STREETS

Residential street types fall into four general categories:

1. linear streets, in the grid pattern, which are plain, straight streets
2. linear streets, in the nongrid pattern, which are curving, winding streets
3. loop streets, which are those that leave a street (such as a collector), go into an area to be served, loop around, and return to the same street on which it originated
4. cul-de-sac streets,[8] which are commonly known as "dead-end streets"

All residential street patterns are composed of these street types, or combinations of them.

Loop streets are the most efficient residential access streets, in terms of dwelling units served per unit of street area, for single-family dwelling unit sites. They are more efficient than cul-de-sac streets (unless the cul-de-sac is less than 150 feet [50 meters] in length).

Loop streets that are no more than 500 feet [150 meters] long are the only access streets that can be advantageously planned for one-way traffic. Their shortness precludes inconveniences, and the direct return to the original street minimizes confusion.

There are a number of alternative designs used for the closed end of cul-de-sacs. Some of these are shown in Figure 16.13.

The bulb turnaround is the most frequently found end of a cul-de-sac. AASHTO recommends that the minimum radius for the outer edge of the pavement should be 10 meters [33 feet] in residential areas, but 15 meters [50 feet] in commercial and industrial areas where large vehicles are often present. Ten meters [33 feet] of paving makes quite an expanse of concrete, so some street designers

**Figure 16.13. Alternative Designs
for Ends of Cul-De-Sacs**

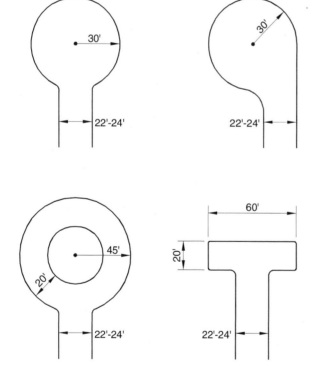

Source: ULI–Urban Land Institute, 1025 Thomas Jefferson St., N.W., Suite 500W, Washington, DC 20007-5201. *Residential Streets.* 2nd ed., pp. 50-51. Used with permission.

recommend islands in the centers of cul-de-sacs; this is visually more attractive, especially if the island has plants maintained in it. AASHTO notes that if an island is placed in the end of a cul-de-sac with a small radius, it should have mountable curbs so that the occasional large truck can turn around. The "T" end for a cul-de-sac is not recommended for residential areas because it requires vehicles to back up in order to turn around. Backing vehicles in areas that may have small children present is not a desirable practice.

Figure 16.13, reproduced from the ASCE-NAHB-ULI book, gives recommended minimum dimensions in feet for cul-de-sac turnarounds; these dimensions are not appropriate for commercial or industrial areas. The end with the offset bulb is easier for drivers to use than the one with the symmetrical bulb, because drivers have one less steering wheel reversal to make. On the other hand, the symmetrical style of bulb is considered by some to be more pleasing to the eye.[9]

RESIDENTIAL STREETS

As described in Chapter 8, there are six classifications of streets used in urban areas. These are:

1. freeways
2. expressways
3. arterials
4. collector streets
5. subcollector streets
6. access streets (such as loop streets and cul-de-sacs)

Arterials, expressways, and freeways are all nonresidential streets, and will not be discussed further in this chapter.

Access streets and subcollector streets are commonly used to provide direct access to low-density residential uses. Collector streets should not be used to provide access to scattered low-density uses, but they may be used to provide access to concentrated urban developments such as apartment clusters, employment centers, and shopping centers.

DESIGN GUIDELINES FOR ACCESS STREETS AND SUBCOLLECTOR STREETS

In residential areas, access streets are intended solely to give access to abutting, low-density residential uses such as single-family homes, duplexes, and townhouses. Access streets are not intended to carry through traffic; subcollector streets should carry very little. The design speed of these streets should be as low as practicable because the streets are sometimes adjacent to concentrations of small children.

Design Speed

Access streets and subcollector streets are designed for movements of 20 mph [30 km/h]. This is a practical compromise between the 0 mph of parked cars and the 25 to 35 mph [40 to 55 km/h] movement on collector streets. Street design should encourage 15 mph [25 km/h] traffic speeds, but be geometrically safe at 20 mph [30 km/h]. Recommended design speeds are given in Table 16.1.

Table 16.1. Recommended Design Speeds for Access Streets, Subcollector Streets, and Collector Streets

Street Type	Terrain Class		
	Level (mph)	Rolling (mph)	Hilly (mph)
Access street	20	20	20
Subcollector	20	20	20
Collector	35	30	25

Source: Reprinted with permission from the publisher, ULI–The Urban Land Institute, 1025 Thomas Jefferson St., N.W., Suite 500W, Washington, DC 20007-5201. *Residential Streets.* 2nd ed. p. 43.

Horizontal Geometry

- Access and subcollector streets should be laid out as near to parallel or perpendicular to one another as possible to assure a maximum number of rectangular building sites.

- The access and subcollector street patterns must preclude use of these streets for through traffic, "shortcut" traffic, and traffic that is avoiding congestion on nearby collector or major streets.

- Straight sections of level streets that are more than 500 feet [150 meters] long will generate traffic speeds in excess of 20 mph [30 km/h]. Because of this, no straight section of any street intended to carry local traffic should be more than 500 feet [150 meters] in length.

- Curves on access and subcollector streets should have a centerline radius of at least 100 feet [30 meters], but no more than 200 feet [60 meters]. Curves of a radius that is less than 100 feet [30 meters] will not be safe at 20 mph [30 km/h]. Curves of a radius that is more than 200 feet [60 meters] will generate traffic speeds in excess of 20 mph [30 km/h]. (See Table 16.2.)

Table 16.2. Desirable Range of Centerline Radius for Access, Subcollector, and Collector Streets

Street Type	Curve Radius	
	Feet	Meters
Access	100-150	30-45
Subcollector	150-300	45-90
Collector	300-500	90-150

Source: Reprinted with permission from the publisher, ULI–The Urban Land Institute, 1025 Thomas Jefferson St., N.W., Suite 500W, Washington, DC 20007-5201. *Residential Streets.* 2nd ed. p. 46.

Vertical Geometry

- As a general rule, access and subcollector streets should not exceed 12 percent grade (although a maximum grade of 8 percent is preferable) where ice and snow will never exist.[10] An 8 percent maximum grade should be observed where winter icing is possible.
- Access streets must be provided with a running grade of at least 0.5 percent for positive surface drainage of storm waters and snow melts.
- Where streets intersect, a street grade of no more than 5 percent (3 percent is more desirable) should exist on each leg of the intersection within 50 feet [15 meters] (100 feet [30 meters] is more desirable) of the intersection of the street centerlines.

Street and Block Length

- The block length resulting from an access street pattern is immaterial, although a maximum block length of 1,000 to 1,600 feet [300 to 500 meters] is commonly accepted.
- Single-access streets (cul-de-sac streets lacking emergency vehicle connections at their ends) should generally be no more than 1,000 feet [300 meters] long. Some jurisdictions limit them to no more than 500 feet long. Longer dead-end streets may be acceptable in low-density subdivisions. As mentioned earlier in this chapter, it is more reasonable to limit the length of a residential cul-de-sac based on the number of dwelling units on it rather than specifying a maximum length for all cul-de-sacs.

Intersections

- Streets should not intersect in such a way as to result in four-way intersections, except where at least two legs of the

Figure 16.14. Minimum Distance Between Street Intersections

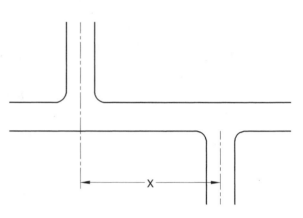

X = at least 150 feet [45 meters] for roads carrying low traffic volumes
X = at least 250 feet [75 meters] for roads carrying high traffic volumes

intersection are short loop or cul-de-sac streets which have little potential for creating cross-intersection traffic.

- Intersections of streets should be at least 150 feet [45 meters] apart, centerline to centerline, for low-volume access streets. For streets that carry higher volumes of traffic (such as collector streets), a separation of centerlines of 250 feet [75 meters] may be more appropriate. (See Figure 16.14.)
- As a general rule, all streets should intersect at 90 degrees. Where a 90-degree intersection angle is impossible, angles of 75 to 90 degrees are acceptable. Under no condition should any street intersection angle of less than 60 degrees be provided.

DESIGN GUIDELINES FOR RESIDENTIAL COLLECTOR STREETS

Collector streets, as the name implies, collect traffic from residential access and subcollector streets, and lead it to arterial streets. The design speed for collector streets is usually 25 to 35 mph [40 to 55 km/h], as they serve local through traffic.[11] These speeds are transitional between the 20 mph [30 km/h] speed of access street traffic and the higher travel speeds of 40 to 45 mph [65 to 72 km/h] for arterial streets.

Although on-street parking on streets carrying through traffic increases the accident potential, decreases traffic speed, and decreases road capacity, many urban collector streets provide parallel parking lanes, where an adequate ROW is available.[12]

Single-family homes, duplexes, row houses, and low-density apartment residential uses should not have direct access from a collector street. The only residential uses that should be provided with direct access from a collector street are high-density, multistory apartment developments on large sites. These uses should be provided with just a few entrance locations, preferably with entrances at least 800 feet apart (centerline to centerline) and at least 800 feet from any other intersecting street (centerline to centerline).

Curves on collector streets should have a centerline radius of no less than 250 feet [75 meters] (except in hilly terrain), but no more than 500 feet [150 meters]. The 250-foot [75-meter] radius is the smallest radius that is geometrically safe at 35 mph [55 km/h]. Radii over 500 feet will generate traffic speeds in excess of 35 mph.

CLEAR SIGHT DISTANCE

Whenever a street intersects a street of higher order in the hierarchy of streets, traffic on the lower order street should be made to stop or yield.[13] It is essential that vehicle drivers entering the higher order street have an unobstructed view of traffic using that street. This means that there should be no visual barriers in what is known as "the clear sight

triangle." Figure 16.15 illustrates the location of this triangle.

Dimension X shown in the diagram should be at least 20 feet [6 meters]. For intersections in which an access street or a subcollector street intersects with a collector street, dimension Y should be at least 300 feet [90 meters]. If the street being intersected is a subcollector, dimension Y should be at least 200 feet [60 meters].

RESIDENTIAL STREET/ LOT RELATIONSHIPS

Property lines of residential lots should be perpendicular to straight street sections and radial to curved street sections. This results in ease of surveying and a maximum number of lots that approximate a rectangular shape, which results in the most efficient lot use.

It is desirable to have side and rear property lines of adjacent residential lots meet at

Figure 16.15. Clear Sight Triangle for Collector, Subcollector, and Access Street Intersections

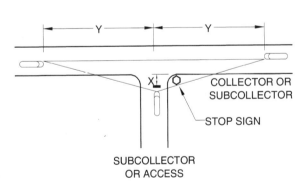

CLEAR SIGHT DISTANCE TRIANGLE
X = 20 feet
Y = 300 feet on collectors
Y = 200 feet on subcollectors

Source: ULI–Urban Land Institute, 1025 Thomas Jefferson St., N.W., Suite 500W, Washington, DC 20007-5201. *Residential Streets.* 2nd ed., p. 73. Used with permission.

common points, to minimize the number of surrounding properties that abut any one property.

Street spacing must reflect the site needs of dwelling unit types and densities. A block width of 200 to 240 feet [60 to 75 meters] between ROW boundaries might be fine for single-family homes at a density of from 4 to 7 DU/ac [1.5 to 3 DU/hectare], but would produce building sites that are unreasonably small for apartment developments at 80 DU/ac [32 DU/hectare] or for single-family homes at 1/2 DU/ac [0.2 DU/hectare].

Residential development built in areas with terrain of over 15 percent slope may require double street frontage (one lot that lies between two streets). This is because:

- Houses built on downhill slopes are often more desirable than those at uphill locations.
- It is easier to construct a house on a downhill slope (i.e., materials handling is easier).
- It is easier to drain wastewater from a house to a sewer located in a downhill street than it is to pump it into a sewer located in an uphill street.
- It is usually easier to develop vehicular access to properties that lie below a street than it is from a street that is at the bottom of a steep lot.

When double-frontage lots (i.e., lots which abut streets in both front and back) are platted in hillside areas, it is good practice to prohibit vehicular access to them from the street which provides the most difficult access.

Where residential uses are planned to abut types of streets that do not permit direct access for those residential uses, a marginal access road may often be provided, or the lots may be oriented in such a manner as to have their rear lot lines abut the road with no provision for access. This results in double street

frontage for these lots. Where this device is used, lots are often made deeper than is common, and construction of a solid wall or fence separating the residential site from the road at the rear lot line is made mandatory. (Refer to Figure 18.5.)

GENERAL GUIDELINES FOR RESIDENTIAL STREET DESIGN

- It is generally desirable to minimize the total length of road, the area of paving, and the total area of street right-of-way in residential areas. This has economic advantages to both the land developer and the local jurisdiction. Remember that land area in right-of-way donated by the developer to the municipality is not taxed and must be maintained, policed, and repaired at public expense.
- It is desirable to minimize the number of intersections between streets originating in a residential area and the perimeter streets bordering it. Remember that at least two access points to each pocket of residential area should be provided for safety reasons. However, even most large superblocks will need no more than six access points to adequately serve the residential traffic load.
- Four-way intersections in the interior or at the perimeter of a residential area should be avoided, except at two facing cul-de-sac or loop streets which produce minimal cross-traffic.
- Steep road grades should be avoided wherever possible. Steep grades result in the confusion of unskilled drivers and in high earthwork costs.
- When two adjacent, large residential areas are not separated by a collector or arterial street, it is desirable to provide at least one minor street to connect the two areas. This is needed for the convenience

of the small amounts of traffic that may flow between these areas.

- All curves on access streets should be segments of circular arcs that are tangent to straight road sections connecting curves. (Spiral curves may be appropriate for very low-density subdivisions.)
- Remember that service and delivery vehicle travel patterns should be efficient. Provide for convenient routes for services such as garbage trucks, letter carriers' trucks, and police cars.
- Access to each lot in a residential area from perimeter streets should not be unduly circuitous.
- Avoid streets that are diagonal to the contours on grades over 8 percent slope because such development results in increased foundation costs and creates cut-and-fill problems in the provision of street access.
- When laying out streets to "follow the contours," remember that the street must have a minimum grade of 0.5 percent for drainage purposes.
- Remember that the overall physical order of a residential development must be clearly evident from street and pedestrian paths, or no sense of visual order will exist.
- Wherever possible, create visually identifiable residential subareas (small areas of "our street" that can be identified by more ways than just the street name).

PARKING IN SUBDIVISIONS

Residential areas require parking space for the cars of residents and their visitors. Zoning regulations usually specify how much off-street parking must be provided for each dwelling unit. The number varies from two off-street spaces per DU for low-density suburban subdivisions, to 1/2 space per DU for

apartment units that are well served by public transit. These zoning provisions are intended to take care of the normal, day-to-day parking demand of the residents; they almost never adequately consider the parking needs of visitors.

Visitor parking is usually provided in the form of parallel parking along the street curb. This on-street parallel parking is usually accommodated by providing a continuous, 7-foot-wide, paved parking lane adjacent to the travelled lane in the street. This parking may be on one or both sides of the street. When this type of parking is provided in residential areas, a space 22 feet long should be allowed for each car (although 20 feet of length is adequate for "end stalls").

Note that 70-foot-wide residential lots for homes fronting on an access street result in provision of two (not three) on-street parking spaces per DU. This is because about 20 feet of curb space in front of the DU must be used for a driveway leading to the off-street parking area (or garage) on the property. If parking is provided on just one side of the street, only one parking space per DU is the result. On-street, parallel parking is expensive to provide because it must be paved to the same high construction standards as the street travel lanes. This type of parking also results in expensive (and often ineffective) street cleaning and snow removal.

On-street parking in bays may be provided directly adjacent to street travel lanes, and may be at 60, 75, or 90 degrees to the centerline of the street. Since vehicles entering or leaving on-street bays interfere with the flow of traffic on the street, this form of parking should be used only on streets with low traffic volumes. This form of parking is usually less expensive to build than on-street parallel parking because the number of spaces provided can be scaled to the demand, and the spaces can be inexpensively paved. These spaces may be public (provided totally within the public ROW) or private (provided on the abutting private property). Unfortunately, parking bays of this type are very difficult to sweep or to remove snow from.

Parking areas should not be located within "clear sight triangles" at intersections, or on the inside curb line of street curves which have a centerline radius of less than 150 feet [45 meters]. Parking of all types should have finished slopes of less than 5 percent grade. They should also have finished grades of at least 1 percent slope, in order to provide adequate drainage.

Guidelines for the design of off- and on-street parking areas are provided in Chapter 11.

Notes

1. Laurence C. Gerckens was the original author of this chapter, but I have modified it substantially. Mr. Gerckens should not be held responsible for errors or omissions.

2. Blocks in the conventional grid pattern of streets are often 400 to 600 feet in length; occasionally, they are 1,000 feet long.

3. An extreme example of a gridiron street converted to a chicane can be found on Lombard Street in San Francisco, where the paved street twists its way downhill. Unfortunately for the local residents, the street is so intriguing to tourists that it has stimulated traffic flow rather than discourage it.

4. Woonerfs are streets that are for the primary use of pedestrians and bicyclists, although slow-speed vehicular traffic is allowed to weave its way through them. They were originated by the Dutch; they are described further in Lynch and Hack (pp. 199, 203, 204), and by Hoyle (p. 14).

5. In some circumstances a street can be blocked by flooding, snow, a fallen tree, or even a fire. This is often considered to be an acceptable risk if only a few residences are located on a long, dead-end street, but it becomes unacceptable when many homes are located there.

6. ASCE-NAHB-ULI, pp. 54, 55.

7. An exception to this rule is found when a block includes buried "flag lots." These are described in Chapter 18.

8. Their name comes from the French, and means "bottom of the sack."

9. For further information on the design of cul-de-sac turnarounds, see ASCE-NAHB-ULI (pp. 49-51) and AASHTO (pp. 443-335).

10. See also Table 10.8.

11. See Table 16.1.

12. AASHTO, p. 474.

13. ASCE-NAHB-ULI, p. 73.

Recommended Reading

Lynch, Kevin and Gary Hack. *Site Planning.* 3rd ed. Cambridge, MA: MIT Press, 1984. See Chapter 7, "Access," pp. 193-221.

Sources of Further Information

[AASHTO]—American Association of State Highway and Transportation Officials (AASHTO). *A Policy on Geometric Design of Highways and Streets.* Washington, DC: AASHTO, 1994.

[ASCE-NAHB-ULI]—American Society of Civil Engineers, National Association of Home Builders, and the Urban Land Institute (ASCE, NAHB, and ULI). *Residential Streets.* 2nd ed. Washington, DC: Urban Land Institute, 1990.

Hoyle, Cynthia L. "Traffic Calming" (Planning Advisory Service Report No. 456). Chicago: American Planning Association, 1995. This report deals with techniques to reduce vehicular traffic in residential areas. It discusses, among other topics, traffic diverters and one-way streets.

Kone, D. Linda. *Land Development.* 8th ed. Washington, DC: Home Builder Press (National Association of Home Builders), 1994. See Chapter 8, "Residential Streets."

17

The Subdivision Process

BACKGROUND

Many states allow local jurisdictions (such as cities and counties) to enact and administer subdivision regulations. These regulations set forth the procedures to be followed for the review and approval of a subdivision, and usually establish the development standards that must be met. The state laws relating to subdivisions are often titled something like "The Subdivision Map Act." The local laws are generally called "Subdivision Regulations" of such-and-such a jurisdiction. These local regulations are usually more detailed than are the state requirements, and are tailored to fit local needs and standards. Anyone who engages in the land subdivision process should be familiar with both the state and local regulations.

While residential subdivisions are probably best known to the general public, there are other kinds as well (such as subdivisions to create office parks, industrial areas, and sites for other nonresidential uses). In fact, most states require that a subdivision plan be prepared and approved whenever one parcel of land is divided into a number of new parcels. (Many states have established the creation of four new parcels as the triggering point that requires the formal subdivision process.)

WHY WE HAVE SUBDIVISION REGULATIONS

The need to regulate the development of subdivisions became evident when it was found that the dictum of "let the buyer beware" did not satisfactorily protect individual land buyers or the interests of the general public.

The general purposes of subdivision regulations are to:

- assure that lands divided and sold as "building sites" are, in fact, suitable for the intended purposes (that is, not submerged properties off the coast of Florida nor plots of land in the California desert far from roads and water)
- assure that suitable and agreed-upon, on-site improvements, such as roads and utilities, will be installed
- assure that reasonable and equitable contributions will be made by the subdivider for off-site improvements, the need for which is generated by development of the subdivided lands (which may be facilities such as off-site roads, off-site schools, off-site parks, off-site sewage disposal facilities, and downstream flood protection structures)
- assure that accurate surveys of the properties are prepared and recorded, and

that survey monuments are accurately installed.

- establish a method of property descriptions (such as lot and block numbers) which will provide accurate, economical, and convenient legal descriptions of properties that are sold or transferred
- assure that fraudulent practices will not be used in the division, sale, or transfer of properties
- assure that lands will be developed in accordance with the general plans adopted by the local communities
- assure that "the public health, safety, and welfare" will be protected

THE LAND SUBDIVISION PROCESS

The subdivision process is often long and complex. In most cases, it is initiated under the sponsorship of a land developer who owns (or has an option to purchase) a tract of land.

The land developer should have on their staff, or should contract with, appropriate professionals to participate in the following phases of the land subdivision process:

- market analysis
- subdivision design (such as the design of land uses, streets, utility systems, and site grading; and the layout of lots and blocks)
- site development (grading and installation of streets and utilities)
- building construction
- public relations
- marketing and sales

The subdivision design process usually consists of three distinct phases. The first phase is the preparation of a "preliminary subdivision map," which is a draft subdivision plan indicating what the land developer wishes to do. Most, but not all, jurisdictions require the preparation and review of this map as an integral part of the subdivision process. The preliminary map may be prepared by anyone who has some basic design skills, and who has knowledge of the local government's subdivision requirements and review procedures. It should be remembered, however, that if the very first concepts of the subdivision are dull and pedestrian, this may set the tone for later design studies. Although amateurs and novices are allowed to prepare preliminary subdivision maps, it is likely that the land developer would be better served by skilled designers at this critical stage.

The second phase is the preparation and formal review of a "tentative subdivision map." This is a substantial refinement of the "preliminary map"; it shows in greater detail what the land is to be used for, how it is to be divided, and what improvements (such as streets and utilities) are to be installed.

The professional qualifications required for those who prepare tentative subdivision maps vary from state to state. Official requirements aside, many of us hold the view that, especially on large subdivisions, a team of people with a variety of skills is desirable. Engineers and surveyors are certainly essential, but they may benefit from contributions that landscape architects, urban planners, architects, soils engineers, attorneys, environmental review specialists, and other professionals can make.

The tentative map is usually reviewed by the local planning commission, and may be approved, approved subject to specific conditions, or denied by them. Once approved, it represents a commitment on the part of local government to approve the final subdivision map, if it is substantially in compliance with the tentative map, and the subdivider meets the conditions of approval that were specified. The tentative map, if approved, is valid for only a limited time span (usually one, two, or three years). The developer, in many states, is permitted to request an extension of time for the tentative map. The validity of the tentative map usually lapses if the subdivider does not file for the approval of a "final map" prior to the expiration date of the tentative map. Approval of the tentative map does not commit the developer to proceed with the subdivision; they have the option of dropping the subdivision or proceeding with it.

The third phase is the preparation, review, acceptance, and recordation of a "final subdivision map." This is a precisely engineered map that describes in specific detail the boundaries of the blocks and lots that are to be created. Accompanying this final map are agreements and (usually) bonds that guarantee the installation of the agreed-upon improvements. This map must be officially approved by the local legislative body and recorded in its official records. Final subdivision maps are usually prepared by registered civil engineers and/or licensed land surveyors.

A SUMMARY OF THE SUBDIVISION DESIGN PROCESS

Here, in brief, are some of the steps that are often included when a subdivision is being planned. The work involved in Phase I will be discussed at greater detail later in this chapter.

Phase I: Preparation of a "Preliminary Subdivision Map"

1. Make a *site analysis.* This involves examining the characteristics of the site such as slope, drainage, vegetation, existing structures, and zoning. It also includes review of conditions in the surrounding area that may influence the development of the site such as nearby land uses, land values, population characteristics, road access, and availability of utilities.

2. Identify the *goals of the land developer.* What type of development do they wish to build? How many dwelling units are they seeking?

3. Review the general plan and zoning regulations of the local jurisdiction. What future development do they show for the property?

4. Talk with staff people in the local planning and engineering offices. What opportunities do they see for development of the property? Of what limitations (physical, economic, or political) to its development are they aware?

5. Make one or more *concept plans* of possible site development. Select the best one, or the best parts from several plans, for further refinement.

6. Develop the selected concept plan into a *preliminary subdivision map* by showing major and minor streets, major grading required, improvements to be installed, etc. Lot lines should be sketched in so that you can make a count of the approximate number of dwelling units that the development will yield.

7. Make preliminary *cost estimates* of developing the subdivision.

8. *Review the preliminary map with the land developer.* Does it represent what they are looking for? Do the preliminary cost estimates indicate that it will be financially feasible?

9. If the preliminary map appears to show a feasible and desirable subdivision, *review it with appropriate agencies* in local government. If the map is not feasible or desirable, go back to Step 3, or perhaps to Step 2, and start again.

Phase II: Preparation of a "Tentative Subdivision Map"

1. *Consider the comments on the preliminary map* received from the agencies and the people who reviewed it. These comments may:

   A. improve the design of the subdivision;

   B. make it more politically acceptable locally;

   C. clarify the procedural steps needed to get approval of the tentative map; or

   D. be so demanding as to make the subdivision financially infeasible.

2. *Assemble (or have prepared) appropriate maps and data* concerning the site. (Much of this may have been completed in the situation analysis section of the preceding phase.)

3. Transform the preliminary subdivision map into a revised and more *precise subdivision map*. Show in greater detail the land uses, streets, lot lines, utilities to be installed, and grading of the site.

4. *Prepare impact analyses* of the revised plan such as environmental impacts, traffic impacts, and effect on the local economy. (This step may not be required in some jurisdictions.)

5. Make accurate *estimates of the development costs* based on the revised plan.

6. Make an *economic feasibility analysis* based on the cash flow anticipated from development costs and financial returns from sales or leases. If the subdivision is found to have financial problems, make revisions to the design of the project.

7. *File the tentative map* with the appropriate governmental agencies for review and approval.

Figure 17.1 is an example of a tentative subdivision map.

Phase III: Preparation of a "Final Subdivision Map"

In most states, the preparation of final subdivision maps is restricted to work by registered civil engineers or licensed land surveyors. It involves preparation of maps that are both accurate and precise. Fortunately, computer programs, linked to computer graphics, now make this task far easier than it was a few years ago. An example of a final subdivision map is shown in Figure 17.2.

A MORE DETAILED REVIEW OF PHASE I: PREPARATION OF A "PRELIMINARY SUBDIVISION MAP" (as applied to a residential subdivision)

Make a Site Analysis

A site analysis is an essential part of the subdivision design process; it will enable you to anticipate what type of development the site can support. It should also inform you about potential problems with the site, thereby letting you avoid nasty surprises in the future.

A site analysis is concerned with the site itself, its immediate environment and, to some degree, the entire jurisdiction in which the site is located.

Site analysis consists of gathering information about the site and its environment, and analyzing it. The topics that are usually appropriate for inclusion in a site analysis are listed below. Most of the subjects are needed for the preparation of a good preliminary subdivision map. It should be recognized, however, that sometimes a land developer does not yet own the site of the proposed subdivision, but has only an option to buy it. If this is the case, they will be reluctant to spend money on new surveys. It is true that, in some

Figure 17.1. An Example of a Tentative Subdivision Map

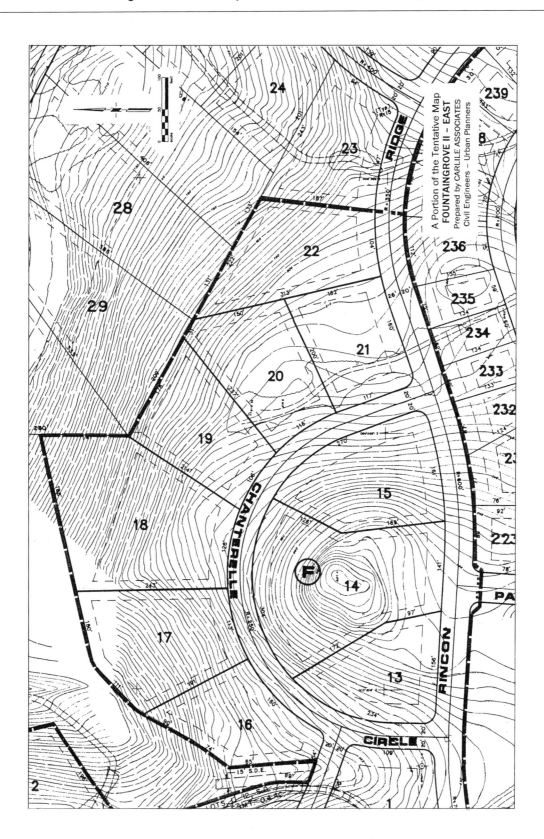

Figure 17.2. An Example of a Final Subdivision Map

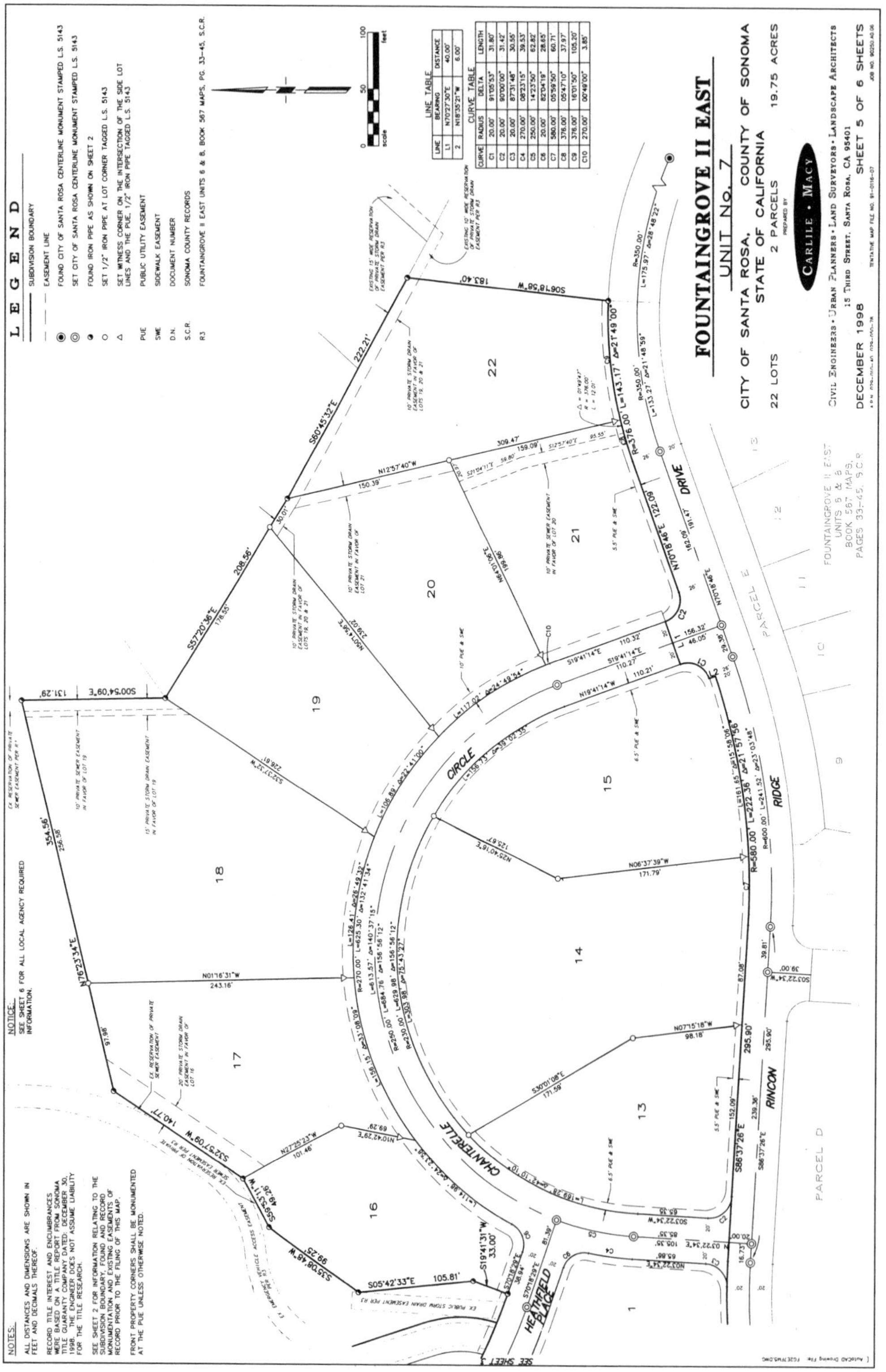

cases, some of the surveys listed below may be postponed until the tentative map stage. Therefore, be very careful that surveys which determine the basic feasibility of the subdivision are not omitted.

Basic information concerning the site

- *Legal description and map of the property.* You need to be sure just where the boundaries of the property are. You should also review a copy of the title report on the property to ascertain if there are any easements over the land (and, if they exist, where they are), and any deed restrictions which may limit how the property may be used.
- *A topographic map of the property.* Note that all maps of the site should usually be at the same scale. If the land developer already owns the land, it would benefit them to have an accurate topographic map prepared, at an appropriate scale (such as 1 inch = 200 feet). If the developer does not yet own the land, in some cases an enlargement from a USGS topographic map may be sufficient for use in preparing a *preliminary* subdivision map. (These enlargements are very definitely *not suitable* for preparing tentative maps.)
- *Aerial photographs of the site.* These should be at the same scale as the topographic map.

Physical conditions of the site

- *Slope map.* You should prepare one (see Chapter 3 for preparation procedures).
- *Location and analysis of existing structures on the property.* Which appear to be candidates for retention and which for removal? Are any of them registered historic buildings?
- *Map of utilities on the site.* Show utilities such as water supply lines, sewer lines, storm sewers, telephone lines, and electric power lines.
- *Soils map of the site.* The U.S. Department of Agriculture's Soil Conservation Service has prepared soils maps of many parts of the country. See if they have one which includes your subdivision site.
- *Soils analysis of the site.* It may be important to have a soils report made of the site in order to identify any potential soils problems. If your subdivision will rely on septic tanks for sewage disposal, it is *essential* that soils testing be done and percolation tests be made in some potential building sites. (See Chapter 5.)
- *Geologic report of the site.* If the site is in an area that may have geologic hazards (such as earthquakes or landslides), a report prepared by a recognized engineering geologist may be a very good investment.
- *Drainage analysis.* Identify wetlands (areas that are permanently or seasonally covered with water). Identify drainage channels and flowing streams. Review available history of flooding on the property.
- *Vegetation analysis.* Prepare a map of vegetation on the site. (The appropriate degree of detail for this map will vary from site to site.) A generalized map can be prepared using data from aerial photographs, augmented by on-site inspection.
- *Climatological data.* It may be useful to collect information on climate (such as rainfall, snowfall, and seasonal temperatures). Some of this information will be needed when the storm drainage system of the subdivision is designed. When you come to the tentative map stage, you may wish to have an investigation made of the microclimates of the site, if you are working with a very large subdivision.

Inspection of the site

If you are granted access to the site, it is important to make an inspection of it, in person. Don't rely on topographic maps, aerial photographs, or the impressions and recollections of others as your only sources of site information.

- *Walk the site.* Don't just drive around the perimeter of the site in a car; get out and hike around on the site in order to get a good feel for it.
- *Mark the location of notable features on a map of the site.* This could include rock outcroppings, areas with attractive views, and wooded areas. Note especially the areas that may be difficult to develop or verge on being unbuildable. If there are streams or seasonal watercourses, make a note of them on your map.
- *Take some photographs of the site.* These will be useful later on when you are back in the office and are trying to remember details about the site.

Off-site factors

- *Utilities which serve the site.* Map the location of these off-site utility lines and get information on their capacities. Get information on how much reserve capacity they have which may be available for use by your proposed subdivision.
- *Identify the location, capacity, and existing traffic flow on roads that are important for access to your subdivision.* Do they have enough reserve capacity to accommodate traffic that will be generated by your subdivision?

Some of the following topics may be more appropriate for the Market Analysis people on your land developer's team to investigate, rather than for you to worry about.

- *Land uses in the vicinity of your site.* What are they? Will they be compatible with the land uses planned for your site?
- *Housing in the vicinity of your subdivision.* What is its general character? What is its condition? What is the typical sales price?
- *Shopping centers.* Where are they? Will they attract the residents of the new subdivision? Should the subdivision include new shopping facilities?
- *Community facilities* (such as schools, libraries, hospitals, and parks). Where are they? What are they like? Are they conveniently located for use by the potential residents of your subdivision? Will it be desirable (or required by the local jurisdiction) to have some new community facilities located on the site of the subdivision?
- *Public transportation.* Do any transit routes serve the subdivision site? How can design of the new subdivision take advantage of this service?

Regulations to be reviewed

- *Zoning of the property and the lands surrounding it.* What land uses are presently permitted? If it is appropriate to request that the zoning be changed, what are the procedures to be followed? How long does the process take?
- *General plan of the community.* How are the site and nearby properties depicted in the general plan? Are there any recommendations in the plan that would influence the planned future use of the site? If it is appropriate to request that the general plan be amended, what are the procedures to be followed? How long does the process take?
- *Subdivision regulations.* What steps are required in the subdivision review proce-

dure? What documents are to be submitted at this step? How long does the subdivision review procedure take?

- *Are any sites or buildings on the property on the National Register of Historic Places,* or on a similar state register?
- *Are there any wetlands on the site* that would be subject to Section 404 of the Clean Water Act of 1977?
- *Is the site a habitat for any endangered species?* Is the site therefore subject to the Endangered Species Act of 1973?
- *Have any hazardous wastes been deposited on the site,* so that it may now be subject to the Resource Conservation and Recovery Act (RCRA) and the Comprehensive Environmental Response, Compensation and Liability Act (CERCLA)? Are there any buried fuel tanks on the property that may be leaking?
- *Is any of the site in a flood zone,* and therefore subject to the National Flood Insurance Act of 1966, which is administered by the Federal Emergency Management Agency (FEMA)?
- *Is the site subject to coastal zone regulations,* under the Coastal Zone Management Act of 1972, or by state regulations?
- *Will residential construction on the site be subject to a state or metropolitan planning agency's fair-share housing allocation program?*
- *Will impact reports (such as environmental, traffic, and economic) be required?* Which agencies require them? How long a period of time must be provided for public review and comment?

Review the Goals of the Land Developer

You need to have a clear understanding of what your client's goals are. Your developer, after consulting with their market analyst, may have decided on one or more of the following goals:

- Maximize financial profit.
- Build an attractive, ecologically sound development that will be well respected by the local community.
- Build a gated community that will attract the high-income, socially elite crowd.
- Provide affordable housing for middle-income families.
- Provide subsidized housing for low-income families.
- Provide a range of housing types and prices for a wide range of buyers.
- A mix of some of the above.
- None of the above.

Prepare Concept Plans

- Review the site data and conditions (presumably you have just done this) .
- Review the goals of the developer (presumably you have just done this, too).
- Identify potential design concepts.
  — Show the location of major streets and arterials that appear to be essential for the development. These will probably be dictated by the external street pattern and topography of your site.
  — Identify the housing types you are going to consider.
  — Identify the basic pattern for the placement of the residences. Will they be on cul-de-sacs or on loop streets? To do this, you are going to decide on a basic type of residential street pattern (cul-de-sacs or gridiron).
  — Consider what nonresidential uses (if any) are appropriate (and may be mandated by local regulations) to include in the plan. These may include such facilities as schools, parks, convenience shopping areas, and other community facilities. (See

Chapter 20 for a discussion of planning for community facilities.)

- Prepare a sketch plan showing the major circulation routes and land uses. The depiction of land uses need not be detailed but may be shown in somewhat amorphous blobs.

- Estimate the potential yield of the site in dwelling units. This is done by measuring the area of each blob of land use (in acres) and multiplying its area by the number of dwelling units per acre (DU/ ac) for the type of housing being proposed in that blob. (Note that measuring blobs of land uses will give you only approximations. Later on, when you prepare a preliminary subdivision map, you will need to make much more specific estimates, which will be needed to estimate financial feasibility and for compliance with local regulations.)

- Select a small area to use as an illustration of the type of development possible. In this prototype area show the block and lot lines, and the placement of typical buildings.

- It is recommended that you make studies of several alternative design concepts so that you and your client can consider the advantages and disadvantages of each.

- Review the alternative concept plans with the land developer. They will possibly wish to review the alternative plans with the people who will be doing the marketing of the development.

Transform the Selected Concept Plan into a Preliminary Subdivision Map

- Design all the major streets and arterials. Carefully show their alignments and profiles.

- Add the local streets that will serve the residential areas.

- Draw in all lot lines to get an accurate count of the probable number of dwelling units the site will yield.

- Identify which areas will need to be graded, and make a preliminary calculation of the amount of cut and fill that will be required.

- Make a preliminary design of the major elements of the utility systems that will be required such as trunk sewers, major water mains, and major storm drains. (It is not necessary to show the service lines to individual lots.)

Prepare Cost Estimates Based on the Preliminary Subdivision Map

This cost estimate should be generally accurate, although not necessarily precise in detail. The estimate is to be used by the developer to ascertain whether or not the subdivision appears to be financially feasible. If the cost estimates indicate that an excessive investment would be required when compared with anticipated revenues, then a redesign of the subdivision at this stage is indicated.

Review the Preliminary Map with the Developer

Review the preliminary subdivision map and the cost estimates with the developer, and with other members of the development team. It is quite possible that suggestions for modification of the design will be made, in order to make it less costly to develop or more suited to the current real estate market. You will, of course, revise the map as needed and appropriate.

Review the Revised Preliminary Subdivision Map with Local Agencies

The local agencies will probably include the planning commission, the city (or county) engineer, and perhaps engineers from local utility companies.

It is up to the land developer to consider when and how to discuss the plan with special interest groups and the general public.

UNDERTAKING PHASES II AND III

Phase II: Preparation of a "Tentative Subdivision Map"

The job of preparing a tentative map consists of refining the general design of the subdivision, and doing the necessary engineering analysis and design. This is the stage of the subdivision process that really benefits from the application of basic design skills and imagination.

Phase III: Preparation of a "Final Subdivision Map"

The preparation of a final subdivision map is primarily a job for experienced civil engineers and land surveyors.

Recommended Reading

Bookout, Lloyd W., Jr. *Residential Development Handbook.* 2nd ed. Washington, DC: Urban Land Institute, 1990. See Chapter 5, "Plan Preparation and Processing"; read pp. 193-230; pp. 231-254 are optional.

Sources of Further Information

Colley, Barbara C. *Practical Manual of Land Development.* 3rd ed. New York: McGraw-Hill, 1998. See Chapter 3, "Site Analysis," and Chapter 4, "Maps and Plans."

Katz, Peter. *The New Urbanism.* New York: McGraw-Hill, 1994.

Kone, D. Linda. *Land Development.* 8th ed. Washington, DC: Home Builder Press (National Association of Home Builders), 1994.

Lynch, Kevin and Gary Hack. Site Planning. 3rd ed. Cambridge, MA: MIT Press, 1984. Suggest review of Chapter 9, "Housing."

18

Single-Family Subdivisions

STREETS SERVING SUBDIVISIONS

Streets constitute a defining framework for residential areas, which is clearly visible to all. Chapter 8 reviewed "the hierarchy of streets." That text described a variety of types of streets and identified their functions. A brief review of the subject is provided below, with emphasis on how these roads are used to serve subdivisions.

Freeways are intended for high-speed traffic between major segments of metropolitan areas or for interregional travel. No access to adjacent properties is permitted from freeways. They are not intended to carry local traffic and they are noisy. It is preferable to have no residential uses within 1/4 mile of freeways, because of the noise pollution and the air pollution from engine exhausts.

Expressways are streets which are intended to carry substantial amounts of through traffic. Their function is somewhat similar to that of freeways, but they often have at-grade intersections and do not have completely restricted access from adjacent properties. Access from major activity centers is usually permitted if it is properly engineered. Access to individual residences is always prohibited except in case of extreme hardship.

Arterial streets are intended to carry traffic between communities and activity centers, and to connect communities and activity centers to freeways and expressways. Access to adjacent properties is usually permitted only to major traffic generators such as shopping centers, office centers, or major apartment complexes. Parking is usually restricted along major arterial streets. Access to single-family homes from arterials should always be prohibited for three reasons:

1. Turning movements into and out from single-family homes would be seriously disruptive of traffic flow on the arterial.

2. The residents of single-family homes would run a relatively high risk of collision when turning into or out from their properties.

3. The residents would probably be very discontented with living adjacent to a busy street, and would probably complain (justifiably) about the dangers and nuisances they have to endure.

Collector streets are principal traffic arteries within commercial or residential areas. As such, they often carry high volumes of traffic between arterial streets and local access streets. They are intended as distributors of traffic, rather than as routes for through traffic. Parking along collector streets is usually restricted or limited. Traffic entering collector streets is often required to stop at stop signs; it is occasionally regulated by traffic signals. Access from collector streets to major traffic generators is usually permitted, but access to single-family residences should generally not be allowed.

Subcollector streets provide for the passage of traffic between collector streets and access streets. Subcollectors are intended to carry a low volume of traffic. Like the access street, it may provide access to some residential lots.

Access streets, as the name implies, are intended to provide access to adjacent properties. They should be designed to carry no through traffic. The low volume of local traffic that they do carry should move at low speeds. Parking along access streets is usually permitted. Examples of access streets are cul-de-sacs, loop streets, and streets in a blocked-grid pattern.

Another form of access street which should be mentioned is the "woonerf" (a form of street that was developed in the Netherlands and is used in some of their larger cities). It is designed to be shared by pedestrians, bicyclists, and slow and cautiously moving motor vehicles. The roadway for motor vehicles is usually quite narrow and winding.[1]

SOME GENERAL GUIDELINES CONCERNING STREETS IN SUBDIVISIONS

Review of the characteristics of the types and functions of streets above can lead to some generalized guidelines for subdivision design:

- Keep through traffic out of residential neighborhoods. The subdivision designer should make it convenient for traffic to pass around residential areas, and diffi-

cult (or impossible) to pass through them.
- Create a sense of visual organization in the street system. It should be relatively easy for strangers to comprehend how the street system is organized, so that they can easily find a destination, and then find their way back to the collector street and arterial street system.
- Design access streets to promote slow vehicular speed (15 to 20 mph is appropriate). This can be done by avoiding long, straight stretches of road including curves, corners, and cul-de-sacs, and making the access roads quite narrow.
- Provide adequate sight distances along all streets and at intersections.
- Avoid steep road grades, if possible. Make sure that adequate sight distances are provided on vertical curves.
- Remember that service vehicles must have good access to residential areas and individual residences. Consider the drivers' needs for garbage trucks, moving vans, fire engines, mail carriers, ambulances, and police cars. This implies that adequate turnaround spaces should be provided at the ends of dead-end streets, and generous turning radii should be provided at turns and corners.
- *Never* allow direct access to single-family homes from an arterial street or a collector street.
- Provide access to a single-family home from a subcollector street only if you are sure that the street will never carry a significant volume of traffic.

BLOCK AND LOT PATTERNS FOR SUBDIVISIONS

Designers who are preparing a "concept plan" or a "preliminary subdivision map" for a specific site have probably:

- Reviewed the characteristics of the site itself (such as slope, vegetation, existing development, and available utilities) and of the area surrounding the site.
- Conceptualized the development believed to be appropriate for the site. From this it is probable that a concept has been developed for the appropriate size of the blocks and lots (e.g., very large blocks for conventional, low-density uses; small blocks and lots for higher density residential uses such as townhouse developments; small blocks for the "New Urbanism" concept of development).
- Reviewed the relationship of the site to nearby freeways, expressways, arterials, and collector streets.

Now is the time for designers to ask several questions:

- How is the site going to be accessed by the community? Would it be appropriate and desirable for any of the nearby streets to extend into or through the site?
- Is the site large enough to develop as a "neighborhood" or as a significant part of a neighborhood? (See Chapter 15.)
- Does the land developer insist on a conventional subdivision, or will they consider some nontraditional development patterns?

The next steps are to:

- Locate the major street pattern that will form the basic circulation system for the site (that is, show arterials and collector streets).
- Establish the basic block pattern. A review of Chapter 16 will identify these major alternatives:
  — superblocks
  — gridiron pattern (unsuitable for hillside terrain)
  — altered-grid pattern (also unsuitable for hillside terrain)
  — radial
  — linear

The last two patterns utilize nongrid collector street or subcollector streets, with cul-de-sac and loop streets attached.

In establishing the block pattern design, compromises have to be made among these goals:

- maximum yield in number of building sites
- maximum "environmental charm"
- minimum disruption of existing important trees
- minimum development cost
- maximum traffic safety
- minimum "visitor confusion"
- maximum pedestrian convenience
- creation of a human-scale development with a variety of housing types (as proposed by the "New Urbanists") versus the application of the traditional development patterns which produce rather homogeneous subdivisions

BLOCK SIZES AND SHAPES

Block length is usually determined by convenience to pedestrians (if blocks are too long, pedestrians may have to walk very circuitous routes, unless pedestrian cut-throughs are provided). Block length often ranges from 400 to 1,200 feet. Local subdivision ordinances often specify maximum block lengths.

Minimum block lengths are rarely specified in subdivision ordinances, but short blocks require extensive road construction; they are therefore quite uneconomical.

Block width is usually determined by the depth of individual building lots. Typically there are two lots, back to back, in a block. If each lot is 150 feet deep, then the width of the block becomes 300 feet.

CONVENTIONAL LOT SIZES AND SHAPES

Low-Density, Rural Residential Lots

The typical area of these lots might be 10 acres or more. The length of frontage a lot has on a road is not very important for lots of this size. More important is the relationship of the building site to natural features such as creek frontage, open fields, and stands of trees.

Medium-Density, Single-Family Residential Lots

The typical lot size might be from 5,000 to 20,000 square feet. The frontage a lot has on a street is usually important, and the minimum length is usually specified by local subdivision ordinances. Lots should have a width that makes them usable for a typical house, with adequate side yards.

Lot depth should be about two or three times the lot width in order to provide private, open space on the lot for the residents.

Each lot should have some relatively level area that can be used for "outdoor living" by the occupants of the house.

Row House and Townhouse Development

Lot width is determined by the design of the structure that is planned to go on it. If 25-foot-wide row houses are planned, the individual lots should be 25 feet wide.

For row houses, the depth of each lot is equal to the depth of the front yard, plus the building depth, plus the depth of the rear yard.

Townhouses, as defined in Chapter 13, typically have a row house-type structure, but the homeowners share condominium ownership of facilities that are provided in common (such as landscaped areas in the front and back of townhouses, parking areas, and recreation areas).

Figure 18.1. Flag Lots (or "Panhandle Lots")

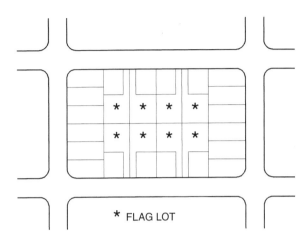

The size of an individually owned townhouse lot is usually equal to the depth of a small front yard (large enough for an entryway), plus the depth of the building, plus the depth of a small, private, rear yard.

Townhouse design requires the provision of adequate sites for the buildings, and very careful design of the common areas.

NONCONVENTIONAL LOTS

Flag Lots (or "Panhandle Lots")

Flag lots (shown in Figure 18.1) are usually buried in a block behind conventional lots. These nonconventional lots often have a street frontage that is just wide enough to provide an adequate driveway from the public street back to the building site. Flag lots are usually created as a means of utilizing land that might otherwise be left undeveloped; their use allows a subdivider to increase the yield of building sites in a subdivision.

The building site of a flag lot is usually made relatively large in size (i.e., larger than the adjacent conventional lots) in order to make an attractive setting for a house. Flag lots can provide very desirable environments if they are developed with skill and taste. On the other hand, they have the potential of being considered undesirable "leftovers" if the building site lacks privacy, or is so small and cramped that it is impossible to build an attractive home on it. It is quite possible that flag lots became popular in America during the era when coach houses were divided off from large, old mansions, and used as quaint living quarters for small families.

Pie Lots

Pie lots (shown in Figure 18.2) are often platted at the curves of subdivision streets, and have the general form of a slice of pie.

Pie lots on the outside of a street curve have narrow street frontages; those on the inside of

Figure 18.2. Pie Lots

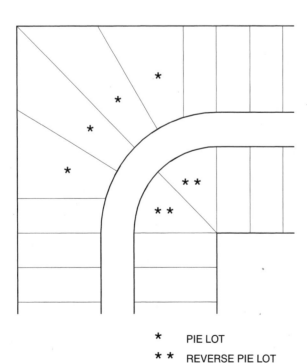

*	PIE LOT
* *	REVERSE PIE LOT

the curve have wide frontages and are sometimes called "reverse pie" lots.

Most jurisdictions establish minimum lengths of street frontage for pie lots, in order to provide space for driveways, off-street parking, and attractive entrances to the houses that will be built on the lots.

It is often desirable to provide more land area in reverse pie lots than is found in conventionally shaped lots, in order to provide private and usable rear yards for the occupants of the houses built on them.

Zero-Lot-Line Lots

There are some advantages to building single-family homes with one of their exterior walls immediately adjacent to one lot line. This pattern eliminates a narrow and usually unusable side yard on one side of the house, and requires that the other side yard be quite wide and thereby more attractive and usable.

The side of the house that is adjacent to the lot line usually has no windows or other openings in it, in order to protect the privacy of the occupants of the adjacent house (and to comply with local building code requirements).

It is necessary to provide an easement over a narrow strip of the adjacent lot which will permit the homeowner to maintain the wall of the house that is on the shared property line. Houses built on zero-lot-line lots (shown in Figure 18.3) should be especially designed so that they do not suffer from the requirement of having one windowless wall, and so that they can take advantage of the side yard which is wider than usual.[2]

"Z" Lots

In the 1980s, some land developers utilized a subdivision pattern in which individual lots had a shape somewhat similar to the letter Z (see Figure 18.4). They found that they could develop more attractive and usable rear yards

Figure 18.3. Zero-Lot-Line Development

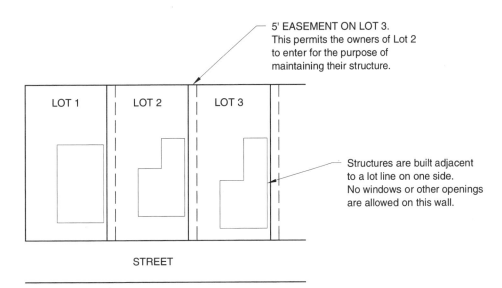

5' EASEMENT ON LOT 3.
This permits the owners of Lot 2
to enter for the purpose of
maintaining their structure.

Structures are built adjacent
to a lot line on one side.
No windows or other openings
are allowed on this wall.

**Figure 18.4. "Z" Lots With
Zero-Lot-Line Development**

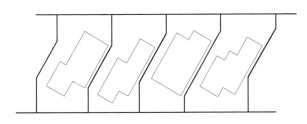

for their houses while at the same time achieving a somewhat higher residential density. In some cases, they utilized zero-lot-line housing; in other cases, they used conventional house design. Experimentation with this lot pattern continues in some areas today.

Double Frontage Lots

A double frontage lot (shown in Figure 18.5) is one which has frontages on streets at both the front and rear property lines. (Lots backing on alleys are not generally considered to be double frontage lots.)

Double frontage lots are generally considered undesirable, probably because detached, single-family homes usually have a front yard (which provides a neatly maintained public front) and a rear yard (which tends to be a private place and is often used for whatever the residents desire). Double frontage lots tend to upset this pattern.

Double frontage lots are, however, designed into subdivisions where single-family homes are built on lots that are adjacent to arterial streets on one end and have access to local access streets on the other. When this pattern occurs, it is essential that access to the arterial street be prohibited by deed restriction. It is common practice for the subdivider to erect substantial fences or walls on the property line adjacent to the arterial street, in order to prevent access to the street, provide a sense of privacy on the rear portion of the lots, provide protection from the intrusion of strangers from the arterial, and mitigate the noise level generated by traffic on the arterial.

CLUSTER DEVELOPMENT

Cluster development permits dwelling units to be built relatively close together on relatively small lots, in exchange for the retention of surrounding open space.

For example, a 20-acre parcel of land, which has conventional zoning that permits the construction of single-family homes on a 20,000-square-foot lot, might yield 35 dwelling units, which would occupy about 16 acres and require about 4 acres of streets. If a cluster development option were available, it might be possible to build 35 dwelling units, each with a lot area of 5,000 square feet. This housing would take up about 4 acres of land and require about 1 acre of streets, leaving 15 acres of open space. (Note that compromises between the developer and the governing jurisdiction can sometimes be negotiated con-

cerning the yield of dwelling units and the amount of open space to be preserved.)

Cluster development is potentially advantageous to land developers because it reduces the length (and thereby the cost) of streets and utility lines, while retaining the same yield of dwelling units. Cluster developments are often very attractive, from a visual point of view, and therefore may be quite marketable.

Open space that is designated in a cluster development may be in the form of some terrain preserved with its natural form and vegetation, or a golf course, or a storm water retention basin, or some other open space use, depending upon the wording of the local zoning regulations.

Cluster developments are advantageous to communities that wish to preserve open space and save desirable natural features which may be in that open space.

There are some caveats concerning cluster development. One is that some effective and reliable method of maintaining the open space on a permanent basis must be established (usually done though a homeowners' association). A second is that cluster development does not necessarily appeal to all potential home purchasers. There are many people who will spurn houses on small lots, even if they are surrounded by an attractive natural environment; some people prefer conventional houses on large lots.

Cluster development can be used to good advantage for developments of detached, single-family homes; townhouses; multifamily structures; or for some combination of the above.

The general procedure for planning a cluster development is to first analyze the proposed site, while keeping in mind the local regulations concerning its possible development. After that, it is appropriate to make a number of alternative site planning studies to

Figure 18.5. Double Frontage Lots

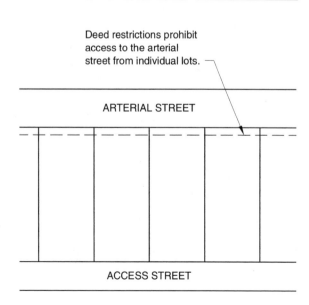

Deed restrictions prohibit access to the arterial street from individual lots.

ARTERIAL STREET

ACCESS STREET

see how the site might be best developed to the satisfaction of the owner and the local community.

Consider a hypothetical example: If you are preparing some concept plans for a 64-acre site that has considerably rugged terrain, some gullies that are subject to flooding, and some groves of trees that should be preserved, you might consider cluster development. Assume that the local regulations indicate a low-density development of 1 dwelling unit per 4 acres of land. If this is the case, some of your development alternatives are indicated in Table 18.1. These range from 16 large, private building sites at 4 acres each with no common open space, down to 16 small building sites with lots of common open space. Four alternative schemes are shown in Figure 18.6, in a very schematic manner. (The diagrams and calculations ignore the area required for streets and problems concerning their design.)

SITING SINGLE-FAMILY STRUCTURES

The procedure for locating a structure on a building site cannot be reduced to a simple set of guidelines. Siting a building involves:

- deciding which design goals should be considered

- deciding which of the goals are of primary importance, and which are of minor importance
- doing design studies to determine which building pattern, size, and location satisfies, to a reasonable degree, the important design goals

Factors often considered in locating a residential structure on a site include:

- accessibility of the building from the adjacent road (especially important in hillside areas)
- provision of usable private yard areas
- view from the structure
- privacy on the site and within the structure
- protection from undesirable natural elements (such as wind, noise, and distasteful views)
- preservation of attractive natural features on the site (such as trees and creeks)
- avoidance of natural hazards (such as steep slopes, unstable lands, and areas subject to flooding)
- avoidance of natural conditions that may increase construction costs (such as rock outcroppings, high water table, and shrink-swell soils)
- solar access for buildings to be placed on the site

Table 18.1. Development Options for a 64-Acre Site Using Cluster Development Patterns

Gross Area of Site (acres)	Number of DUs	Building Site Area per DU (acres)	Area Required for DUs (acres)	Area Remaining as Open Space (acres)
64	16	4	64	0
64	16	2	32	32
64	16	1	16	48
64	16	1/2	8	56

- DU = dwelling unit

**Figure 18.6. Schematic Representation of Alternative Development Patterns
for a 64-Acre Site When Using a Cluster Development Option**

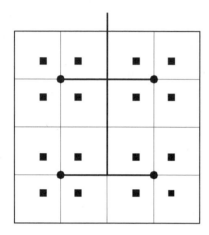

16 DU on 4-acre sites,
leaving no common open space

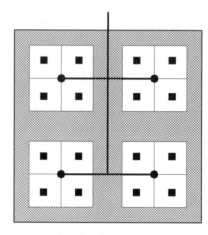

16 DU on 2-acre sites,
plus 32 acres of open space

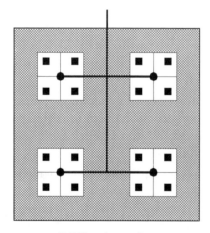

16 DU on 1-acre sites,
plus 48 acres of open space

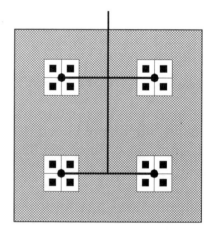

16 DU on 1/2-acre sites,
plus 56 acres of open space

- relationship to community facilities and other amenities (such as adjacent open spaces, golf courses, and flood basins)
- functional considerations (Where will residents park their cars? Where will visitors park? Where will the garbage cans be stored?)

- convenience of access for construction equipment during the building process
- access routes to the site for emergency vehicles (especially fire-fighting equipment and ambulances)
- economic implications of site design (Is one design more costly to build than

another? If so, does it produce a product that is substantially more valuable in the marketplace?)

PROVIDING COMMUNITY FACILITIES IN SUBDIVISIONS

Community facilities are those areas and facilities in a subdivision that are available for use by the residents of the subdivision but are not on the private building lots. These may be structures privately built on private land (and privately maintained), or privately built structures which are turned over to a public jurisdiction for ownership and maintenance.

Chapter 20 discusses planning for community facilities in greater depth.

Typical community facilities that are sometimes found in large subdivisions and in planned-unit developments are:

- tennis courts
- swimming pools
- paths
- golf courses (for very large subdivisions)
- children's play areas
- clubhouses
- exercise rooms
- saunas
- undeveloped open space
- open space used as a storm water retention basin
- lakes, ponds, and waterfronts

Whoever owns the land and structures of a community facility must pay for its maintenance but can control who uses it. If the facility is publicly owned, almost any member of the general public must be allowed to use it.

Questions to be considered by the land developer concerning community facilities should include:

- What type of facility is appropriate?
- How large should it be?
- Who is to own and control its use?
- If it is to privately owned, what provisions will be made to assure its maintenance? (Usually a legal corporation, such as a homeowners' association, must be formed. This association must have legal powers to collect fees for the maintenance and operation of the facilities.)

Notes

1. See Lynch and Hack (pp. 199, 203, 204) for a further description of woonerfs.
2. Bookout discusses zero-lot-line houses at greater length; see pp. 157-158 in his text.

Recommended Reading

Bookout, Lloyd W., Jr. *Residential Development Handbook.* 2nd ed. Washington, DC: Urban Land Institute, 1990, pp. 141-172.

Sources of Further Information

American Society of Civil Engineers, National Association of Home Builders, and the Urban Land Institute (ASCE, NAHB, and ULI). *Residential Streets.* 2nd ed. Washington, DC: Urban Land Institute, 1990.

De Chiara, Panero, and Zelnick, editors. *Time Saver Standards for Housing and Residential Development.* 2nd ed. New York: McGraw-Hill, 1994.

Kone, D. Linda. *Land Development.* 8th ed. Washington, DC: Home Builder Press (National Association of Home Builders), 1994.

Lynch, Kevin and Gary Hack. *Site Planning.* 3rd ed. Cambridge, MA: MIT Press, 1984. Suggest review of Chapter 9, "Housing."

Untermann and Small. *Site Planning for Cluster Housing.* New York: Van Nostrand Reinhold, 1977.

CHAPTER

19

Multifamily Developments

INTRODUCTION

The *procedures* for the design of multifamily developments are very similar to those used for single-family subdivisions.

It is usual in the design and review of multifamily developments to go through the same three-step process of preparing and reviewing a preliminary (or "preapplication") subdivision map, a tentative subdivision map, and a final subdivision map that is used for single-family subdivisions. Chapter 17 describes that process.

One topic concerning procedures used for multifamily developments that may differ from that used for single-family subdivisions relates to final subdivision maps for condominium apartment buildings. It is probable that each state has its own procedures for filing final subdivision maps for condominium apartments. If you are going to be involved with a condominium project, it might be wise to review your state's subdivision map requirements for them.

There are three other differences to be noted. These relate to building design, site planning, and the provision of community facilities.

The design of single-family houses for subdivisions is an important subject, to be sure,

but it is not a terribly complex one. The design of structures for apartment development borders on the critical, however. If buildings are found to have awkward floor plans, if they are considered ugly, or if they are excessively expensive for what the occupants have to pay for them, the development may not be as successful as the land developer hopes. It is therefore important for the developer to engage the services of a thoroughly competent architect to design proposed new apartment buildings.

Site planning for single-family homes is important, of course, but for apartment buildings it is even more so. Multifamily developments must have site plans that function very well, provide a safe environment, provide an attractive setting, and are economical to install and maintain. Once again, it is important for the land developer to engage the services of a thoroughly competent landscape architect to prepare a good site plan and supervise its installation.

"Community facilities" include items such as recreation areas and meeting rooms. Residents of single-family homes sometimes require less in the way of community facilities than do the residents of apartments, because they may have the space and the inclination

224

to provide their own facilities on their own property. Apartment dwellers, on the other hand, find it impossible to provide their own private swimming pools and tennis courts; these facilities are often provided and maintained by the apartment building owners, and used by all the structure's occupants.

When planning a multifamily development, one should consider these questions:

- Which community facilities will be provided nearby by public agencies that will be truly attractive to apartment residents, and therefore need not be provided by the developer or by individual apartment owners?

- Which facilities should be built on site by the developer for shared use by the residents of the development?

- Which facilities will be in, or attached to, individual dwelling units for the exclusive use by their occupants?

Answers to these questions will be helpful in determining the cost of development and the attractiveness of the development.

Planning for community facilities is discussed in Chapter 20.

ROADS IN MULTIFAMILY AREAS

Roads serving multifamily areas are similar to roads serving single-family areas, with the following important exceptions:

- Large areas of multifamily development can generate great amounts of traffic, especially during peak hours. Roads serving multifamily areas therefore often need to have a large carrying capacity in order to accommodate this traffic, and therefore should be in the arterial or collector category.

- Large multifamily sites (perhaps of 10 acres or more) often can be allowed to have direct access to collector streets and arterials.

- Some large multifamily developments are well served by mass transit. For these areas, the peak-hour carrying capacity of their access roads and the capacity of their parking lots may be reduced if it can be shown that the residents will probably utilize the available mass transit.

- The traffic generated by large residential developments may warrant the installation of additional left-turn lanes and new traffic signals on streets serving the project. If needed, these are usually installed at the land developer's expense.

Large residential developments often generate potential traffic flow problems. It is usually in the interest of land developers, and of the local jurisdiction, to make sure that these problems are avoided or mitigated. It is therefore a frequent and very desirable practice to employ a qualified traffic engineer to participate in the planning of large projects.[1]

PARKING IN MULTIFAMILY AREAS

It should be noted that off-street parking is a major determinant in the design of areas for multifamily housing. When you get a concentration of people, you usually also get a concentration of cars. These cars, when parked, take up a great deal of space. This space requirement for parked cars is usually a major factor in the design of apartment developments; it becomes a "form-giver." Parking is not usually a form-giver for low-density, single-family home areas; it is somewhat of a form-giver for townhouses; and is almost always a strong form-giver for apartment development.

Parking takes space and money; each car requires about 350 square feet of area for access and storage space. The current cost of constructing parking areas (in 1999) runs between $1,000 and $2,000 for at-grade parking, 7 times as much for aboveground parking in a structure, and 10 to 15 times as much for below-ground structures.

The relationship between parking areas and the place of residence of apartment development occupants is extremely important. The connection between the two should be as short as possible, and clearly safe to traverse at all hours of the day and night.

Some parking space should be provided on site for visitors to the occupants of large residential developments.

While it is usually considered aesthetically pleasing to have large areas of parked cars screened from view by earth berms, trees, and bushes, it is also very important to have parking areas clearly visible for security patrol purposes (i.e., controlling personal safety, limiting theft, and reducing vandalism).

Off-street loading areas should be planned in conjunction with on-site circulation and parking. Plan ahead for situations such as passenger drop-off, delivery trucks, moving vans, and garbage pick-ups.

For some large developments, it may be desirable to provide screened parking spaces for short-term storage of travel trailers, RVs, and boats on trailers. On the other hand, it is usually considered desirable to avoid long-term storage of these vehicles on the premises.

Guidelines for the design of off-street and on-street parking areas are provided in Chapter 11.

BLOCK AND LOT PATTERNS

The design of lots and blocks for multifamily developments is similar to that of single-family subdivisions, with the following exceptions:

- The lots are substantially larger, to accommodate the larger buildings and their accompanying parking areas. The lots are generally much wider and

deeper than are lots for medium-density, single-family homes.
- The blocks are often larger because of the larger lots and buildings.
- Because the blocks and lots are larger, the design of pedestrian circulation facilities may be more of a problem (i.e., more paths cutting through blocks may be appropriate, rather than relying solely on sidewalks adjacent to the streets).
- Some of the streets serving multifamily areas may be collector streets rather than local access streets.

When large developments are being planned involving a number of large apartment buildings, it is usually desirable for the designers to make sure that the overall project can be developed in stages. Each stage should have features such as good access to the buildings, an adequate street system, adequate utilities, and appropriate amenities for the residents. This makes it more feasible to finance each stage separately and, if found to be desirable, to sell separately.

SITING APARTMENT STRUCTURES

Locating a multifamily building on a site is considerably more challenging and complex than is site design for single-family subdivisions.

Factors concerning the siting of single-family homes in subdivisions were discussed in Chapter 18. Most of these same factors should be considered in siting apartment structures in large-scale developments. There are, however, some changes of emphasis that are appropriate here and there. These factors are discussed below, with commentary on how they might be adapted to apply to apartment developments.

- *Accessibility of the building from the adjacent road.* For single-family homes, this is a simple problem of providing access from a local access road to a private garage or parking space. For apartment buildings, the problem may be more complicated, and involve vehicular access from a collector street to large communal garages, or to large open parking lots, and then pedestrian access from the parking areas to the residential areas.

- *Provision of usable, private, open space areas.* For apartment buildings, this is often possible only for ground-floor occupants. For those living above the ground floor, consideration should be given to building private balconies, or developing usable, private, open spaces on rooftops.

- *View from the structure.* This is probably much more important in apartment buildings than it is in single-family homes.

- *Privacy.* Both visual and sound privacy are very important in apartment buildings; it is usually more difficult to achieve this in apartments than it is in single-family homes.

- *Protection from undesirable natural elements.* As in single-family homes, protection from wind, noise, rain, snowfall, icing, and excessive sun is important. In those apartments that are to be built in dense urban areas, thought should also be given to protection from road noises, which can be considerable.

- *Preservation of attractive natural features on the site.* This is as important in multifamily areas as it is in single-family areas.

- *Avoidance of natural hazards* such as unstable slopes and areas subject to flooding. Consideration of this factor can be joined with the following topic.

- *Avoidance of natural conditions that increase construction costs* such as rock outcroppings and a high water table. Careful site

planning is needed to minimize these dangers.

- *Solar access.* Sunshine in apartments is very important for aesthetic, environmental quality, and visual relief purposes. It may also be possible to utilize some of the advantages of solar heating in an apartment structure.

- *Relationship to amenities and public facilities.* This is a very important consideration in apartment structures because many of these are not feasible to include in individual living quarters; they must be shared with the other occupants of the buildings. Planning the amount, location, and conditions of use for the amenities may have a great bearing on occupant satisfaction.

- *Functional considerations* (e.g., circulation within the buildings, garbage collection, and off-street loading). The larger the structure, the more important this factor becomes.

- *Convenience of access for construction equipment.* This topic may be of importance if large cranes will be needed for building tall structures, if heavy building materials will be delivered to the site, or if large pieces of mechanical equipment will need to be incorporated into the buildings.

- *Access to the site for emergency vehicles.* This is especially important for fire, police, and emergency medical care vehicles.

- *Economic implications of site design.* The same questions should be raised for apartment construction as for single-family subdivisions: Is one design more costly to build than another? If so, does it produce a product that is substantially more valuable in the marketplace?

The following site design factors, which are not present in single-family subdivisions, should also be considered when designing multifamily housing:

- *The location and design of parking areas for use by building residents.* Are they safe and secure? Are they conveniently located? Is access to them by way of routes which are well lit and safe?
- *The location of visitor parking areas.* Are they conveniently located? Are they of adequate size? Is access to them convenient and safe?
- *Pedestrian circulation patterns.* Are they convenient, attractive, and safe?
- *Safety issues.* Will there be assurance of personal safety in corridors, elevators, parking lots, recreation areas, and other public areas?[2]

Notes

1. A useful reference for those who design large projects which will generate considerable traffic is *Transportation and Land Development* by Stover and Koepke.

2. See *Defensible Space* by Oscar Newman.

Sources of Further Information

De Chiara, Panero, and Zelnick, editors. *Time Saver Standards for Housing and Residential Development.* 2nd ed. New York: McGraw-Hill, 1994.

De Chiara, Joseph, and John H. Callender. *Time Saver Standards for Building Types.* 3rd ed. New York: McGraw-Hill, 1990.

Engstromm, Robert and Marc Putnam. *Planning and Design of Townhouses and Condominiums.* Washington, DC: Urban Land Institute, 1979. See Chapter 8, "Mid-Rise and High-Rise Design."

Marcus, Clare Cooper, and Wendy Sarkissian. *Housing as if People Mattered.* Berkeley, CA: University of California Press, 1986. A constructive and detailed guide for designing large-scale, medium-density family housing. While the book is strongly oriented towards making public housing more livable, it contains many valuable guidelines for private housing as well.

Newman, Oscar. *Defensible Space.* New York: Collier Books, 1973.

Stover, Virgil G., and Frank J. Koepke. *Transportation and Land Development.* Englewood Cliffs, NJ: Prentice-Hall, 1988. Prepared for the Institute of Transportation Engineers.

20

Community Facilities

INTRODUCTION

A community facility is generally considered to be a building or site which is owned and operated by a local governmental agency, and is used to provide services to the public. In some instances, the term may apply to the operations of a private nonprofit agency. Examples of community facilities include schools, parks, libraries, and hospitals. A more complete set of examples of community facilities is provided in Table 20.1.

There are three major parts to the process of planning for a new community facility:

1. defining the function and size of the facility, and identifying its optimal location

2. getting community acceptance for the facility in the identified location

3. planning the financing of the facility

Discussion of the third part is beyond the scope of this book; much of it is sometimes considered under the heading of "Capital Improvements Planning."

The second part is usually the most difficult, because it involves what is often referred to as the "Not In My Back Yard" (NIMBY) syndrome. This subject is discussed later in this chapter.

The first part is, to a large degree, a technical analysis. It should not, however, be undertaken by those who are politically insensitive. Discussion of this topic is the major theme of this chapter.

It should be emphasized that the three phases of the process should not be completely separated from each other. Experience has shown that public information and public participation during the planning process are essential foundations for public acceptance, and public acceptance is very important in any city that wishes to build a new community facility.

A GENERIC PROCESS FOR PLANNING COMMUNITY FACILITIES

With so many forms and functions of community facilities (see Table 20.1), it is not possible within the space and time constraints of this chapter to review and discuss each one separately, and to prescribe a planning process that is appropriate for each. We will have to settle on a "generic planning process" that may be used as a starting point for planning community facilities in general. This process should, of course, be modified to suit the circumstances of each proposed application. The

Table 20.1. Examples of "Community Facilities"

EDUCATIONAL
  Elementary schools (K-6)
  Junior high schools
  High schools
  Community colleges

SOCIAL SERVICES
  Day-care centers for preschool children
  Day-care centers for the elderly
  Shelters for homeless people
  Shelters for battered women
  Halfway houses for drug addict rehabilitation
  Halfway houses for prisoner rehabilitation
  Halfway houses for the mentally disturbed
  Halfway houses for the mentally retarded

CULTURAL
  Libraries
  Bookmobiles
  Museums
  Auditoriums

RECREATIONAL
  Parks
    Passive recreation areas
    Active participant sports areas
  Recreation programs
  Sports centers
    (such as stadiums for spectator sports)
  Small boat harbors
  Riding, hiking, and bicycle trails

GOVERNMENTAL BUILDINGS
  Government office buildings
  Post offices
  "Corporation yards"
    (for the storage of materials and equipment)

HEALTH CARE
  Local health clinics
  Community hospitals
  Regional hospitals
  Emergency health services
  Long-term care facilities

PUBLIC SAFETY
  Police stations
  Fire stations
  Jails
  Reform schools for juveniles
  Court buildings
  Civil defense facilities
    Natural disasters
    Military actions

PUBLIC UTILITIES
  Water supply
    Filtration plants
    Reservoirs
    Elevated storage tanks
  Sewage disposal plants
  Storm drainage facilities
    Channels
    Retention basins
  Flood protection facilities
    Dikes
    Flood basins
  Solid waste management
    Landfills
    Transfer stations
    Incinerators
    Waste-to-energy plants
    Hazardous waste depositories
    Recycling centers

OTHER
  Open space preserves
  Cemeteries
  Harbors
  Animal shelters

major steps in the process are outlined in Table 20.2.

The steps in this generic process are discussed in greater detail in the following text.

Step 1. Prepare a Situation Assessment

"Prepare a situation assessment" is popular technical terminology that means "find out what's going on." In order to find out what's going on, it is suggested that you ask the following questions:

- What is the assignment? What type of community facility is to be built? Whom is it to serve? Who is to operate it? Have any decisions already been made concerning its location?

Table 20.2. A Generic Process for Planning Community Facilities

Step 1. Prepare a situation assessment.

Step 2. Review design standards, location criteria, and the experiences of others.

Step 3. Make a preliminary economic analysis.

Step 4. Identify potential sites; screen out the unsuitable ones.

Step 5. Prepare sketch plans for possible development of sites remaining in consideration; make preliminary impact assessments of these sites.

Step 6. Review the preceding studies with your client and other interested parties; identify sites that merit further consideration.

Step 7. Prepare preliminary development plans, impact analyses, and economic analyses of sites remaining in consideration.

Step 8. Review the plans and analyses with your client and other interested parties.

Step 9. Request that your client reach a decision concerning site selection and development plans.

Step 10. If your client approves a development plan for a site, they may then choose to authorize the preparation of working drawings for buildings and site development, and the preparation of a specific financing program.

- Who is your client? Who has asked for the study? Who will make the important decisions concerning the location, design, and financing of the facility?
- Who are the "interested parties" related to the proposed community facility? Who will be served by it? Which groups in the community may benefit from its construction? Which groups may be adversely affected?
- What is your role in the planning process? (As you may know, some professionals, such as urban planners, are reasonably well qualified to make studies of the functions and locations of community facilities, but relatively few are qualified to design them.)

While you may be very helpful in identifying many of the characteristics and location of, let us say, a city hall, are you qualified to design one? How far are you expected to go in the design of the proposed community facility? When and how do you bring in qualified design professionals such as civil engineers, landscape architects, and architects?

Step 2. Review Design Standards, Location Criteria, and the Experiences of Others

What federal, state, or local laws or regulations (or financial grant programs) affect the planning of the location, construction, or operation of the community facility?

Can you find any information in libraries available to you concerning the location, design, or operation of the type of facility in which you are interested? Is there a large university library that has this information? Has the American Planning Association published any of their "Planning Advisory Service" reports on your subject?

It is a good idea to interview the people who will be operating the facility upon its completion, and see if they have any sources of information, or any strong preferences for the location or design of the facility.

Have any nearby jurisdictions planned and built a community facility similar to the one in which you are interested? If so, talk with the people who were involved with its planning and with those who are operating it, and find out what they think they did right and what they think they did wrong.

Perhaps this is the time to consider one of the basic decisions your community must make: Is it preferable to build one large centralized facility, or several smaller decentralized facilities? For example, does your jurisdiction need one large, fully equipped, centrally located fire station, or would it be preferable to build four small, minimally equipped, decentralized stations? The same question about the basic design approach may be asked about many other types of community facilities such as libraries, schools, and health clinics.

Step 3. Make a Preliminary Economic Analysis

It is often useful to make approximations of what the cost of acquiring and operating a proposed new community facility might be before a decision is made to build it. Interested citizens like to know this information, and city councils must have it before committing support for a project. So, it may be appropriate for you to get *approximate* cost estimates for:

- *Site acquisition.* How large a site is needed? What is the range of local land costs, in dollars per square foot?

- *Site development.* What is the approximate cost of new roads, utilities, site preparation, and landscaping?

- *Building construction.* How large a building is contemplated, and what is the range of local building costs, in dollars per square foot?

- *Annual operating costs.* How much will be needed to budget for staffing? How much for items such as materials and supplies?

- *Annual revenues to be produced.* Any user fees anticipated? Any subventions and grants? Any increase in the local tax base?

At this stage of your study, you certainly can't (or shouldn't attempt to) make precise economic estimates. You might consider reporting ranges of costs and income, giving "probable highest" and "probable lowest" figures. These estimates will not be perfect, but they will serve the local citizens and decision makers far better than no estimates at all.

Step 4. Identify Potential Sites; Screen Out the Unsuitable Ones

The first thing you need to do in this step is to identify what characteristics a site for your community facility *must* have if it is to be considered suitable. A review of the design standards and location criteria developed in the preceding step should help you here.

Factors that are often appropriate to consider are:

- relationship of the site to the population the facility is intended to serve (measured in travel miles or travel time)
- minimum site size required
- maximum affordable land cost
- availability of road access and utilities
- physical characteristics of the site such as maximum slope and danger from flooding

You should then map the location of the potential sites that have already been identified by others, plus any additional ones you can find that appear to meet your selection criteria.

The next step is to apply your site-selection criteria to the identified potential sites. When doing this, you may choose to use a simple *pass/fail* screening procedure, in which you eliminate from further consideration all sites that do not meet your established criteria.

If you have many sites under consideration, you may choose instead to use what has been called a "graduated screening" procedure. When using this method, for each separate screening factor (such as land cost) you establish what you consider to be an "excellent," "good," "fair," or "poor" rating, and then evaluate and rate each site under consideration. Those sites that are assigned mostly "fair" or "poor" ratings are obviously less suitable for your community facility than are those that are assigned predominately "excellent" and "good" ratings. (For a further discussion of this and other rating methodologies, see Anderson (1987).)

Step 5. Prepare Sketch Plans for Possible Development of Sites Remaining in Consideration; Make Preliminary Impact Assessments of These Sites

A sketch site plan is a quickly made, preliminary graphic representation of how a site might be developed for the selected community facility.

In this step, you are primarily interested in examining how well the facility you are considering can fit on each of the sites that are still in the running. In order to do this, you should:

1. delineate the boundaries of each site on a map
2. sketch on the map of each site the size and possible shape of all structures being considered
3. show possible vehicular circulation patterns that would be required on the site and on nearby streets

4. review the relationship of the sketched site development to the surrounding properties

In order to prepare these sketch plans, you will have to apply many of the skills you have learned from studying the preceding chapters of this book.

Discussion of the sketch-planning process will be found in Chapter 11 of the Kaiser, Godschalk, and Chapin book, and in Task 3.5 of the Anderson (1995) book. Both of these references apply to general land-use planning, but can easily be adapted to planning for a single-function land use such as a community facility.

The second part of this step is to make a preliminary impact assessment of each of the sites for which you have prepared a sketch plan. In this procedure, you will identify various aspects of the local setting, which may include the natural environment, the man-made environment, the local economy, local social conditions, transportation facilities, public utilities, other community facilities, and local government finance.

You will then make a quick analysis of how you think the community facility you have shown in your sketch plans would impact the various aspects of its surrounding environment. Make your analysis verbally with terse terms such as "strongly beneficial," "somewhat beneficial," "no effect," "somewhat detrimental," "strongly detrimental," or "does not apply." You can then write a brief summary of the apparent probable impacts that can be expected from each of the sketch plans. Please note that this analysis does *not* constitute a formal environmental impact assessment which might be required in some states; the analysis is intended only as part of your site screening and selection process.

References that discuss the impact assessment process are: Anderson (1995), pp. 106-109; Kaiser, Godschalk, and Chapin (1995),

Chapter 17; and Schaenman (1976), entire book.

Step 6. Review the Preceding Studies With Your Client and Other Interested Parties; Identify Sites That Merit Further Consideration

The title to this step seems to tell most of the story. It is an important step for several reasons. First, it is often desirable to get input from people who may have information of which you are not yet aware. Second, it is a wise policy to keep your boss, and other interested parties, informed about how the study is going. Also, reviewing the work done to date with your client may bring about some change of focus or direction of the study; it is better to learn about this now.

The term "other interested parties" used above may cover a wide range of groups. Among these are often found:

- homeowners' associations that are apprehensive about the impact of any new development on their areas, especially on their property values
- individual businesses that are interested in the possible impact of the proposed new development on their markets
- environmental groups that are concerned about the natural environment in general, and particularly about the preservation of wildlife habitats
- other groups or individuals that are concerned about the effects of urban growth on the character of the existing community and, especially, the traffic problems that new development may generate

It may be appropriate at (or, preferably before) this step to review current literature that deals with Locally Unwanted Land Uses (LULUs) and the Not In My Back Yard (NIMBY) responses that they stir up. One suggested source is *New Approaches to Resolving Public Disputes* by Denise Madigan.

This step should result in reaching some consensus concerning which one of the several sites being considered should receive further concentrated design studies and analysis.

Step 7. Prepare Preliminary Development Plans, Impact Analyses, and Economic Analyses of Sites Remaining In Consideration

If you do not have design skills, now is probably the time to enlist the help of one or more qualified design professionals. How many and what kind depend upon the type and complexity of your project.

This step requires the preparation of a well-designed development plan for the community facility for each site under consideration; back-of-the-envelope sketches just won't be sufficient here. The plans have to be complete enough so that they clearly convey to observers where the facility could be located, how big it might be, and how it might relate to its surroundings. These plans should be detailed enough to provide a basis for cost estimates for site acquisition, building construction, site development, and required equipment.

This step also requires that an economic analysis of the proposed facility be made. This involves considering the costs of acquiring and developing the site, and the costs of operating it. This may involve investigating how the project is to be financed. Will it be paid for through the jurisdiction's capital improvement program? Will it involve a bond issue? Will it involve establishing a special assessment district, wherein the local property owners pay for the facility? Are there any grant programs from the state or federal levels that can be of assistance? Will user fees help pay for its operation and maintenance?

Step 8. Review the Plans and Analyses With Your Client and Other Interested Parties

Step 9. Request That Your Client Reach a Decision Concerning Site Selection and Development Plans

If all is going perfectly, these two steps constitute the last phases in the plan preparation, review, and selection process. The chances are, however, that your client will suggest some design changes be made before a decision is made to proceed with the project, so expect some delays.

Step 10. If Your Client Approves a Development Plan for a Site, They May Then Choose to Authorize the Preparation of Working Drawings for Buildings and Site Development, and the Preparation of a Specific Financing Program

Once again, the name of this step seems to describe what actions are appropriate at this stage of the planning process.

The job of preparing working drawings, which are to be used for the construction of the community facility, should be given to qualified design professionals.

The job of preparing a financing program for the construction and operation of the facility should be given to someone who is well qualified in budgetary matters.

THE "NIMBY SYNDROME"

The "Not In My Back Yard" (NIMBY) syndrome mentioned earlier is virtually always present when a new location for a community facility is proposed. The number of people who will protest a community facility location depends upon how objectionable the facility is, and how many people believe that they will be adversely affected by it.

Even relatively innocuous community facilities (such as ornamental parks) are objected to by those who live immediately adjacent to them (even though they may be welcomed by those who live 200 feet away). At the other end of the scale, clearly obnoxious or dangerous facilities (such as the storage of radioactive wastes) stir up NIMBY reactions in entire states, and even in nations.

The following objections are frequently raised when a new location is proposed for a community facility:

- "The people who will use the facility will be objectionable." These people may be identified in the minds of the protestors as:
  - noisy teenagers
  - senile elderly
  - the unwashed poor
  - people from out-of-town
  - people who practice strange religions
  - people who are not American citizens
  - miscreants of many and various sorts
- "The facility will generate noise and traffic." The sources for this may be:
  - noise from loud radios and loud people
  - automobile traffic, and cars with squealing tires and blaring radios
  - truck traffic
- "The facility will be ugly." It may be the view of some protestors that:
  - The building will be too massive.
  - The building will be of an inappropriate and ugly architectural style.
  - There will be noticeable signs and lights.
  - It will stick out like a sore thumb.
  - It won't fit into the neighborhood.
- "The facility will be used at objectionable hours."

MEETING THE OBJECTIONS

Some objections may be very real and valid; others may be unwarranted. Nevertheless, *all* objections (valid and invalid alike) are real in the minds of some people and must be seriously considered. To do otherwise would be a disservice to the public, and would probably have adverse political repercussions.

The NIMBY syndrome is discussed here, not for your interest and amusement but because it is a very real problem that must be dealt with by those who are planning community facilities.

There appear to be four major ways of dealing with the NIMBY problem:

1. Locate the community facility where it isn't in anyone's backyard; where there is no one nearby to complain. Consider undeveloped rural areas and nonresidential areas. This course of action may, of course, result in a location that is far away from the people it is intended to serve, thereby reducing its usefulness.

2. Acknowledge that the proposed community facility may have some "minor detrimental affects" on nearby areas, but point out that the overall good for the larger community far outweighs the inconvenience that it may cause for a few people. Get political support from the larger community that will overpower the voices of the few malcontents.

   This is a pretty dangerous tactic. It implies in the minds of some that rule by the majority is going to ride roughshod on the rights of people who hold minority views, or that the rich and privileged plan on ignoring the rights of a small group of disadvantaged citizens. If the tactic is used, it must be clearly demonstrated that the "minor detrimental effects" are truly minor,

and that effective measures will be taken to mitigate them.

3. Pay for the anticipated economic damages. If residents in an area have objections to a facility, buy their houses at a current, fair market value, and resell them at a price that acknowledges the adverse economic impact of the proposed community facility. (Sometimes the properties will be sold back to the original property owners.) This technique has been widely employed in areas near airports that are adversely impacted by aircraft noise.

   This procedure can take care of the economic complaints that people may voice, but it really doesn't do much for the quality of life of those who choose to remain in the area.

4. Identify the causes of the complaints and produce a facility design that mitigates the identified problems. For example, if noise is a problem, get a large site and retain an acoustical engineer to assist with the facility design. If parking is a problem, get a large site and provide ample parking areas.

   Be sure to bring in the complainers, and show them what your designers are doing to mitigate their problems. Work with the affected people, and make a bona fide effort to solve their problems.

   This course of action will probably increase construction costs and will undoubtedly prolong the site-selection process, but it may result in identifying a location and a facility design that is acceptable to the community.

Sources of Further Information

Anderson, Larz T. "Seven Methods for Calculating Land Capability/Suitability" (Planning Advisory Service Report No. 402). Chicago: American Society of Planning Officials, 1987.

Anderson, Larz T. *Guidelines for Preparing Urban Plans.* Chicago: Planners Press, American Planning Association, 1995.

De Chiara and Koppleman. *Urban Planning and Design Criteria.* 2nd ed. New York: Van Nostrand Reinhold, 1975. See Chapter 10, "Educational Facilities," Chapter 11, "Neighborhood and Community Facilities," and Chapter 12, "Parks and Recreation."

Goodman and Freund. *Principles and Practice of Urban Planning.* Washington, DC: International City Managers' Association, 1968. See: Chapter 8, "Governmental and Community Facilities," by Frank So.

Kaiser, Edward J., David R. Godschalk, and F. Stuart Chapin, Jr. *Urban Land Use Planning.* 4th ed. Urbana, IL: University of Illinois Press, 1995. See Chapter 15, "Integrating Community Facilities with Land Use."

Madigan, Denise. *New Approaches to Resolving Public Disputes.* Cambridge, MA: National Institute for Dispute Resolution, 1990.

Schaenman, Philip S. *Using An Impact Measurement System to Evaluate Land Development.* Washington, DC: The Urban Institute, 1976.

EXERCISE:
SLOPE ANALYSIS (for Chapter 3)

Figure A.1 is a topographic map, at a scale of 1:2,400 (1 inch = 200 feet), with a contour interval of 10 feet. You should make several photocopies of it for use in this exercise. In this exercise you will:

- Make a slope scale.
- Prepare a slope analysis of the map provided to you.
- Plot the route of a trail that follows prescribed slopes while going from Points A to B to C to D.

Part I: Make a Slope Scale

For the purposes of this exercise, make a slope scale on a 3 × 5 inch file card (or on some equally convenient material) with categories of 0 to 5 percent, 5 to 10 percent, 10 to 15 percent, 15 to 30 percent, and over 30 percent, using the procedures provided in Chapter 3.

Part II: Prepare a Slope Analysis

Using your slope scale, mark on one copy of the topographic map the areas that are in each slope category (for example, the areas that are between 10 and 15 percent slope).

After you have categorized the slopes of all the areas on the topographic map, you are ready to rationalize the boundaries of those areas. This is done by placing a second copy of the topographic map over the copy that has the slope analysis on it and, using a light table (or a well-lit window), producing what appear to be reasonable and logical boundaries of lands in each of the slope categories.

Part III: Coloring the Slope Map

The "rationalized" map should be colored, using a carefully selected range of colors. For this exercise, it is suggested that you use the following Prismacolor pencils:

0 to 5 percent	#916	(canary yellow)
5 to 10 percent	#940	(sand)
10 to 15 percent	#942	(yellow ochre)
15 to 30 percent	#943	(burnt ochre)
over 30 percent	#947	(burnt umber)

You will find that if, after the map is colored, you apply a distinct black line (dark pencil or ink) between the various slope areas, the map will become considerably more legible.

Part IV: Designing Trails

Show the route of a hiking trail that is to go from Point A to Point B to Point C, and then to Point D.

Between Points A and B, the trail is to go downhill at a slope that does not exceed 5 percent.

Between B and C, the trail is to be level.

Between Points C and D, the slope of the trail is to go uphill, at a grade which does not exceed 10 percent.

Show the route of the trail on a clean copy of the topographic map (not the slope map you just prepared).

You can complete this exercise by taking your slope scale and:

1. Start at Point A (elevation 280 feet); mark where you will hit the 270-foot contour if you go downhill at 5 percent. (As you know, on a 5 percent slope you will lose 5 feet of elevation for every 100 feet of horizontal distance; on the same slope, if you go 200 feet you will lose 10 feet of elevation.) Next, mark the point at which you will hit the 260-foot contour. Continue until you reach Point B, which is at an elevation of 200 feet. Next, connect the marks you have made on the contour lines with a line to represent the location of your trail.

2. Trace the location of a trail that goes from Point B to Point C without changing elevation. (*Hint:* This implies that you stay pretty close to the 200-foot contour line.)

3. Show the location of a trail that goes from Point C (elevation 200 feet) up to Point D, which is at 280 feet. This trail is to have a continuous uphill slope of 10 percent. (What is the required horizontal distance travelled between 10-foot contours if the slope of the trail is 10 percent?)

You may recall that many trails in mountainous terrain utilize "switchbacks"; that is, as the trail goes up (or down) a slope, it changes direction, forming a zigzag pattern. You may choose to use this design feature.

Figure A.1. Topographic Map for Slope Analysis Exercise

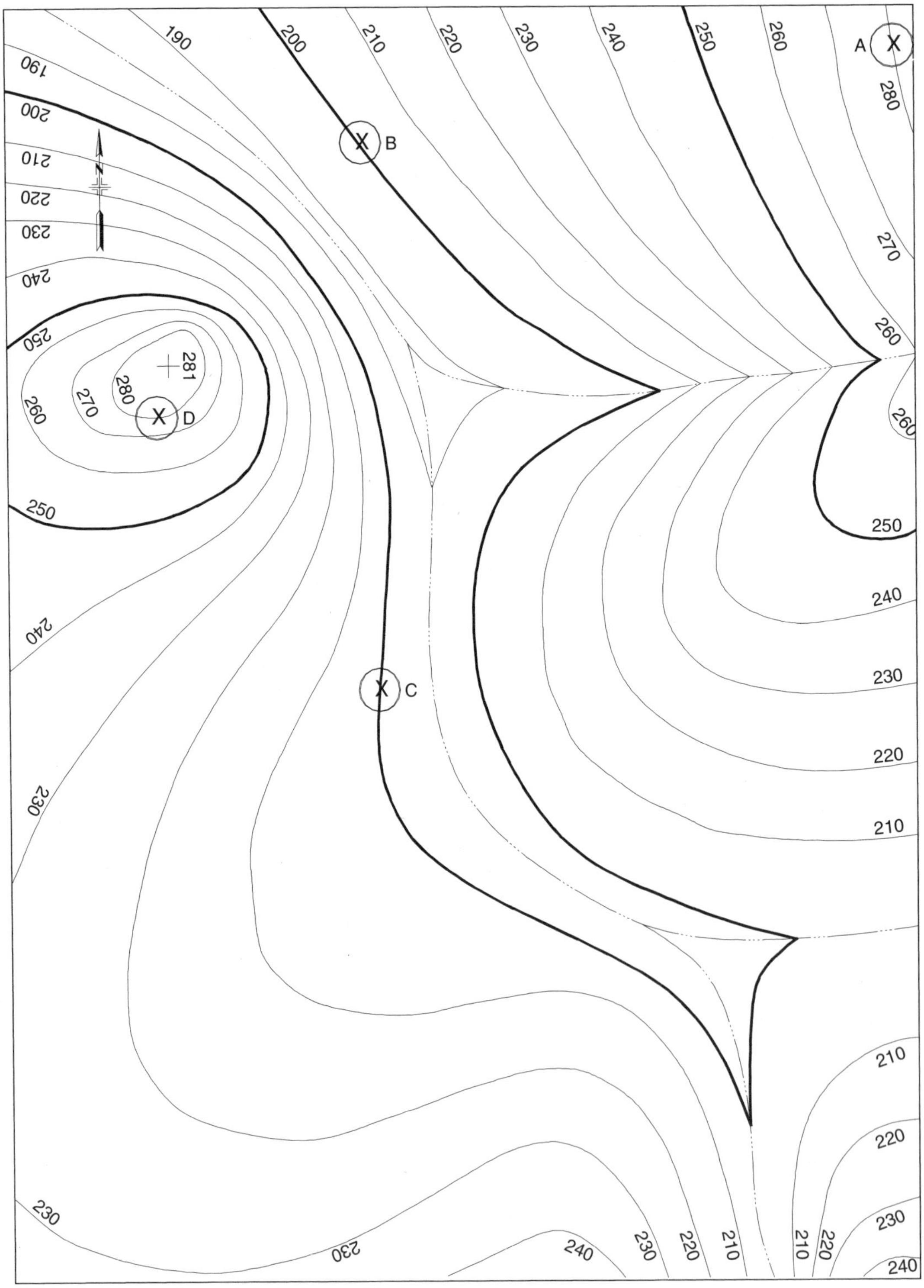

SCALE 1" = 200'

EXERCISE:
DETERMINE THE SERVICE AREA OF A WATER TANK (for Chapter 4)

Given:

- A water tank has its outlet 90 feet above grade, and is located on terrain which has a uniform slope of 4 percent.
- Water weighs 62.4 pounds per cubic foot. This yields a pressure of 0.433 pounds per square inch (psi) for each foot of water depth.
- A minimum water pressure of 20 psi is required in all buildings, at water fixtures which are 10 feet above ground level.
- You are to assume a line loss of water pressure due to friction of water moving in the pipes equivalent to a loss of 5 feet of elevation for every 1,000 feet of pipe length. (This is equivalent to 2.2 psi per 1,000 feet.)
- Water pressure of 100 psi (at ground level) is permissible before a pressure-reducing valve must be installed.

Required:

A. For what distance *at the same elevation* as the foundation of the tank can buildings be served, while maintaining the required water pressure?

Answer:

B. For what distance *uphill* from the water tank can buildings be served, maintaining the required water pressure?

Answer:

C. For what distance *downill* from the water tank can buildings be served, maintaining a minimum pressure of 30 psi inside the building (10 feet above ground level)?

Answer:

D. At what distance *downhill* from the tank should a pressure-reducing valve be installed if a maximum pressure (at ground level) of 100 psi is to be maintained?

Answer:

Show diagrams of the problems and your calculations on a separate page; attach it to this page.

EXERCISE:
DESIGN A SEWER SYSTEM FOR A SUBDIVISION (for Chapter 5)

You are provided with a copy of a map of a proposed subdivision (see Figure A.2), drawn at a scale of 1 inch = 200 feet. You are to show a recommended sanitary sewer system for the subdivision on a copy of this map.

Assume that there are existing sanitary sewer trunk lines at the northwest and southeast corners of the property. The manholes at these locations have invert elevations of 555 and 545 feet, respectively.

The lots in the subdivision are to be developed with apartment buildings, with 16 dwelling units per lot. The outlines of the proposed apartment buildings are shown on your map. The figures shown inside the building outlines are the invert elevations of the "house laterals" as they leave the basements of the structures.

For the purposes of this exercise, you are to use the following design guidelines:

1. Manholes must be installed at the end of every sewer line, and at every change of direction in excess of 10 degrees (in either a vertical or horizontal direction) of the sewer line.
2. Manholes are to be placed no further apart than 500 feet, and should be placed no closer than 300 feet, if reasonably feasible.
3. Manholes should be placed in street rights-of-way, if possible. However, if it is found to be necessary, they may be placed along property lines between lots.
4. The minimum gradient of the sewer line is 0.25 percent; the maximum gradient is 6.20 percent.
5. The sewerage system is for sanitary sewage only. Storm waters will be accommodated in a separate sewer system.
6. The minimum invert elevation of any portion of a sewer line should be 4 feet below the surface of the ground.
7. It is undesirable to exceed an invert elevation of 12 feet below the surface of the ground because of excavation costs.

Assume that all the soil in the subdivision is suitable for construction purposes, and that the depth to bedrock does not present any trenching problems for the sewer lines.

You need not calculate the amount of sewage to be generated by buildings in this subdivision or the size of pipes to carry the sewage.

Sketch the general location of the house laterals (in *red*). Make it possible for sewage to drain from the basement level of each building into a nearby sanitary sewer. You need not calculate the slope of each house lateral; just be sure that the invert elevation at the basement appears to be higher than the invert elevation of the sewer line into which it drains.

Draw your recommended network of sewer lines on your map with a solid *red* line. Manholes are to be shown as small circles.

Show the elevation of the surface of the ground at each manhole in *black;* show the invert elevation of each manhole in *red*.

You may, if you find it appropriate, have the invert elevation of the pipe leaving a manhole lower than the invert elevation of the pipe entering the manhole.

Calculate the slope of each section of the sewer line between manholes and show the resulting figures on your plan. These calculations should be performed using Table A.1.

Show the direction of sewage flow in your sewer system with small *red* arrows.

Factors to be considered in evaluating your design:

1. All building sites must be adequately served by sanitary sewers.
2. No lots may have house laterals that flow uphill to connect with sewer lines.
3. The length of sewer lines is minimized.
4. The number of manholes is minimized.
5. No unneeded sewer lines are recommended.
6. All sewer lines have at least the minimum required gradient (i.e., 0.25 percent), but do not exceed the maximum allowable gradient (i.e., 6.20 percent).
7. At no point is the invert elevation of a sewer line less than 4 feet beneath the surface of the earth.
8. No excessively deep trenches are required (i.e., none over 12 feet deep).
9. The drawing is neatly executed.

Figure A.2. Design of a Sewer System

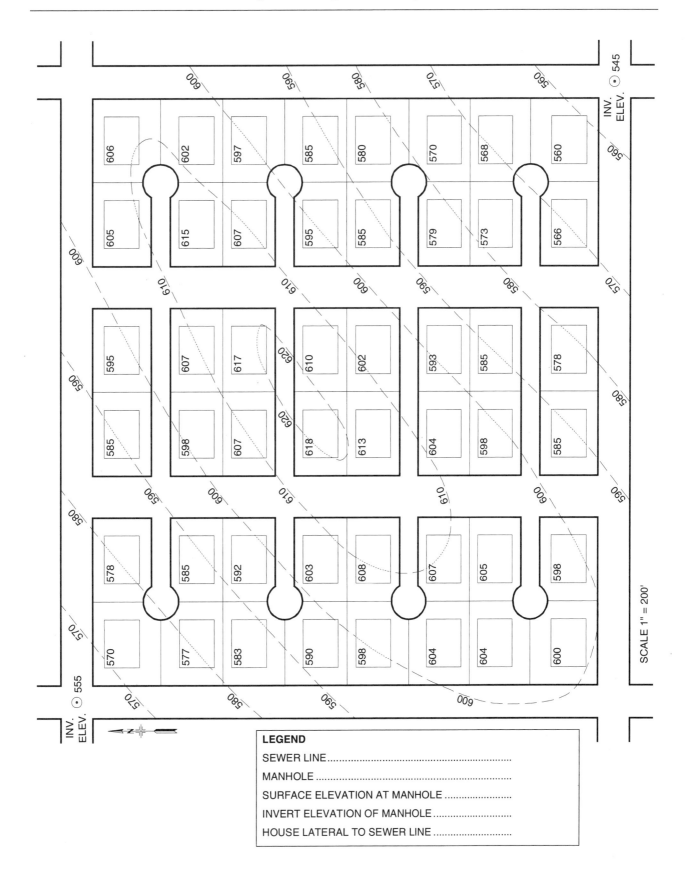

LEGEND

SEWER LINE..

MANHOLE ....

SURFACE ELEVATION AT MANHOLE ....

INVERT ELEVATION OF MANHOLE ....

HOUSE LATERAL TO SEWER LINE ....

Table A.1. Tabular Summary: Design a Sewer System for a Subdivision

| Manholes | | | | | Sewer Lines | |
| Upper | | Lower | | | | |
Identification Number	Invert Elevation	Identification Number	Invert Elevation	Difference in Elevation	Distance Between Manholes	Slope %
				TOTAL		

Total number of new manholes: _____
Total length of sewer lines: _____

EXERCISE:
DEFINE DRAINAGE BASIN BOUNDARIES AND COMPUTE WATER RUNOFF (for Chapter 6)

You are provided with a copy of a segment of a USGS topographic map for Peddlers Hill, California (see Figure A.3).

1. What is the scale of the map?

    Map ratio = 1: ____

    Linear scale 1 inch = ____ feet

    What is the contour interval of the map?

    You will note that much of the area shown on the map is drained by Cat Creek, which flows towards the southwest. Tributary streams to Cat Creek flow along the bottom of Dark Canyon, Loggers Delight Canyon, and Sugar Pine Canyon.

2. Mark on your map in *red* the boundaries of each of the three drainage basins of the creeks in Dark Canyon, Loggers Delight Canyon, and Sugar Pine Canyon. To delineate a drainage basin:

    A. Mark on the map the obvious ridges of land between the drainage basins that appear to be the dividing lines between drainage basins.

    B. Go to the location on the map where it is apparent that water flows out of the drainage basin you are investigating (i.e., identify the *outlet point*). In this case, use the points where streams from the three canyons you are analyzing meet Cat Creek. Then draw a line starting at the outlet point going uphill *perpendicular to the contours* until you meet the ridge lines you drew in Step A.

    Next, follow the ridge lines as far uphill as you can, being sure to keep the line you are drawing perpendicular to the contours. Go back to the outlet point and draw a line going uphill on the other side of the stream, using the same procedure as outlined above. Continue this line uphill until it meets the first line you drew.

    When the lines you have drawn enclose an area on the map, you will have delineated a drainage basin. All rain that falls on the land in this drainage basin will flow downhill, and exit the basin at the outlet point.

3. Make a grid overlay (on mylar or tracing paper) with 500 x 500 foot grids. Tape it on top of your topographic map so that it will not shift as you are using it. Note that each grid has an area of 250,000 square feet, which equals 5.74 acres.

4. Identify which grids drain into each basin. When doing this, use the "all-or-nothing-at-all" technique. That is, count as *in* all grids which are entirely in a drainage basin, plus all those that are 50 percent or more in the basin. You are to count as *out* all those grids which are entirely out of the basin, as well as those which are less than 50 percent in the basin. Be sure you don't allocate the same grid to two adjacent drainage basins. Do not, under any circumstances, get bogged down by counting "half grids" or "quarter grids."

5. Count the number of grids that are in each drainage basin.

6. Fill in Table A.2.

Table A.2. Areas of Drainage Basins

Drainage Basin	Number of Grids	Area in Acres (grids × 5.74)
Dark Canyon		
Loggers Delight Canyon		
Sugar Pine Canyon		
TOTAL		

7. Compute the water runoff from each canyon, using the "rational equation," which is $Q = CIA$ (see Chapter 6). In this equation, A = the area of the watersheds in acres; you are to assume that $C = 0.20$, and that $I = 3.00$ inches per hour.

8. Consider the matter with "significant figures." In using the equation $Q = CIA$, which factor has the fewest significant figures? How many does it have? In view of this, how many significant figures should there be in your answer?

9. Fill in Table A.3.

Table A.3. Runoff from Drainage Basins

Drainage Basin	Calculated Runoff (cubic ft. per second)
Dark Canyon	
Loggers Delight Canyon	
Sugar Pine Canyon	
TOTAL	

Figure A.3. A Segment of the Peddler Hill (California) USGS Map

CONTOUR INTERVAL 40 FEET

EXERCISE:
TRAFFIC ASSIGNMENT (for Chapter 8)

Part I: Calculating the Number of Trips Generated

You are given the street network illustrated in Figure A.4, which consists of Nodes (A, B, C, D, E, F, G, H, I, and J), and Links (A-B, C-D, D-E, etc.). You are to compute the amount of traffic generated at each node, and assign it to the links in the street network. All of the trip-generation figures given below are for the *morning peak hour*.

1. Incoming traffic entering the network at Node A is 3,000 vehicles eastbound. Traffic interviews indicate the following driver destinations:

   From A to B   =   55 percent   =   ____ vehicles
       A to C   =   5 percent   =   ____
       A to E   =   10 percent   =   ____
       A to F   =   10 percent   =   ____
       A to H   =   5 percent   =   ____
       A to I   =   15 percent   =   ____
               100 percent   =   3,000 vehicles

2. Incoming traffic entering the network at Node B is 2,000 vehicles westbound. Destinations of this traffic are:

   From B to A   =   50 percent   =   ____ vehicles
       B to C   =   5 percent   =   ____
       B to E   =   10 percent   =   ____
       B to F   =   10 percent   =   ____
       B to H   =   5 percent   =   ____
       B to I   =   20 percent   =   ____
               100 percent   =   2,000 vehicles

3. Traffic leaving a single-family, residential development at Node C is based on the following:

   250 acres of single-family, residential development at 4 DU/ac = _____ DUs.

   Each dwelling unit generates 0.8 vehicle trips during the morning peak hour; therefore, the 250-acre development generates _____ vehicle trips in the morning peak hour.

   The trip distribution of this traffic is as follows:

   From C to A   =   20 percent   =   ____ vehicles
       C to B   =   25 percent   =   ____
       C to E   =   30 percent   =   ____
       C to F   =   5 percent   =   ____
       C to H   =   0 percent   =   ____
       C to I   =   20 percent   =   ____
               100 percent   =   ____ vehicles

4. Traffic outbound from the office center at Node E is 20 vehicles. Distribution of the trips from this source is:

   From E to A   =   20 percent   =   ____ vehicles
       E to B   =   35 percent   =   ____
       E to C   =   10 percent   =   ____
       E to F   =   5 percent   =   ____
       E to H   =   20 percent   =   ____
       E to I   =   10 percent   =   ____
               100 percent   =   20 vehicles

5. Traffic outbound from the shopping center at Node F amounts to 40 vehicles, distributed as follows:

   From F to A   =   15 percent   =   vehicles
       F to B   =   25 percent   =   ____
       F to C   =   15 percent   =   ____
       F to E   =   30 percent   =   ____
       F to H   =   5 percent   =   ____
       E to I   =   10 percent   =   ____
               100 percent   =   40 vehicles

6. Traffic generated by the "Planned Apartment Community" at Node H during the morning peak hour is to be calculated by completing Table A.4.

7. Trip distribution from the "Planned Apartment Community" at Node H during the morning peak hour is:

   From H to A   =   20 percent   =   ____ vehicles
       H to B   =   25 percent   =   ____
       H to C   =   5 percent   =   ____
       H to E   =   30 percent   =   ____
       H to F   =   5 percent   =   ____
       H to I   =   15 percent   =   ____
               100 percent   =   ____ vehicles

8. The morning peak-hour trips generated at the industrial park at Node I is 10 cars, 5 of which go directly to Node A, and 5 of which go directly to Node B.

Figure A.4. Schematic Diagram of a Road Network

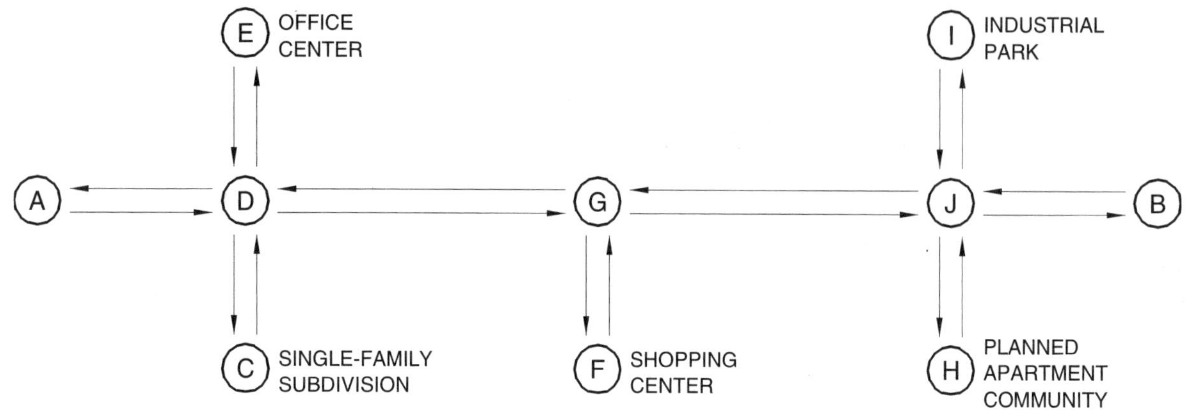

Table A.4. Traffic Generation from the Planned Apartment Community

Type of Building	Area (acres)	DU/Acre	DUs	Vehicle Trips/DU	Trips Made
High-rise apartments	10	100		0.5	
6-story apartments	10	40		0.5	
3-story apartments	20	20		0.8	
Townhouses	30	10		1.0	
TOTAL	70				

• DU = dwelling unit

Part II: Preparing a Trip Table

You are to fill in Table A.5.

Check your work by "cross-footing" your table (add the totals from the *rows*, and then add the totals of the *columns)*. If the totals are not the same, you have made an error in addition.

Total of rows   = ____
Total of columns = ____

Part III: Plotting the Traffic Flows

1. Use Table A.5 to identify the number of vehicle trips that have their *origin* at n = Nodes A, B, C, E, F, H, and I. Enter the numerical values in the appropriate fat arrows on Figure A.5.

2. Do the same to identify the number of vehicle trips that have their *destination* at the same nodes. Enter the values in the appropriate fat arrows on Figure A.5.

3. By analysis of the individual directional flows from each origin, and to each destination, calculate *all* the missing flow figures. Enter these figures in the appropriate narrow flow arrows on Figure A.5.

4. Calculate the traffic flow between Nodes D and G, and between G and J. Enter the figures in the appropriate fat arrows on Figure A.5.

5. Calculate the total *two-way* traffic at Nodes A, B, C, E, F, H, and I. Enter the appropriate figures in the boxes provided on Figure A.5.

Table A.5. Trip Table

Origin	Destination									
	A	B	C	D	E	F	G	H	I	TOTAL
A	—									
B		—								
C			—							
D				—						
E					—					
F						—				
G							—			
H								—		
I									—	
TOTAL										

Figure A.5. Traffic Flows at Nodes D, G, and J

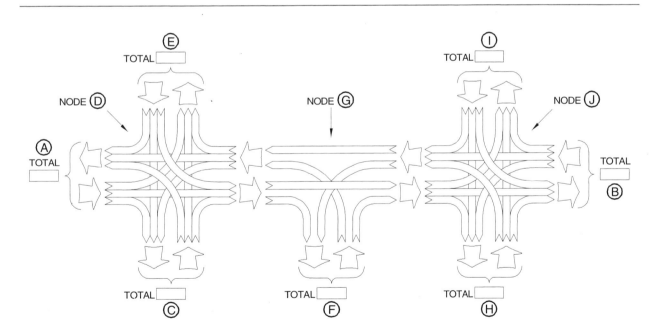

You are provided with a topographic map (see Figure A.6) which has a scale of 1 inch = 200 feet, and a section of profile paper (see Table A.6).

Design a road that runs from Point A to Point D. Tangents of the road are to pass through Points B and C. (These points are identified on the topographic map.)

The design speed of the road is to be 30 mph. The maximum grade of the finished road is to be 8 percent.

1. Calculate the minimum safe radius for turns on the road. Show your calculations on a separate page. Assume that the Factor e (factor for the superelevation rate) is 0.08 feet per foot, and that Factor f (factor for side fraction) is 0.16.

2. For the purposes of this exercise, use a 300-foot radius for the curve between lines AB-BC, and a 500-foot radius for the curve between lines BC-CD.

3. Draw the centerline of your proposed road on the topographic map. Label stations every 100 feet. (Do not compute the lengths of the road along the curves in this exercise; estimate their length by scaling them.) Identify all "points of curvature" (PC) and all "points of tangency" (PT).

4. Plot the profile of the centerline of the proposed road on the profile paper, as it would appear on the surface of the *existing* ground.

    The horizontal scale on the profile paper is to be 1 inch = 200 feet, and the vertical scale is to be 1 inch = 20 feet. The elevation of the start of the proposed road is to be at 500 feet.

5. Plot the profile of the centerline of your proposed road on the same sheet of profile paper, as it would appear after the terrain has been graded to accommodate it. Your road is to have:

    *   a 5 percent uphill slope between stations 0+00 and 4+00

    *   a 1 percent downhill slope between stations 4+00 and 8+00

    *   an 8 percent downhill slope between stations 8+00 and 13+50

    *   an 8 percent uphill slope between station 13+50 and Point D

    Mark these grades on your profile.

6. After you have established the grades for your recommended road, design vertical curves for those locations where a change of grade is planned.

    *   Use Table 10.11 to select the appropriate "factor K." Use the minimum value of K for the assigned design speed.

    *   Show your calculations on a separate sheet of paper.

    *   Plot the vertical curves on the profile of your recommended road. Draw to scale, and show the dimensions of the length L of each vertical curve, and the distance E between the apex of the tangents and the surface on the recommended street.

    *   In this exercise, round off the length L to the next highest multiple of 50 feet. When calculating E, use this rounded figure for L. One-half of the distance L is to be on each side of the apex of your vertical curves.

7. Some common errors that should be avoided are:

    *   failure to label centerline stations correctly

    *   failure to identify and give dimensions of L and E on the profile

    *   failure to draw E to scale on the profile

    *   failure to give the correct elevation of the stream bed at station 13+50

    *   failure to use "rounded up" figures for L in your calculations for E, and when drawing the profile of your proposed road

    *   excessive foreshortening of arc lengths along the curve with a radius of 500 feet (the length of the chord of 100 feet of arc of a circle which has a radius of 500 feet is 99.9 feet)

Figure A.6. Topographic Map for the Road Design Exercise

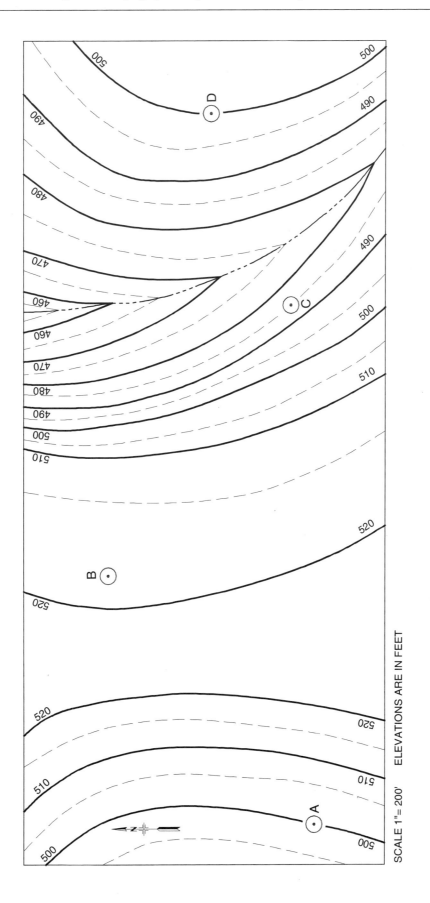

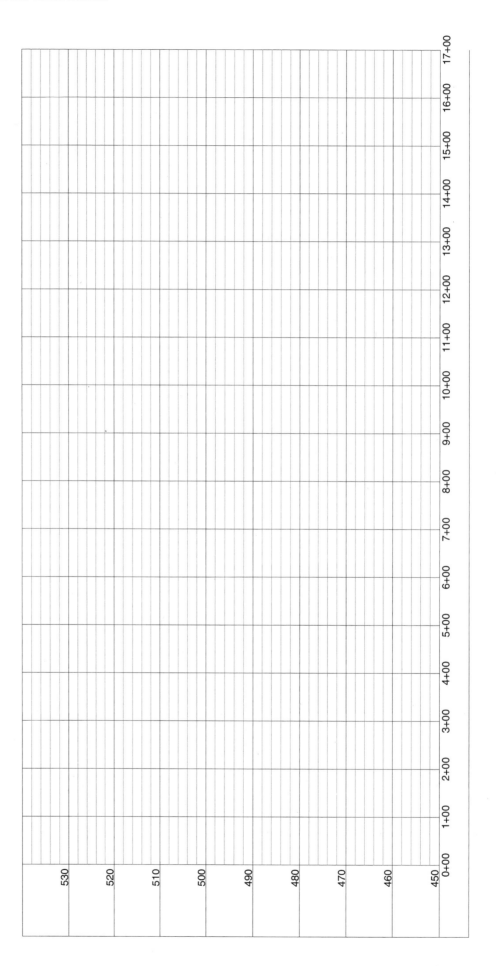

Table A.6. Profile Paper for the Road Design Exercise

EXERCISE:
DESIGN TWO PARKING LOTS (for Chapter 11)

You are to prepare two alternative parking lot layouts for a parcel of urban property. The first alternative is to show how the property can be developed using 90-degree parking; the second alternative is to use 60-degree parking.

The property measures 130 feet on the street frontage, and has a depth of 150 feet. It is located on a collector street, adjacent to the Central Business District (CBD) of a medium-sized city. There are walls on three sides of the site. The lot has a slope of 1 percent towards the street, and has no soils or drainage problems.

Design Standards

You are to use the design standards provided in Table 11.3, except as noted below:

1. Parking stalls are to be at least 9 feet wide.

2. No more than one entrance and one exit, or one combined entrance-exit, is to open onto the street.

3. Internal circulation may have one- or two-way aisles (or a combination thereof).

4. One-way aisles are to have a minimum width of 12 feet, and two-way aisles 24 feet. (When an aisle is to be used for maneuvering space, as well as for circulation, it may need to be wider than these minimums.)

5. The minimum inside radius (r) of turns is to be 15 feet.

6. The minimum outside radius (R) of turns is to be 29 feet.

7. Two spaces for parking for the physically handicapped are to be provided, each with a stall width of 13 feet.

8. Landscaping along the front of the lot is encouraged, but is not mandatory.

9. Cars are to be parked by their drivers (not by attendants) for a short term (not all day).

10. "Dead" parking spaces are to be avoided.

11. Your drawing is to give key dimensions of typical stalls and aisles, so that a semi-skilled worker could lay out the parking lot design.

12. Parking stalls alongside walls or fences should be increased in width by 2 feet, to make it easier to open the adjacent car door.

Preparing a Base Map of the Site

Your first step is to prepare a base map of the property for use in your design studies. This map should be at a scale of 1 inch = 20 feet (thus the lot itself, which has a width of 130 feet and a depth of 150 feet, will have mapped dimensions of 6-1/2 × 7-1/2 inches). This will easily fit on a sheet of 8-1/2 × 11 inch paper.

Figure A.7 shows, at a reduced scale, what your base map should look like. At the lower edge of the map, you should provide space to indicate the number of stalls provided in your design, and the gross lot area per stall.

It is recommended that you prepare one well-drafted, original base map, and then make photocopies of it for use as preliminary study maps, and for your final design maps.

Figure A.7. Parking Lot Site

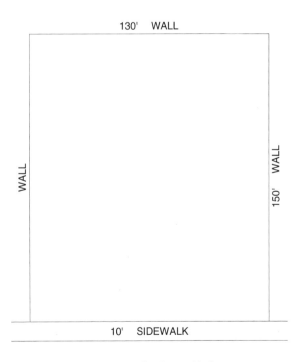

Number of stalls provided: _____
Lot area = 19,500 sq. ft.
Lot area per stall: _____

Recommended Design Procedure

1. Using Table 11.3, which recommends design standards, you are to decide on the basic configuration of the parking lot (i.e., how many aisles, how many rows of stalls).

2. Lay out your circulation system by drawing in the aisles and the required radii of the turns.

3. Draw in individual parking stalls. You may find that you will want to make each stall a bit larger than the minimum required dimension, in order to utilize all available space. Or, you may wish to make some stalls extra wide for handicapped drivers, or in areas adjacent to walls.

4. Draw in any landscaping to be provided.

5. Provide required dimensions on the drawing, and arrows indicating the direction of traffic flow.

How Your Designs May Be Evaluated

1. Ease of circulation within the parking lot

2. Efficient utilization of space

3. Neatness of presentation (note that the use of a tee-square, triangles, and a pencil compass is essential)

4. Compliance with design standards

EXERCISE:
CALCULATE AND DIAGRAM LAND AREAS REQUIRED FOR SIX HYPOTHETICAL CITIES
(for Chapter 14)

The objective of this exercise is to give the reader experience in working with residential density figures. In this exercise, you are to design six cities, each with 5,000 dwelling units in it.

Part I of the exercise requires you to calculate the land area required for each of six hypothetical cities, each of which has a different density of residential development. This is to be done by completing Table A.7. It should be noted that the assumptions concerning population and nonresidential uses in the table do not reflect conditions that are found in new cities; the figures provided were selected to make the computations simple.

Part II of the exercise requires you to prepare a graphic representation of the cities that were described statistically in Part I. The purpose of this is to demonstrate the impacts that alternative densities of development have on the spatial requirements of urban development. The city designs that are to be produced need not reflect good urban design; they should reflect space requirements, not necessarily design skills.

Part III of the exercise employs the equation set forth in Chapter 14 concerning the relationships among residential density, building height, and building coverage. This is intended to show how residential density affects the second and third dimensions of urban design, namely the area covered by buildings and building height.

Part I: Calculate the Land Areas Required for Six Cities

Instructions: Fill in the blank spaces in Table A.7. The column for 10 DU/ac has been completed to serve as a guide for completing the other columns.

Note that all the areas of land uses and all the densities are reported in *gross* (rather than *net*) terms (that is, the area of local streets is included along with the area of the adjacent land use).

Part II: Prepare Diagrams of Six Cities

Assignment: Draw a schematic diagram of each of the six cities analyzed in Part I of this exercise, at a scale of 1 inch = 2,000 feet.

Objective: To graphically illustrate the impact that density of development has on the land area required for a city.

STEP 1
Calculate the gross area required for each city, and calculate the dimensions of this area if the city were to have a rectangular form.

Example: A city with a gross residential density of 10 DU/ac has an area of 813 acres (see line 16 of Table A.7).

813 acres × 43,560 square feet/acre = 35,414,280 square feet (this can be rounded off to 35,000,000 square feet).

If the shape of the city is square, the length of each side of the square is the square root of the area of the city. The square root of 35,000,000 square feet is 5,916 feet, or about 6,000 feet.

If you don't care for square cities, you can have a rectangular one, such as 4,000 feet × 8,750 feet or 5,000 feet × 7,000 feet, or even a circular one, with a radius of 3,340 feet.

Note: For the lowest density city (1 DU/ac), it is strongly recommended that you develop a rectangular city, with a dimension of 14,000 feet along one side. If you do not heed this advice, you will have a hard time plotting your city on an 8-1/2 × 11 inch sheet of paper.

STEP 2
Calculate the area required in each city for schools, commercial uses, employment centers, and parks.

Each *school* requires 5 acres (see line 9 of Table A.7).

5 acres × 43,560 square feet/acre = 217,800 square feet = 220,000 square feet.

If the school site is square, its dimensions will be about 470 × 470 feet. Alternatively, it can be rectangular, such as 300 × 730 feet, or 400 × 550 feet.

(See line 8 of Table A.7 for the number of 5-acre school sites required in each city.)

Commercial uses also require 5 acres per city.

Employment centers require 50 acres per city.

50 acres × 43,560 square feet/acre = 2,178,000 square feet = 2,200,000 square feet. If the area for employment centers is square, its dimensions will be 1,500 × 1,500 feet. Alternatively, it may be rectangular, such as 1,000 × 2,200 feet.

Parks require 25 acres per city. 25 acres × 43,560 square feet/acre = 1,089,000 square feet = 1,000,000 square feet. If the park is square, its dimensions will be 1,000 × 1,000 feet. If it is to be rectangular, its dimensions might be 500 × 2,000 feet.

Table A.7. Land Areas Required for Six Cities (each of which has 5,000 dwelling units)

		1.0	5.0	10	20	40	80
(1)	Net residential density (DU/ac)	1.0	5.0	10	20	40	80
(2)	Net lot area per DU (in square feet)			4,356			
(3)	Acres of land required for residential buildings			500			
(4)	Assumed persons per DU	3.4	3.2	2.8	2.4	2.2	2.0
(5)	Total population (number of DUs × persons per DU)			14,000			
(6)	Assumed elementary school children per DU	1.0	0.8	0.6	0.4	0.2	0.1
(7)	Elementary school population			3,000			
(8)	Number of schools required (at 1 school per 500 pupils)			6			
(9)	Area required for schools			30			
(10)	Area for commercial uses (at 1 acre per 1,000 DUs)			5			
(11)	Area for employment centers (at 10 acres per 1,000 DUs)			50			
(12)	Area for parks (at 5 acres per 1,000 DUs)			25			
(13)	Net developed areas (sum of lines 3, 9, 10, 11, and 12)			610			
(14)	Assumed percent of gross area used for streets	20	20	25	30	35	40
(15)	Factor used to divide net area to get gross area (percent)	80	80	75	70	65	60
(16)	Gross area of the city (acres)			813			
(17)	Gross density of the city (DU/ac)			6.2			
(18)	Gross density of the city (persons per acre)			17			

- DU/ac = dwelling units per acre

STEP 3

Calculate the size that the cities will be when mapped at 1 inch = 2,000 feet. To do this, complete Table A.8.

STEP 4

Plot your cities on sheets of 8-1/2 × 11 inch paper. You may place several cities on each sheet of paper, if you have room for them. Plot the cities at a scale of 1 inch = 2,000 feet (the scale that is used on USGS quads).

Plot within each city the areas required for: schools (show individual sites); commercial uses (show one 5-acre site); employment centers (show one 50-acre site); and parks (show one 25-acre site).

Try to illustrate a reasonable spatial relationship between your land uses. Show some major arterial streets in your cities (but no minor local streets), and show how your land uses would be related to these streets.

STEP 5

Apply color to the plans of the cities. It is recommended that you use the following colors for the land uses in your cities:

Residential areas .... yellow
Schools .... blue
Commercial uses .... red
Employment centers .... grey
Parks .... green
Streets .... black

Part III: Calculate Building Height

Assignment: Using the equations developed in Chapter 14 relating to the interrelationships of building density, height, and coverage, calculate the average building height that would result in each of your six cities. Base your calculations on the residential densities in Table A7 (line 1), and on the assumptions set forth in Table A.9.

The appropriate equation from Chapter 14 to use is:

$$\text{Number of stories} = \frac{(\text{floor area square feet per DU}) \times (\text{DU/ac}) \times 100}{(43{,}560 \text{ square feet per acre}) \times (\text{coverage in percent})}$$

Table A.8. Dimensions of Cities When Mapped

Residential Density of the City (DU/ac)	Area of the City (acres)	Area of the City (sq. ft.)	Dimensions of the City (feet)	Dimensions of the City When Mapped (inches)
1.0				
5.0				
10.	813	35,000,000	7,000 × 5,000	3.5 × 2.5
20.				
40.				
80.				

- DU/ac = dwelling units per acre

Table A.9. Average Building Height in Cities

Net Residential Density		Assumed Coverage in %	Average Floor Area per DU (sq. ft.)	Average Building Height (stories)
(DU/ac)	(sq. ft./DU)			
1.0		4.5	2,000	
5.0		9.0	1,600	
10.	4,356	16.	1,400	1.99
20.		22.	1,200	
40.		31.	1,000	
80.		31.	1,000	

- DU/ac = dwelling units per acre

EXERCISE:
DESIGN A SUBDIVISION (for Chapter 18)

You are to prepare a subdivision plan for a 44-acre parcel of urban land. The property is bounded on the north and south by arterial streets, and on the east and west by collector streets. You are to design a subdivision of single-family homes for this property. Each building lot is to have a width of at least 75 feet, and a net lot area of at least 10,000 square feet (typical lots should be 75 × 135 feet; pie-shaped lots must have a frontage of at least 40 feet).

Observe recommended design standards and practices wherever possible. (*Note:* this will not always be possible. You may have to compromise the standards concerning the 500-foot maximum length of a straight road, and for the distance between the entrance to the subdivision and the intersection of the boundary streets.) You may utilize a grid pattern of streets, a modified grid pattern, loop streets, cul-de-sac streets, curvilinear streets, or any combination thereof.

No lots in your subdivision are to face arterial streets or collector streets. This means that some of the lots will face local residential streets, but their rear yards will abut arterial or collector streets.

Your subdivision is to include only streets and single-family home building sites. For this exercise, we are excluding such niceties as schools, parks, and shopping centers.

Your design should be neatly executed, using pencil lines and drafting instruments. If you have curvilinear streets, draw the curves in them using a compass (not a French curve). At all curves, the same center point should be used for the inside radius of the right-of-way (ROW), the street centerline radius, and the outside radius. Show with a dot the center point of the radius of all curves.

Show the boundaries of all street rights-of-way and all lot lines. You need not show sidewalks or the edge of the paving. Put dimensions on a few typical lots; you need not dimension all of the lots in the subdivision.

In order to keep this exercise simple, all street rights-of-way in your subdivision are to be 50 feet wide.[1] At T intersections and 90-degree turns in streets, the minimum inside radius at the property line is to be 20 feet. If you have bulbs on the ends of cul-de-sacs, their diameter at the property line should be 80 feet.[2]

Assume that the property is eminently suitable for subdivision development, and that there are no problems such as flooding, drainage problems, bedrock close to the surface, clay deposits, a high water table, landslides, or earthquake faults. For the sake of clarity, contours have been omitted from your base map.

Preparing a Base Map of the Site

Your first step is to prepare a base map of the property for use in your design studies. This map should be at a scale of 1 inch = 200 feet. The site measures 1,200 × 1,600 feet; its size, when drawn to scale, will be 6 × 8 inches. (This will easily fit on a sheet of 8-1/2 × 11 inch paper.)

Figure A.8 shows, at a reduced scale, what your base map should look like. Your map should include a north

Figure A.8. Base Map for Designing a Subdivision

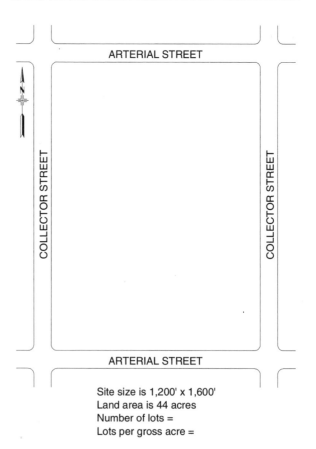

Site size is 1,200' x 1,600'
Land area is 44 acres
Number of lots =
Lots per gross acre =

point and an indication of map scale. There should also be space to record the number of lots in the subdivision, and the gross density of the subdivision, in lots per gross acre.

Recommended Design Procedure

1. Draw, at the same scale as your base map (1 inch = 200 feet), three small templates on mylar tracing film (or vellum tracing paper) which show streets with building lots along both sides of them. The templates should be for:
    *   a 90-degree turn in a street
    *   a T intersection
    *   a bulb cul-de-sac

    Figure A.9 illustrates what these templates should look like.

2. Make some photocopies of the blank base map and use some of them to sketch out alternative street patterns (or, use tracing paper over a copy of the base map). At this stage use freehand sketching; don't spend your time with engineering drawing. The templates you prepared in Step 1 will show you about how much land you will need between streets.

3. Select what appears to be a reasonable street pattern, and start making a refinement of it on a clean base map. Use engineering drawing techniques to draw in the centerlines of your streets. When these appear to be reasonable and workable, draw in the edges of the street ROW. Next, draw in the lot lines.

Basis For Evaluating Your Design

*   probable attractiveness and charm of the resulting subdivision
*   efficient use of land (i.e., maximum yield of building sites)
*   traffic safety
*   probable ease of residents and visitors in comprehending the street pattern
*   neatness of presentation
    *   — line quality
    *   — appropriate use of a compass and straightedge
    *   — adequacy and neatness of dimensions

Notes

1. 50 feet is excessively wide for a local access street, but that width is specified here because it is easier to draw than a narrower street.

2. This dimension is also excessive.

Figure A.9. Templates for Subdivision Design (drawn at scale 1" = 200')

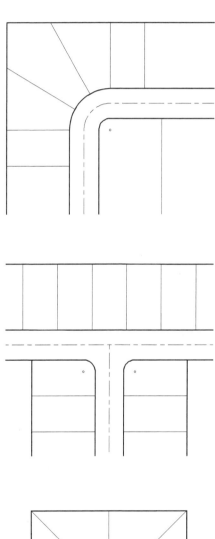

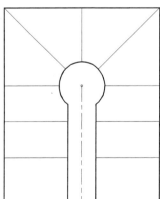

Appendix B

Using This Book as a Classroom Text

Instructors who use this text for their classes will certainly not be able to cover all of the material in one 3-credit hour course which lasts for 12 weeks. Some instructors may choose to cover the text material in a sequence of courses; others may choose to pick and choose which material to cover in a single course.

When this book is used in the classroom, please note:

- Before class, each student should read the assigned chapters in this text, *and* the text materials listed at the end of those chapters under the heading of "Recommended Reading." (The material under the heading of "Sources of Further Information" is optional reading.)
- During class, the instructor should review the subjects of the assigned readings, clarify any issues that are raised, and augment the text as they find appropriate. The instructor should then review any exercise that is to be assigned, to make sure that the students understand what they are supposed to do and how to do it. (Experience has shown that students learn substantially more from the exercises than they do from sitting in a lecture hall and having a topic described to them.)
- After class, each student should complete an exercise, if one is assigned for the topic of the day.

The "Recommended Readings" should be considered as essential parts of the course materials. The instructor is urged to put them on a time-limited reserve in the school library, so that they will be available to all class members, not just the ones who can check them out of the library first.

"Sources of Further Information" augment other course materials, and are listed for use by students (and instructors) who wish to delve further into the subject matter of each chapter. It is also very desirable to have many of these texts put on a time-limited reserve in the school library.

RECOMMENDED TOOLS AND SUPPLIES

It is recommended that each student have the following materials available when doing the exercises, which are an integral part of the coursework:

- 30-60-90 degree triangle (about an 10-inch size)
- 45-degree triangle (about an 8-inch size)
- access to a drafting table, or an 18 × 24 inch drafting board
- tee-square (about 24 inches long)
- drafting pencils (grades H, 2H, and Eagle Drafting)
- drafting tape (one small roll; *not* masking tape)
- engineer's scale, triangular, 12 inches long (*not* an architect's scale; *not* a metric scale)
- pencil compass which opens to a radius of about 5 inches (purchase of a set of drafting instruments is *not* recommended)
- a simple, hand-held calculator
- colored pencils, such as Prismacolor (preferred), in the following hues:

	Prismacolor #
true blue	903
olive green	911
canary yellow	916
poppy red	922
black	935
sand	940
yellow ochre	942
burnt ochre	943
dark umber	947

Appendix C

Derivation of Equations Which Relate Building Height, Density, and Coverage

ASSUMPTIONS

- There is a residential building on a building lot.

- The number of dwelling units in the building are of uniform size and are uniformly distributed throughout the building.

- All floors of the building have equal areas.

Figure C.1. Schematic Diagram of a Multistoried Building Constructed on a Building Lot

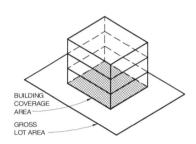

BUILDING COVERAGE AREA

GROSS LOT AREA

We can describe the area of the building lot that is covered by the building in two different ways:

(1) building coverage area $= \dfrac{\text{gross floor area in the building in feet}^2}{\text{number of stories}}$

and (2) building coverage area $=$ gross lot area in feet$^2 \times \dfrac{\text{coverage in percent}}{100}$

If we equate (1) with (2),

(3) gross lot area in feet$^2 \times \dfrac{\text{coverage in percent}}{100} = \dfrac{\text{gross floor area in feet}^2}{\text{number of stories}}$

We can then divide both sides of the equation by the number of dwelling units in the building:

(4) $\dfrac{\text{lot area in feet}^2}{\text{DU}} \times \dfrac{\text{coverage in percent}}{100} = \dfrac{\text{floor area/DU in feet}^2}{\text{number of stories}}$

from which we can derive:

(5) number of stories $= \dfrac{\text{floor area/DU in feet}^2 \times 100}{\text{lot area in feet}^2/\text{DU} \times \text{coverage in percent}}$

But we know from our definitions that:

(6) lot area in feet^2/DU $= \dfrac{43,560 \text{ feet}^2/\text{acre}}{\text{density in DU/acre}}$

Substituting equation (6) in equation (5) we get:

(7) number of stories $= \dfrac{\text{floor area in feet}^2/\text{DU} \times \text{density in DU/acre} \times 100}{43,560 \text{ feet}^2/\text{acre} \times \text{coverage in percent}}$

Transposing terms in equation (7) we get:

(8) density in DU/acre $= \dfrac{\text{number of stories} \times \text{coverage in percent} \times 43,560 \text{ feet}^2/\text{acre}}{\text{floor area in feet}^2/\text{DU} \times 100}$

and

(9) coverage in percent $= \dfrac{\text{floor area in feet}^2/\text{DU} \times \text{density in DU/acre} \times 100}{43,560 \text{ feet}^2/\text{acre} \times \text{number of stories}}$

261

EQUATIONS FOR FLOOR AREA RATIO (FAR)

By definition:

$$(10) \quad \text{FAR} = \frac{\text{floor area in feet}^2/\text{DU}}{\text{lot area in feet}^2/\text{DU}}$$

From equation (4) we can say that:

$$(11) \quad \text{lot area in feet/DU} = \frac{\text{floor area in feet}^2/\text{DU} \times 100}{\text{number of stories} \times \text{coverage in percent}}$$

Substitution equation (11) in equation (10) yields:

$$(12) \quad \text{FAR} = \text{number of stories} \times \frac{\text{coverage in percent}}{100}$$

Index

"Z" lots, 218-219
zero-lot-line lots, 218
subdivision design exercise, 258
subdivision map examples, 207, 208
subdivisions
   final subdivision map, 206, 208, 213
   off-site factors, 210
   preliminary subdivision map, 205, 212
   regulations, 210-211
   subdivision design process, 205-213
   subdivision process, 203-213
   tentative subdivision map, 204, 206-207, 213
   why we have subdivision regulations, 203-204, 210-211
superblocks, 194-195
superelevation, 110, 113
superelevation runoff, 111, 113

telephone service, 72
tentative subdivision map, 204, 206-207, 213
terrain
   effect on traffic flows, 95
   maximum street grades, 116
   related to design level of service, 108
topographic maps, 9, 10, 12, 209
topography; influence on storm water runoff, 67-68
townhouses, 156, 159
traffic assignment exercise, 247
traffic counts, 85
traffic diverters
   chicanes, 190-191
   cul-de-sac streets, 190-191
   rumble strips, 190-191
   speed bumps, 190-191
   traffic circles, 190-191
   woonerfs, 190-191
traffic engineering, 80
traffic signals, 96
transit
   advantages, 138-139, 143
   alternative forms, 147-148
   construction costs, 142
   definition, 139

disadvantages, 143-144
feasibility, 144-146
goals, 146
issues in, 146-147
planning procedures, 148-149
systems, 83-84, 139-140
trip-end density, 139, 144-146
vehicles
   costs, 142-143
   speeds, 141-142
   types, 140-141
transportation planning
   branches, 80
   definitions, 80
   diagram of the planning process, 82
   models, 81-84, 86
   planning process, 81-82, 85
   scope, 79-80
transportation routes; effect on city location, 5
treatment plants; wastewater, 53
trip assignment, 84
trip attraction, 81, 85
trip-end density, 139, 144-146
trip generation, 81, 85
   sample rates, 83
triplexes and fourplexes, 159
trucks; effect on traffic flows, 95

UBC (Uniform Building Code), 164
underground utility lines, 62
urban form; influences by
   landforms, 3
   slope, 24-27
   storm drainage, 61-63
   utility lines, 71
   wastewater management, 57
   water supply, 36-37
urban location; *see* city location
USGS (U.S. Geological Survey)
   ESICs (Earth Science Information Centers), 20-21
   internet address, 21
   maps, general description, 16
   orthophoto quadrangles, 16
   topographic mapping, 16
utility lines
   electric, 71-72
   influences on urban form, 71
   in residential areas, 73

natural gas, 72
related to urban development, 73-74
serving subdivision sites, 209-210
spatial relationships among, 39, 41, 72-73
telephone, 72
underground, 62

V/C ratio (volume-to-capacity ratio), 98, 99, 101-102
vegetation
   analysis, 209
   influence on storm water runoff, 66, 68
vertical curves, 115, 119
vertical geometry in road design, 107, 115, 122, 198
visualizing slope, 22-23

wastewater
   definitions, 45-46
   flow amounts, 48-49
   flow types, 48
wastewater management
   alternative forms, 58-59
   in relation to urban development, 57
wastewater planning, 51-54
wastewater treatment
   primary, 47
   secondary, 47-48
   tertiary, 48
water-borne transport; influence on city location, 5
water demand
   for agriculture, 37
   for fire fighting, 38
   for industrial use, 37-38
   general, 37-38
   per capita demand, 37-38
water distribution
   basic distribution systems, 35-36, 38-40
   calculating service areas, 41-43
   relationship of water lines to sewer lines, 39, 41
water pressure
   desirable domestic water pressure, 38